Showcasing globalisation?

Manchester University Press

Showcasing globalisation?
The political economy of the Irish Republic

Nicola Jo-Anne Smith

Manchester University Press
Manchester and New York

distributed exclusively in the USA by Palgrave

Copyright © Nicola Jo-Anne Smith 2005

The right of Nicola Jo-Anne Smith to be identified as the author of this work has been asserted by her in accordance with the Copyright, Designs and Patents Act 1988.

Published by Manchester University Press
Oxford Road, Manchester M13 9NR, UK
and Room 400, 175 Fifth Avenue, New York, NY 10010, USA
www.manchesteruniversitypress.co.uk

Distributed exclusively in the USA by
Palgrave, 175 Fifth Avenue, New York,
NY 10010, USA

Distributed exclusively in Canada by
UBC Press, University of British Columbia, 2029 West Mall,
Vancouver, BC, Canada V6T 1Z2

British Library Cataloguing-in-Publication Data
A catalogue record for this book is available from the British Library

Library of Congress Cataloging-in-Publication Data applied for

ISBN 0 7190 6992 0 *hardback*
EAN 978 0 7190 6992 5
ISBN 0 7190 6993 9 *paperback*
EAN 978 0 7190 6993 2

First published 2005

14 13 12 11 10 09 08 07 06 05   10 9 8 7 6 5 4 3 2 1

Typeset
by SNP Best-set Typesetter Ltd., Hong Kong
Printed in Great Britain
by CPI, Bath

To Mum, Dad and Ian

Contents

List of figures — *page* viii
List of tables — x
Preface and acknowledgements — xi
List of abbreviations — xii

Introduction — 1

1 The globalisation debate — 10

2 Economic performance (1): Ireland the 'Celtic tiger'? — 36

3 Economic performance (2): a 'showpiece of globalisation'? — 63

4 The trajectory of the Irish state (1): 1921 to 1987 — 97

5 The trajectory of the Irish state (2): 1987 to 2004 — 119

6 The dynamics behind policy change (1): the international economic context — 140

7 The dynamics behind policy change (2): the political discourse of globalisation — 167

Conclusion — 197

Select bibliography — 202
Index — 209

List of figures

1.1	Ratio of merchandise trade to GDP in current prices, 1913 and 1995	*page* 14
1.2	Share of world merchandise trade by 'triad' countries, 1948–2002	14
2.1	Irish GDP growth in international perspective, 1990–2000	39
2.2	Volume of GNP and GDP, 1980–2000	41
3.1	Trade openness in selected OECD countries, 2001	65
3.2	Inward foreign direct investment stocks as a share of GDP, 2002	67
3.3	Ireland's net receipts from the EU budget, 1973–2003	72
3.4	Corporate tax rates for selected countries, 2003	73
3.5	Educational attainment, 2001	75
3.6	Science and engineering graduates per 1,000 population, 2000	76
3.7	Migration and natural increase in population in Ireland, 1994–2003	77
3.8	Spending as a percentage of GDP on active labour market policies, 1985–97	79
3.9	Participation rates, 2002	79
3.10	Workdays lost to industrial disputes in Ireland, 1986–2003	80
3.11	Workdays lost due to industrial disputes per 1,000 employees, 1992–2001	81
5.1	Government expenditure in Ireland (% GNP), 1987–2003	124
5.2	Government expenditure in Ireland (€ million), 1987–2003	126
5.3	Social welfare expenditure compared with inflation in Ireland, 1993–2002	127
6.1	Destination of Irish exports, 1970–99	149
6.2	Foreign direct investment inflows to Ireland by geographical location, 2002	154
6.3	Foreign direct investment stocks in the Irish economy by geographical origin, 2002	155

7.1	Public opinion in the EU of globalisation and European membership	184
7.2	Opinion poll support for Fianna Fáil by social group, 1969–97	187

List of tables

1.1	World total of foreign direct investment and international production, 1982–2002	page 11
1.2	Social expenditure and tax revenue, 1980–98	16
2.1	Irish economic performance, 1990s	40
2.2	Irish and East Asian growth rates, 1960–99	42
2.3	Irish economic growth, 1997–2003	45
2.4	Human and income poverty, 1990–2001	50
2.5	Percentage of persons lacking basic deprivation items in Ireland, 1994–2001	51
2.6	Percentage of persons below relative income poverty lines in Ireland, 1994–2001	51
2.7	Percentage of persons below 1994 relative income standards in Ireland, 1994–2001	52
3.1	Exchequer balance and debt in Ireland, 1987–2002	83
4.1	Expenditure of central government by purpose of expenditure and economic category in Ireland, 1965–6 to 1984	108
4.2	Government spending and debt in Ireland, 1980–6	112
5.1	Distribution of gross hourly and weekly earnings in Ireland, 1987–94	123
5.2	Overall government expenditure and social protection expenditure in Ireland, 1999 and 2002	125
6.1	Openness of small EU economies, 1960	148
6.2	Ireland's trade by geographical origin, January–March 2005	151
6.3	Foreign direct investment inflows to Ireland by geographical origin, 1987–98	153

Preface and acknowledgements

This book has its origins in my doctoral thesis, which I undertook in the Department of Political Science and International Studies at the University of Birmingham. While the book represents a considerably revised and updated version of the thesis, the core arguments remain the same. My greatest academic debt is therefore undoubtedly to Colin Hay, who, as my lecturer, PhD supervisor and now colleague, has consistently gone beyond the call of duty to give me enormous support, advice, feedback and encouragement. I would also like to acknowledge the tremendous help given to me by Matthew Watson, who has been extremely generous with both his time and his ideas; my work would look very different without his input. While a great many other people have helped me along the way, I would particularly like to thank Mick Moran, Dan Wincott, David Marsh, Peter Kerr, Donna Lee, Michelle Pace, Nicola Hothi, Karina Pawlowska, Mikko Kuisma, David Hudson, George Taylor and Ronnie Munck.

More generally, I would like to thank the Department of Political Science and International Studies at the University of Birmingham, which has provided a wonderfully supportive and intellectually rewarding environment to research and teach in. In addition, I am extremely grateful to all at Manchester University Press for their support and help throughout the writing of this book, and to the Economic and Social Research Council for their continued funding of my research. I would also like to thank the various people in Ireland who have helped me, not least those who agreed to spend their valuable time being interviewed.

Last but by no means least, I am indebted to my family and friends – above all my parents and my partner, Ian.

List of abbreviations

ABT	An Bord Tráchtála
ASEAN	Association of South East Asian Nations
CAP	Common Agricultural Policy
CBFSAI	Central Bank and Financial Services Authority of Ireland
CPA	Combat Poverty Agency
CSO	Central Statistical Office
EMS	European Monetary System
EMU	European Monetary Union
ESRI	Economic and Social Research Institute
FDI	foreign direct investment
HEA	Higher Education Authority
IBEC	Irish Business and Employers Confederation
ICTU	Irish Congress of Trade Unions
IDA	Industrial Development Agency
IFSC	International Financial Services Centre
IPE	international political economy
NCC	National Competitiveness Council
NCPP	National Centre for Partnership and Performance
NESC	National Economic and Social Council
NIEC	National Industrial and Economic Council
OECD	Organisation for Economic Co-operation and Development
OEEC	Organisation for European Economic Co-operation
PCW	Programme for Competitiveness and Work
PESP	Programme for Economic and Social Progress
PPF	Programme for Prosperity and Fairness
PNR	Programme for National Recovery
P2000	Partnership 2000: Employment, Competitiveness and Inclusion
SEA	Single European Act
SEM	Single European Market

Introduction

Why globalisation?

> Globalisation is in danger of becoming, if it has not already become, the cliché of our times.[1]

'Globalisation' may be a cliché, but it is a dangerous one. While there is considerable debate about the nature, extent and impact of globalisation, it is nevertheless widely assumed to alter the scope for social and political choice radically. Indeed, it is seen by some to mark the end of the nation-state, of social democracy, of geography and even of history itself.

Yet the concept delivers very little in analytical terms. Despite the enormous academic literature on globalisation, it remains highly ambiguous and illusive. Most often it is used as a rather vague umbrella term for a variety of diverse phenomena ranging from Maastricht to McDonalds. It is rarely (if ever) used to signify processes or tendencies that can actually be described as 'global'. Indeed, globalisation is often presented as if it were somehow synonymous with change itself.[2] Those who attempt to question whether globalisation actually exists thus find themselves (wrongly) characterised as claiming that nothing has changed in recent years by critics seeking to easily discredit their arguments.[3]

Moreover, 'globalisation' is used not only to describe contemporary developments but also to explain them. It is globalisation that is the agent of change; globalisation that serves to shape the terrain of political possibility. But globalisation is not an actor and so cannot actually 'do' anything. Although intended as a convenient shorthand, the term 'globalisation' tends to obscure rather than illuminate the dynamics of change by implying that social and political outcomes are somehow predetermined by exogenous forces beyond the control of human actors.[4]

Despite – or perhaps because of – the concept's illusive nature, it remains not just the subject of considerable academic debate but also highly influential in political terms. Whether or not globalisation actually exists, the power of the *idea* of globalisation is considerable. If political decision-makers believe in globalisation, it may serve to shape policy outcomes irrespective of its 'real' existence. Indeed, in acting as if it were a material reality, policy-makers may actually create the very conditions they attribute to globalisation itself.[5] It is for this reason that the critical analysis of 'globalisation' remains extremely important.

Why Ireland?

Given the enormous debate about the impact of globalisation on national policy-making, it is surprising that so few authors seek to examine specific national contexts in detail.[6] Yet such an approach can reveal a great deal about the dynamics of change in contemporary political economies. For, while states may be exposed to common external pressures, the existence of distinctive institutional and cultural environments means that they may respond in different ways and achieve different outcomes.[7] This highlights the need not only to consider how these common external pressures might be conceptualised (and, in particular, whether they can be characterised in terms of 'globalisation') but also to explore how they impact upon particular national systems. The use of country case studies can therefore be particularly instructive in the analysis of globalisation.

The Irish Republic is perhaps *the* test case for globalisation. Not only is Ireland hailed as the most globalised country in the world,[8] but its rapid economic growth in the 1990s is widely cited as evidence of how nations can flourish in the new global economy. Indeed, having become famous as the 'Celtic tiger', the Republic is now widely regarded as a model economy for other countries to follow. In this sense, Ireland has become for many something of a 'showpiece of globalisation'.[9]

Such claims have not gone unquestioned in the Irish academic literature. Various commentators have sought to challenge the assumption that globalisation has been good for Ireland.[10] However, despite this normative divergence, there has been surprisingly little attempt to question globalisation in analytical terms. A range of authors has explored *how* and *why* Ireland has been globalised, but no one has challenged the view *that* Ireland has been globalised. Indeed, it seems to

INTRODUCTION

be regarded as self-evident that a small, open economy such as Ireland's should be subject to the forces of globalisation. In this sense, it is not globalisation *per se* that is questioned by these authors but rather the extent to which its impact is detrimental to Ireland's economic and social development. Thus, even the critics perceive globalisation to restrict the social and political choices available in contemporary Ireland. The book ahead seeks to question this conventional wisdom by examining whether the Irish Republic – supposedly the most globalised country in the world – is indeed subject to the external imperatives of 'globalisation'.

Key aims

The principal aim of this volume is to examine what, if anything, globalisation can reveal about the Irish case and, indeed, what the Irish case can reveal about globalisation. In fact, there is surprisingly little dialogue between the globalisation and Irish literatures. Globalisation theorists debate the impact of globalisation on national economic management, yet few attempt to examine specific country case studies in detail. Similarly, authors specialising in the Irish case emphasise the significance of globalisation, yet few seek to engage systematically with the globalisation literature. The book ahead thus seeks to engage with and contribute to both literatures by investigating whether the Irish Republic can really be considered a 'showpiece of globalisation'.

In so doing, the book addresses four central issues. The first relates to how globalisation might be defined. It is a key contention here that if the concept is to have any meaning at all it must refer to processes or tendencies that are (or at least are becoming) truly 'global'.[11] This means that 'globalisation' cannot simply be used as an umbrella term for various factors unless such factors are becoming genuinely global in scope. This relates to the second issue: that the existence of such global tendencies cannot simply be assumed, but must instead be shown empirically. Whether or not Ireland's political economy can indeed be characterised as global is thus an open, empirical question rather than an intuitive one.[12] The third issue relates to a rather more fundamental theoretical point: even if Ireland's political economy can be *described* in terms of globalisation (which is an open, empirical question), does this mean it can also be *explained* in these terms? A key problem with the term 'globalisation' is that it invites reification: it implies something that is *doing* rather than being *done*, as if it were somehow an actor in its own right.[13] Yet, while contexts may present constraints on and/or opportunities for change, they cannot exhibit causal properties. Rather, it is the conduct of agents that is ultimately responsible for existing social conditions.[14] This highlights the need to be explicit about questions of structure (that is, context) and agency (that is, conduct), in order to avoid presenting a false dualism between the two.[15] Finally, this leads to the fourth issue: that is, the role of ideas. Whether or not globalisation exists in 'real' terms, ideas about globalisation may nevertheless play an important role in shaping the conduct of political decision-makers in Ireland. After all, human actors do not have perfect knowledge of the world in which they live but must instead interpret their context – and these interpretations may be wrong. In turn, it is these interpretations rather than the context itself that informs the way in which actors behave.[16] Thus, the political discourse of globalisation should be treated as an important object of analysis in its own right.[17]

It should be noted that while the volume is explicitly concerned with the globalisation controversy, it also seeks to engage with much broader debates about the dynamics of change in contemporary political economies. In particular, it emphasises the need to unpack processes of economic and policy change, highlighting their complexity and contingency. In so doing, the book adopts a diachronic and processual approach to change by examining Ireland's economic and policy trajectory over time. It also emphasises the need to explore the dynamic interaction between a range of spheres, including the national and international, the economic and the political, the structural and the agential, and the material and the ideational. Thus, while the volume is most clearly located within the political economy literature on globalisation, it also engages with a variety of literatures such as international relations, political sociology and economic history.

Methodology and sources

The methodology adopted in this book is inclusive rather than exclusive, employing both qualitative and quantitative methods. As Devine notes, the crucial question is not whether particular methods are 'better' or 'worse' than others *per se*, but rather whether they are appropriate to the theoretical and empirical questions addressed.[18] As this volume explores a broad range of issues and questions, it has entailed the use of a wide variety of primary and secondary sources. These include statistical data from both national and international bodies, party political manifestos, official policy documents, parliamentary debates, ministerial speeches and news journalism. In addition, a series of semi-structured interviews with high-ranking policy-makers, economic advisers and opinion formers in Ireland was undertaken for the research.[19] The methodology employed has been underpinned by the principle of triangulation, which essentially refers to the need to corroborate information by checking the accuracy of a particular source through reference to other sources.[20] In turn, this methodology has itself illuminated the sheer complexity of issues involved in this research.

Outline

The structure of this volume reflects its aims: to consider what can be understood by the term 'globalisation' and to test its utility in the study of political economy through analysis of the Irish case.

Chapter 1 provides an overview of the globalisation debate and considers what (if anything) the concept can offer in the analysis of social and political change. The chapter provides an overview of the literature so far, identifying five competing conceptions of globalisation. These are: globalisation as the borderless world; globalisation as a myth; globalisation as a complex (set of) process(es); globalisation as an opportunity and a constraint; and globalisation as a tendency. The chapter then reconsiders the concept of globalisation, and argues that it may be better to dispense with it altogether in analytical terms. The concept, it suggests, is unnecessary, misleading and dangerous. It is unnecessary because globalisation can reveal very little about the actual mechanisms of change producing political outcomes; it is misleading because the focus on globalisation serves to obscure these actual processes of change; and it is dangerous because it serves to shape current perceptions of policy alternatives. By this token, while the concept itself should be rejected, the way in which it is used (that is, its discursive construction) remains an important object of enquiry.

The book then turns to perhaps *the* test case for globalisation – the Irish Republic – in order to examine whether Ireland can indeed be considered a 'showpiece of globalisation'. Chapter 2 explores the nature of Ireland's economic transformation in the 1990s. In particular, it assesses both empirically and conceptually whether the Republic has indeed become the 'Celtic tiger'. In so doing, it engages with alternative claims that Ireland is in fact a 'paper tiger'. The chapter suggests that the picture is rather more complex than this binary distinction between Celtic and paper tiger implies, for Ireland's performance is impressive in some areas but less so in others. Yet this ambiguity is in itself interesting, for it points to the role of interpretation and ideas. The chapter thus also explores the role of discourses about the 'Celtic tiger' and the reasons why such discourses have taken hold. In so doing, it contends that while the 'Celtic tiger' concept is limited in analytical terms, it nevertheless possesses significant discursive power.

After this consideration of the nature of Ireland's transformation in chapter 2, chapter 3 explores the dynamics behind it. While there is significant debate about the reasons for Ireland's improved growth performance, many commentators point to the role of globalisation in shaping Ireland's growth. The chapter assesses such claims through analysis of a range of factors behind Irish economic growth such as trade openness, foreign direct investment, fiscal policy, European Union (EU) membership, human capital, social partnership and industrial policy. In so doing, it argues that there is simply no evidence to suggest that the dynamics behind Ireland's growth can be characterised in terms of 'globalisation'. The chapter also points to the significance of discursive factors in Ireland's success – in particular, the 'Celtic tiger' discourse has helped Ireland to attract inward investment. This complex range of factors means that Ireland can hardly be seen as a 'showpiece' – and certainly not of globalisation.

Chapter 4 turns from the issue of economic performance to that of policy change. Globalisation is often seen to have redefined the role of national economic management, so that states must increasingly prioritise market forces through neo-liberal economic strategies. Such accounts tend to assume not only that nation-states have radically altered course but that this is in itself a response to globalisation. In order to examine these claims, the chapter places the trajectory of the Irish state in historical perspective. It traces the development of Irish economic policy from 1921 (when the Republic was established) up to 1987 (which is widely recognised to mark the beginning of the current political project). In so doing, it rejects 'snapshot' accounts of change (evident in the posing of binary oppositions such as the 'active state' and the 'neo-liberal state'), instead arguing that the trajectory of the Irish state has been highly complex and, at times, contradictory.

Chapter 5 then focuses in on the path of economic policy since 1987. While some authors classify the contemporary Irish state as essentially distributive and developmental, others point to a distinctive shift towards neo-liberalism since 1987. Peadar Kirby, for instance,

INTRODUCTION

suggests that Ireland has been resituated as a 'competition state' in which social justice is subordinated to the needs of the market. In turn, he attributes this to the economic imperatives unleashed by globalisation.[21] The chapter explores this controversy through analysis of key areas of economic policy such as social partnership, public expenditure, industrial policy, privatisation and membership of the EU. While it identifies strong market-oriented tendencies in Irish economic policy, it nevertheless rejects claims that Ireland has been resituated as the model of a 'competition state'. Rather, important counter-tendencies (including a variety of social measures) are also apparent.

Chapter 5 thus explores the dynamics *of* policy change in Ireland; chapter 6 turns to the dynamics *behind* that change. While there is considerable debate about the reasons for policy change in Ireland, many authors nevertheless point to the central role of globalisation in shaping the trajectory of the Irish state. This is underpinned by a tendency to conflate the economic context of policy change with 'globalisation' and, in turn, to assume that policy change occurs as a direct and unmediated response to this context. Questioning such assumptions, chapter 6 explores the role that economic factors have played in shaping the developmental trajectory of the Irish state. These include domestic economic conditions, external trade, foreign direct investment and European integration. The chapter argues that these economic conditions simply cannot be conflated with 'globalisation'. Nor can they in themselves explain the development of Irish economic policy over time, which in turn suggests that other factors have been at work.

This disparity between claims about globalisation and the evidence for such claims invites the question of why globalisation is so widely invoked politically.[22] As argued in chapter 1, the very *idea* of 'globalisation' may in itself play a powerful role in shaping political outcomes. Chapter 7 explores this issue with respect to the Irish case. The chapter argues that ideas about globalisation have indeed come to play a central role in Irish political discourse, yielding real policy effects. In particular, while globalisation is seen as an opportunity for Ireland, it is also regarded as a constraint that drives the need for competitiveness. This in turn played a central role in shaping the responses and strategies of Irish policy-makers in the 1990s. The chapter then considers why such ideas have come to the fore in Ireland. As Schmidt notes,[23] for discourses to be successful they need to perform cognitive, normative, coordinative and communicative functions. The chapter argues that while globalisation discourses in Ireland have successfully performed all four of these functions in the past, the coordinative and communicative elements are beginning to weaken, in turn meaning that the current policy paradigm is becoming increasingly harder to sustain.

Finally, the conclusion provides a summary of these arguments and outlines the implications of the Irish case for other countries within and outside Europe. If the Irish Republic – supposedly the most globalised country in the world – is not in fact subject to the 'competitive imperatives of globalisation', then other nations, too, may have considerably more autonomy than is so often assumed.

Notes

1 D. Held, A. McGrew, D. Goldblatt and J. Perraton, *Global Transformations: Politics, Economics and Culture* (Stanford, CA Stanford University Press, 1999), p. 1.
2 M. Watson, 'International capital mobility in an era of globalisation: adding a political dimension to the "Feldstein–Horioka Puzzle"', *Politics*, 21: 2 (2001), pp. 81–92.
3 See for instance the characterisation of the 'sceptical' position put forward by both Dicken and Giddens – see P. Dicken, *Global Shift: Transforming the World Economy* (New York: Guilford Press, 1998), p. 3; A. Giddens, 'Runaway world: the Reith Lectures revisited – lecture 1' (1999), www.lse.ac.uk/Giddens.
4 C. Hay, 'Globalisation as a problem of political analysis: restoring agents to a "process without a subject" and politics to a logic of economic compulsion', *Cambridge Review of International Affairs*, 15: 3 (2002), pp. 379–92.
5 C. Hay and D. Marsh, 'Introduction: demystifying globalisation', in C. Hay and D. Marsh (eds), *Demystifying Globalisation* (London: Macmillan, 2000), p. 9; B. Rosamond, 'Babylon and on? Globalisation and international political economy', *Review of International Political Economy*, 10: 4 (2003), pp. 616–17; M. Watson, 'Rethinking capital mobility, re-regulating financial markets', *New Political Economy*, 4: 1 (1999), pp. 55–73.
6 L. Weiss, 'Introduction: bringing domestic institutions back in', in L. Weiss (ed.), *States in the Global Economy: Bringing Domestic Institutions Back In* (Cambridge: Cambridge University Press, 2003), p. 2.
7 Ibid., pp. 27–8.
8 For instance, Ireland has ranked first in the A. T. Kearney Globalisation Index for three years running – see 'Measuring globalisation: economic reversals, forward momentum', *Foreign Policy* (March/April 2004).
9 D. O'Hearn, 'Globalisation, "new tigers," and the end of the developmental state? The case of the Celtic Tiger', *Politics & Society*, 28: 1 (2000), p. 73.
10 See for instance K. Allen, *The Celtic Tiger: The Myth of Social Partnership in Ireland* (Manchester: Manchester University Press, 2000); P. Kirby, *The*

Celtic Tiger in Distress: Growth and Inequality in Ireland (Basingstoke: Palgrave, 2002); O'Hearn, 'Globalisation, "new tigers," and the end of the developmental state?', pp. 67–92.
11 D. Wincott, 'Globalisation and European integration', in Hay and Marsh, *Demystifying Globalisation*, p. 175.
12 See also C. Hay, 'What's globalisation got to do with it?' (2003), www.bham.ac.uk/POLSIS/department/staff/publications/hay_inaugural.htm.
13 C. Hay, 'Structure and agency', in D. Marsh and G. Stoker (eds), *Theory and Methods in Political Science* (London: Macmillan, 1995), p. 201.
14 R. Sibeon, 'Anti-reductionist sociology', *Sociology*, 33: 2 (1999), p. 318; C. Hay, 'Structure and agency', p. 201.
15 Hay and Marsh, 'Introduction: demystifying globalisation', p. 13.
16 C. Hay, *Political Analysis* (Basingstoke: Palgrave, 2002), p. 199.
17 C. Hay and N. Smith, 'Horses for Courses? The political discourse of globalisation and European integration in the UK and Ireland', *West European Politics*, 28: 1, p. 125.
18 F. Devine, 'Qualitative analysis', in Marsh and Stoker, *Theory and Methods in Political Science*, pp. 138–41.
19 Interviewees included: the secretary general of the government; the assistant secretary of the Public Expenditure Division in the Department of Finance; the assistant secretary of the Personnel and Renumeration Division at the Department of Finance; the assistant secretary of the Enterprise Competitiveness Division in the Department of Enterprise, Trade and Employment; the assistant secretary general of the Department of Education and Science; a senior representative of the EU Division at the Department of Foreign Affairs; the chief executive of the Industrial Development Agency (IDA); the Director of the Economic and Social Research Institute (ESRI); a senior economist with the Department of Finance Economic Forecasting Unit; a senior European Commission representative in Ireland; the deputy head of economic analysis, research and publication in the Central Bank of Ireland; and the director of economic affairs for the Irish Business and Employers Confederation (IBEC). All interviews were semi-structured and open rather than tightly structured and closed. A broad range of issues was covered, but respondents were asked in particular to elaborate upon Ireland's economic policy and performance since the late 1980s. Interviewees have requested that their names are not directly linked to quotations within the text. As with other qualitative materials used for this research, the interview transcriptions were coded and analysed using QSR NVivo.
20 A. Bryman, *Social Research Methods* (Oxford: Oxford University Press, 2001), p. 509.
21 Kirby, *The Celtic Tiger in Distress*, pp. 143–4.
22 C. Hay and N. Smith, 'Horses for courses?' p. 21.
23 V. A. Schmidt, *The Fuliures of European Capitalism* (Oxford: Oxford University Press, 2002), pp. 277–89.

1

The globalisation debate

Once hailed as the buzzword of the 1990s, the concept of 'globalisation' is still going strong. It has generated an enormous literature across a range of academic disciplines and is frequently appealed to by journalists and policy-makers alike. It is perhaps inevitable that such a ubiquitous term should possess no one clear definition but instead be interpreted in a variety of different ways. But what *is* startling is the sheer diversity of phenomena associated with 'globalisation'. These range from financial liberalisation, European integration and the North–South divide to telephone access, environmental degradation, Hollywood films and the Big Mac.[1]

Given this lack of clarity, it is worth spending some time examining the different ways in which globalisation has been, and indeed should be, understood. To provide an exhaustive account of the vast and expanding literature on globalisation is clearly an impossible task. Nevertheless, several core conceptions – reflecting rather different perspectives on the meaning, nature and impact of 'globalisation' – can be identified. These are: globalisation as the borderless world; globalisation as a myth; globalisation as a complex process or set of processes; globalisation as an opportunity and a constraint; and globalisation as a tendency. The aim of this chapter is to provide an overview of these different positions and, in turn, to reconsider what, if anything, the concept can offer in the analysis of social and political change.

Globalisation as the borderless world

The original position in the globalisation debate is associated with a range of highly influential authors such as Ohmae, Gray, O'Brien and Reich.[2] While this position has fallen out of favour somewhat within academic circles, it continues to hold considerable sway among policy-making elites. It has been described as the 'first-wave', 'extreme',

THE GLOBALISATION DEBATE

'strong' or 'radical' thesis but is perhaps most widely known as the 'hyperglobalist thesis'. As this position is already well documented it needs only a brief consideration.

As the hyperglobalists famously assert, a new world order has arisen that is truly borderless in character. Indeed, O'Brien argues that we have witnessed 'the end of geography... a state of economic development where geographical location no longer matters'.[3] In particular, the erosion of *economic* borders is seen as crucial, for the 'hallmark of this new globality is the mobile economy'.[4] Flows of goods, capital, labour and information are perceived to move effortlessly across national boundaries. For example, authors point to the dramatic rise in world trade and foreign direct investment (FDI) in the 1980s and 1990s. As table 1.1 shows, between 1982 and 2002 world exports nearly quadrupled (from $2.1 trillion to $7.8 trillion) and the stock

Table 1.1 World total of foreign direct investment and international production, 1982–2002

	Values at current prices ($ billions)			Annual growth rate (%)		
	1982	1990	2002	1986–90	1991–5	1996–2000
FDI inflows	59	209	651	23.1	21.1	40.2
FDI outflows	28	242	647	25.7	16.5	35.7
FDI inward stock	802	1,954	7,123	14.7	9.3	17.2
FDI outward stock	595	1,763	6,866	18.0	10.6	16.8
Cross-border mergers and acquisitions	–	151	370	25.9	24.0	51.5
Sales of foreign affiliates	2,767	5,675	17,685	16.0	10.1	10.9
Gross product of foreign affiliates	640	1,458	3,437	17.3	6.7	7.9
Total assets of foreign affiliates	2,091	5,899	26,543	18.3	13.9	19.2
Export of foreign affiliates	722	1,197	2,613	13.5	7.6	9.6
Employment of foreign affiliates	19,375	24,262	53,094	5.5	2.9	14.2
GDP	10,805	21,672	32,227	10.8	5.6	1.3
Gross fixed capital formation	2,286	4,819	6,422	13.4	4.2	1.0
Exports of goods and non-factor services	2,053	4,300	7,838	15.6	5.4	3.4

Source: UNCTAD, *World Investment Report 2003: FDI Policies for Development – National and International Perspectives* (New York: United Nations, 2003), p. 3.

of FDI rose more than tenfold (with inward stocks now exceeding $7 trillion). Indeed, the estimated value-added of foreign affiliates now accounts for around a tenth of world gross domestic product (GDP).[5]

Conceptualised essentially in economic terms, globalisation is nevertheless believed to have profound political implications. Economic activity, it is argued, now 'defines the landscape on which all institutions, including the apparatus of statehood, must operate'.[6] The hypermobility of goods, capital, labour and information is seen not only to erode national economic borders but also to reduce dramatically the power of national governments. Rather than being able to mediate market forces through regulation and social protectionism, states are now forced to compete with each other in a process of natural selection in which only the leanest survive. For example, the risk of capital flight due to its heightened mobility means that high taxation in order to fund social welfare is now seen as a luxury that no government can afford.[7]

Globalisation is therefore believed to produce a qualitatively novel degree of convergence between nations in terms of their economic strategies. Since globalisation 'eliminates poor performers',[8] programmes which deviate from free-market capitalism are deemed no longer viable. Globalisation is thus seen to represent the triumph of neo-liberalism, the end of social democracy and even the end of the nation-state itself.[9] The collapse of the Soviet Union and the crisis of the East Asian 'developmental states' are seen to reinforce this further, as are the existence of regional trading blocs – 'witness Europe, hurtling towards economic union'.[10] As Castells writes: 'a new brand of leaner, meaner capitalism [is] alone at last in its planetary reach'.[11]

It is worth noting that there is considerable divergence as to whether the ascendancy of global capitalism is a 'good thing' or not. For some, economic liberalism encourages the spread of efficiency and wealth, creating 'a better life for all of us'.[12] For others, globalisation represents the oppression of global capitalism against which there can be no political resistance.[13] Yet, despite this normative divergence, such perspectives are remarkably similar.[14] Both conceive globalisation in highly structuralist terms, affording little or no room for political agency. Indeed, globalisation is *itself* often presented as the agent of change. As Greider writes: 'Imagine a wondrous new machine, strong and supple... Think of this awesome machine running over open terrain and ignoring familiar boundaries... this machine has no wheel nor any internal governor to control the speed and direction. It is sustained by its own forward motion, guided by its own appetites.'[15] In

THE GLOBALISATION DEBATE 13

this sense, globalisation is conceived as a harsh material reality that can be neither resisted nor controlled. The hyperglobalists are therefore simply not interested in the role that ideas may play in shaping change. Quite the contrary: 'The only option people have is to catch up with reality.'[16] In sum, then, the hyperglobalists conceive globalisation as an inexorable economic logic that severely constrains the autonomy of political actors, not least at the national level.

Globalisation as a myth

The hyperglobalists' rather dramatic account of contemporary developments has been challenged by a number of authors such as Hirst and Thompson, Rugman, Wade and Zysman.[17] At first sight, this 'sceptical' (or 'second-wave') approach been quite successful: after all, few authors would now claim to embrace the hyperglobalist thesis. Yet the sceptical thesis has not permeated the globalisation literature as much as it perhaps deserves to. Despite the fact that this position is widely known, its core claims are often sidelined or forgotten altogether in many globalisation accounts. It is thus worth outlining the sceptical thesis in some detail here.

In particular, while the sceptics acknowledge the significance of such developments as financial deregulation, deindustrialisation and flexibilisation, they reject claims that these represent the rise of a new global economic structure.[18] Indeed, they note, in some respects the world economy is actually *less* open and integrated than it was before World War I. In terms of the ratio of trade to GDP, for example, countries such as Japan, the UK and the Netherlands were more open in 1913 than in 1995, whereas France and Germany were only slightly less open (see figure 1.1).

For the sceptics, moreover, 'the world economy is far from being genuinely "global"'.[19] Integration has not occurred across the world or even between the North and South. Hirst and Thompson estimate that just 16 per cent of global FDI flows were received by 54–70 per cent of the world's population in the early 1990s.[20] Indeed, Wade finds that North–South trade has actually fallen as a proportion of total trade.[21] Africa, for example, secured just 2.2 per cent of world merchandise trade in 2002 compared to 4.5 per cent in 1983 and 7.5 per cent in 1948.[22] Instead, the sceptics note that the bulk of trade and investment is concentrated within the 'triad' of North America, Europe and Japan. For example, the triad has accounted for around 80 per cent of the world's outward FDI stocks and around 50–60 per cent of the

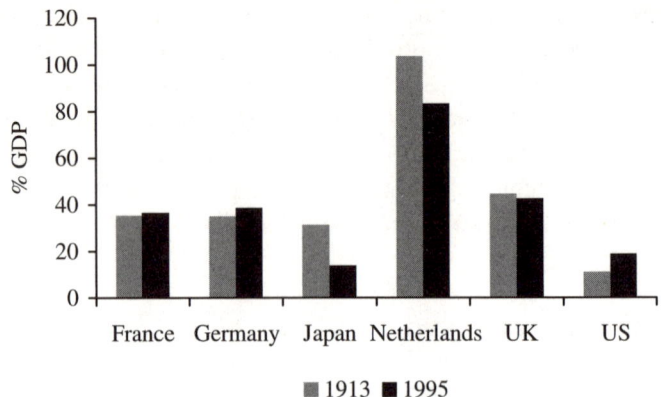

Figure 1.1 Ratio of merchandise trade to GDP in current prices, 1913 and 1995

Note: Merchandise trade refers to exports and imports combined.
Source: Hirst, P. and G. Thompson, *Globalisation in Question: The International Economy and the Possibilities of Governance* (Cambridge: Polity, 1999), p. 2.

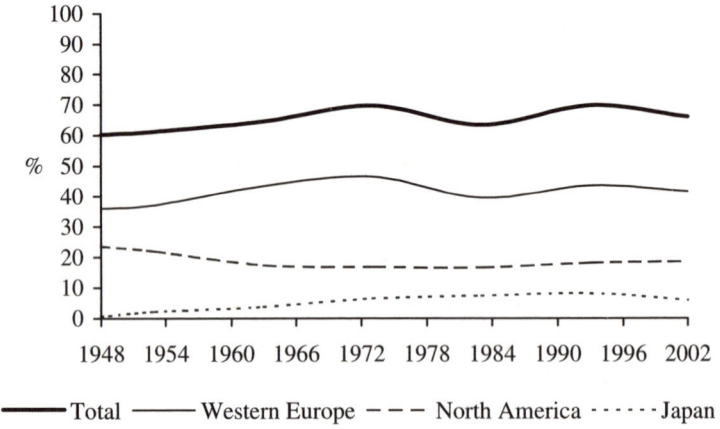

Figure 1.2 Share of world merchandise trade by 'triad' countries, 1948–2002

Note: World merchandise trade refers to exports and imports combined.
Source: calculated from WTO, *International Trade Statistics 2003* (Geneva: World Trade Organisation, 2003), p. 32.

world's inward FDI stock throughout the period 1985–2002.[23] As figure 1.2 shows, triad countries have also accounted for around 60–70 per cent of world merchandise trade throughout the post-war period. Nor can this process of 'triadisation' itself be cited as evidence of globalisation, as the hyperglobalists assume. Rather, the sceptics find that the 'strongest and most intense' trade and investment relations exist *within* the regional blocs rather than *between* them.[24] As they note, regional trade agreements are preferential in nature and thus do not represent genuine free trade. While they may promote trade within the bloc, they also serve to divert trade from outside the bloc.[25] For the sceptics, then, a process of regionalisation is apparent that is quite distinct from – and indeed contradicts – globalisation.

For the sceptics, the concept of free capital mobility is also greatly exaggerated. Rather, capital – and particularly fixed capital such as advanced industrial machinery – is 'strongly rooted in place', not only in physical terms but also in social terms.[26] The cost of 'exit' – with the loss of physical and human resources already invested in a plant – is thus far from negligible. Indeed, Ruigrok and van Tulder conclude (after evaluating the world's top hundred core companies) that 'not one of these can be dubbed truly "global", "footloose" or "borderless"'.[27] Instead, firms remain distinctly multi*national*, operating from a distinct home base. For example, Wade finds that most firms hold the bulk of their assets and employees in their home country, and the few exceptions still hold the largest single bloc of assets and employees there. Moreover, 'both strategic decision-making and innovation are concentrated in the [corporations'] home nations', with most research and development, for example, being undertaken there.[28] Even finance capital is not as mobile as the hyperglobalists assume. For example, Feldstein and Horioka point to a strong correlation between the rate of domestic savings and the rate of domestic investment – something they argue would simply not exist in an era of perfect capital mobility.[29]

For the sceptics, the world economy is far from being globalised; rather it is 'an open international economy that is still fundamentally characterised by exchange between relatively distinct national economies and in which many outcomes, such as the competitive performance of firms and sectors, are substantially determined by processes occurring at the national level'.[30] Claims that the nation-state is in decline are thus 'at best, premature and, at worst, ill founded'.[31] Indeed, the sceptics point to the growth of government in the postwar period. For example, the share of government expenditures in GDP averaged 47 per cent in the mid-1990s, compared to just 21 per cent before World War II.[32]

Nor is there a 'race to the bottom' in terms of costs. As Navarro, Schmitt and Astudillo note, if the hyperglobalists' predictions are correct then the period of deregulation of trade and capital flows (1980–2000) should correspond with a clear convergence towards reduced welfare spending and, indeed, a shift in the funding of welfare from taxes on mobile factors (such as capital) to fixed factors (such as labour). In stark contrast, however, they find that not only has there been an *increase* in both social expenditures and tax revenues as a share of GDP in most Organisation for Economic Co-operation and Development (OECD) countries, but also a rise in the *share* of revenues from taxes on capital during this period (see table 1.2).[33] Moreover, these rising costs are not associated with a decline in economic performance. Quite the contrary: Navarro, Schmitt and Astudillo find that social democratic countries 'fared no worse' than liberal ones in the 1990s, with Norway, Austria and Denmark all growing faster than liberal economies such as Canada, Japan and the UK in the period 1989–99, despite having more extensive welfare states.[34] On these grounds, the sceptics argue, there is simply no evidence to suggest that the future of either social democracy or the welfare state is bleak.

Table 1.2 Social expenditure and tax revenue (selected indicators), 1980–98

	Social public expenditure (% GDP)		Tax revenue (% GDP)		Taxes on corporate profits and capital gains (% total revenue)	
	1980	1997	1979	1998	1979	1998
Austria	23.9	26.2	39.9	44.3	3.5	4.8
Denmark	29.4	30.8	44.0	50.1	3.1	5.6
Finland	18.9	29.5	37.0	46.3	3.7	9.0
France	23.5	29.6	39.8	45.5	4.8	6.0
Germany	25.4	27.7	36.3	37.2	6.0	4.4
Greece	11.5	22.2	24.2	33.5	3.5	6.3
Ireland	17.6	17.9	30.5	32.3	5.7	10.7
Italy	18.4	26.9	44.0	41.1	8.3	7.0
Japan	10.5	14.8	24.6	28.3	20.8	13.3
Netherlands	28.9	25.9	44.0	41.1	5.8	10.6
Spain	16.3	20.9	23.0	34.4	4.9	7.3
Sweden	29.8	33.7	48.8	51.8	3.1	5.7
UK	18.4	21.9	33.5	36.4	7.7	10.9
US	13.9	16.5	26.8	25.7	11.9	9.0

Source: adapted from Navarro, V., J. Schmitt and J. Astudillo, 'Is globalisation undermining the welfare state?', *Cambridge Journal of Economics*, 28 (2004), pp. 133–52.

Hence, for the sceptics, globalisation is a 'myth'[35] – it simply does not exist. Yet, while their position may at first sight appear to be the polar opposite of the hyperglobalist thesis, it should also be noted that the two positions do share some common ground. In particular, like the hyperglobalists, the sceptics conceive globalisation in economic terms – although they reject rather than affirm its existence. As Hirst and Thompson contend, those who adopt a broader approach – to incorporate sociology, cultural studies and social geography – serve to 'dilute' the crucial issue of whether economic processes are indeed undermining the autonomy of national governments.[36] It is for this reason that Hay and Marsh describe the sceptical thesis as 'essentially derivative' of the hyperglobalisation thesis. Both approaches, they argue, focus on the material reality of globalisation, giving little consideration to the role of ideas in shaping outcomes.[37] This is perhaps an exaggeration, for authors such as Hirst and Thompson *do* recognise that ideas about globalisation are highly influential and serve to shape policy outcomes. Indeed, this is a key reason for their desire to question the extreme globalisation thesis: 'These myths still need puncturing before they do impossible damage to both social stability and economic performance.'[38] Nevertheless, Hay and Marsh are right to note that the sceptics do not examine the role of ideas as independent causal variables in their own right, instead choosing to focus on measuring the extent of economic globalisation. In short, then, the sceptical theorists (like the hyperglobalists) are interested in globalisation as an economic logic, but (unlike the hyperglobalists) argue that it simply does not exist.

Globalisation as a complex process

A growing body of literature – encompassing authors from a range of disciplines such as international relations, political geography, international political economy (IPE) and sociology – has attempted to counter the criticisms of the sceptical authors. In so doing, they have tried to reclaim the concept of globalisation by redefining it. Rather than conceiving globalisation as an 'all-encompassing end-state',[39] authors such as Axford, Dicken, Giddens and Held et al. argue that it should instead be seen as multifaceted, multidimensional, interconnected, uneven and contradictory.[40] This complex (or 'transformationist') approach to globalisation has been remarkably successful – at least in terms of its popularity. While few authors would now describe themselves as hyperglobalists, it is widely accepted that globalisation *does* exist but as a highly complex process or set of processes.

For the complex theorists, then, globalisation is 'the most satisfactory descriptive label for the current historical era'.[41] As Dicken notes, while in *quantitative* terms the current level of integration is comparable to that of the pre-World War I era, in *qualitative* terms it is very different. The current era is characterised by 'deep' integration, including the production (rather than just the trade) of goods and services.[42] Globalisation thus represents a 'more complete and penetrating stage of the internationalisation process'.[43] However, this does not mean that the world is now borderless. Rather, the complex theorists emphasise the considerable geographical unevenness of the world economic map, with each activity being grounded in a specific location. Yet this is seen as part and parcel of the globalisation process, which 'represents, above all, a greater tying-in and subjugation of localities . . . [to] global forces'.[44] For instance, Axford agrees that few corporations are truly global but nevertheless points to the 'self-conscious, "global rationale"' adopted by many firms.[45] As Scholte writes, globalisation does not mean the end of geography but instead 'entails a reconfiguration of geography, so that social space is no longer wholly mapped in terms of territorial places'. In this sense, territorial space exists alongside and interacts with global spaces.[46]

Globalisation is therefore believed to entail 'a reconfiguration of power at all levels and the production of new spaces'.[47] The rise of macro-regions is seen to illustrate this. While regional trade blocs may possess defensive qualities, authors such as Held et al. argue that these may nevertheless serve to deepen the impact of globalisation. For example, by promoting liberalisation, trade blocs encourage new members to open up to the global economy as a whole. Thus, while trade and investment flows are indeed concentrated within regional blocs, this is in itself seen as part of the broader globalisation process.[48]

Crucially, this reconfiguration of power is believed to have important implications for national governance. Globalisation, it is argued, has redefined – if not eradicated – the role of nation-states.[49] State power is seen to have shifted not only upwards (to international organisations and movements) and downwards (for example to local pressure groups) but also sideways to market actors (such as multinational corporations).[50] This shift in power from states to markets is believed to heighten competitiveness between nations, so that governments must increasingly prioritise economic rather than social issues. In this sense, while government intervention has grown, globalisation also serves to erode the power and authority of nation-states. Indeed, Cox argues that government has been 'reduced to a question of management'.[51]

This clearly has implications for the role of the welfare state. Authors such as Rhodes and Mény contend that although (European) welfare states are not in demise, they have nevertheless reached an impasse. While welfare spending has indeed increased, it is much lower than one might expect once factors such as demographic pressure have been accounted for.[52] The complex globalisation theorists therefore identify some signs of convergence, although not necessarily towards stark neo-liberalism. For example, Cerny points to the rise of the 'competition state' and Jessop to the 'Schumpetarian workfare state', both characterised by their commitment to competitiveness rather than to redistribution and social inclusion.[53] Crucially, these authors attribute these developments (at least in part) to competitive imperatives unleashed by globalisation such as the heightened mobility of capital flows. As Coates writes, 'globalisation may not have obliterated the space for social reform, but it has definitely squeezed it'.[54]

Yet the complex globalisation theorists also contend that globalisation should not be conceived as primarily economic. Rather, it takes place within a variety of spheres including the cultural, the political, the technological, the ecological and the criminal.[55] Globalisation is thus a highly complex (set of) process(es) rather than an inexorable economic logic. This means that it need not be conceived in purely structuralist terms. Rather, authors point to the role of agents in the globalisation process, including transnational business elites, supranational agencies and even states themselves.[56] Moreover, although some authors (such as Held et al. and Dicken) make no attempt to examine the role of ideas, others (such as Cerny and Cox) do give some consideration to this issue. In particular, they point to the increasingly hegemonic discourse of globalisation, associated with neo-liberal ideology and the logic of competitiveness.[57] Ultimately, though, these discourses are seen to derive from the 'reality' of globalisation itself and, as such, are not treated as objects of analysis in their own right.

Globalisation as an opportunity and a constraint

Along with the complex thesis, another position to achieve considerable prominence is that of the self-titled 'new institutionalists'. As this name suggests, authors such as Hall and Soskice, Garrett, Weiss, Thelen and Scharpf aim to 'bring institutions back in' to the study of globalisation and, indeed, capitalism more generally.[58] For these authors, other approaches have failed to devote sufficient attention to this issue. As Weiss contends, although the hyperglobalist and complex theorists are right to point to the challenges of openness and interdependence, they do not consider in any detail how such pressures are mediated by domestic institutions. Similarly, the sceptical thesis is limited by its focus on measuring the extent of globalisation, for this can reveal little about how national authorities can and do manage the challenges of openness.[59]

For the institutionalists, then, discussions about broader processes of globalisation have generated more heat than light. Instead, analysis should focus on the role of institutions in mediating and managing these processes. While nations may experience common pressures, the existence of different institutional and cultural environments means that they respond in different ways and achieve different outcomes. In this sense, 'domestic institutions, depending on their characteristics, can hinder or enable states to respond to new challenges and accomplish new tasks, thus softening, neutralising, or exaggerating the potentially constraining effects of global markets'.[60]

Indeed, for these authors, globalisation does not just constrain nation-states but may actually enable them.[61] As Hobson notes, many globalisation accounts are limited by an 'either/or' framework: 'either globalisation is all-powerful and states are impotent; or globalisation is weak and states are dominant'. But globalisation may actually create important opportunities for states.[62] While exposure to global markets poses significant challenges for national governments, it also creates instability and insecurity, which can, in turn, encourage governments to develop initiatives in national systems of innovation and social protection.[63] Authors such as Cameron and Rodrik argue that the greater the levels of openness, the greater the incentive for governments to adopt an assertive role. Since countries with open economies are more exposed to external risk, governments are encouraged to increase their intervention in order to protect the economy from unpredictable market forces. These authors therefore identify a clear *positive* correlation between size of government and exposure to international markets.[64]

Indeed, Garrett argues that it is not *despite* but *because of* globalisation that social democratic countries have continued to thrive. This is because globalisation rewards 'coherent' strategies – whether market liberal or social democratic corporatist – but punishes 'incoherent' regimes. Social democratic corporatist regimes can offer significant benefits to business (such as co-operation between employers and employees and a highly skilled workforce) that provide greater returns on investment than would a low taxation environment.[65] In a similar vein, Steinmo argues that the benefits of being in a high-cost location can 'far outweigh the costs'. After conducting more than 50 interviews with corporate executives in the US and EU, he finds that factors such as wage rates, quality of workforce, access to markets, quality of infrastructure and political stability – which can all be positively affected by high taxes – were generally considered more important than low taxes.[66] On these grounds, the institutionalists agree wholeheartedly with the sceptics that there is no 'race to the bottom'. However, unlike the sceptics, this does not lead them to reject globalisation as a 'myth'. Rather, globalisation is associated with continuing – and even growing – *divergence* between market liberal and social democratic regimes.[67]

In this sense, the institutionalists do not question globalisation itself but rather seek to confront 'the monolithic political dynamic conventionally associated with globalisation'.[68] Yet, as Hay notes, it is for this reason that authors such as Hall and Soskice and Garrett only succeed in modifying, rather than dispelling, the globalisation orthodoxy. Rather than being seen to drive a shift towards neo-liberalism, globalisation is assumed to create a bifurcated path (towards market liberalism, on the one hand, and social democratic corporatism on the other). Ultimately, though, it is *globalisation* that is seen to be driving change forward and, indeed, to restrict the parameters of what is politically possible. Moreover, the assumption that social democratic outcomes are dependent upon social democratic institutions leaves little hope for *non*-social democratic countries to pursue a more progressive path.[69] Thus, authors such as Garrett try but ultimately fail to open up genuine space for policy alternatives and, indeed, for political agency.

The institutionalists do give some consideration to the role of ideas, however. The work of Vivien Schmidt is notable in this regard. For Schmidt, factors such as economic vulnerability and institutional capacity cannot in themselves explain policy developments within (European) states. After all, in some countries changes such as membership of European Monetary Union (EMU) have represented a radical shift in long-established policy trajectories that have challenged both the narrow self-interests of large sections of the population and widely held national values. Thus, while economic vulnerability and political institutional capacity may provide both the impetus and the means for a policy shift, they cannot explain 'how policy actors create an interactive consensus for change'.[70] For Schmidt, the role of discourse must also be seen to play a crucial role. Discourses 'matter' not only in ideational terms (by generating the ideas and beliefs about whether a particular policy is both necessary and appropriate) but also in interactive terms (by providing both a common language and framework for elites to construct a policy programme and the means for elites to communicate that programme to the general public). In this sense, 'discourse serves not only to generate the ideas for change . . . but also to legitimate them'.[71]

As we shall see, Schmidt's position has much in common with that of authors such as Hay and Rosamond (discussed below). Yet, in contrast to these authors (and much like the complex theorists), Schmidt appears to assume that discourses of globalisation largely reflect the material reality of globalisation. There can be 'little doubt', she argues, that 'globalisation has been a potent force for change in national economies' (for example by promoting market liberalisation through the internationalisation of trade and finance).[72] In this sense, globalisation is not in itself seen as a discursive construction. Rather, discourses about the need for policy adaptation have arisen 'in response to the pressures of globalisation and Europeanisation'. Indeed, the need for legitimising discourses in order to secure public consent for policy change 'only increases' as globalisation progresses.[73] Once again, then, globalisation is seen as a crucial driving force for change.

It should be noted, though, that not all institutionalist accounts accept the significance of globalisation in this way. For example, Navarro, Schmitt and Astudillo (mentioned earlier) situate themselves within the institutionalist literature and yet are keen to challenge claims that globalisation is responsible for changes in the welfare state.[74] However, while the institutionalist perspective is by no means synonymous with the belief that globalisation has promoted policy change, many prominent institutionalists have nevertheless come to adopt precisely this assumption.

Globalisation as a tendency

It is within this context that authors such as Hay and Marsh have sought to challenge the conventional wisdom that globalisation is driving policy change within (and outside) Europe. In so doing, they seek to 'demystify' the concept by redefining how we see globalisation in the first place. These authors describe themselves as the 'third wave' of globalisation theory but their view might also be labelled the 'contingent globalisation thesis'.

In particular, Hay and Marsh emphasise the need to 'bring the subject back in' to the study of globalisation. In most accounts, they argue, globalisation is treated as 'a process without a subject'; that is, as if it functions independently of the intentions and actions of human subjects.[75] Indeed, globalisation is often assumed to exhibit causal properties of its own, as if it were somehow an actor in its own right. Yet globalisation is not a 'real thing' and, as such, cannot actually *do* anything. For Hay and Marsh, then, globalisation must be seen as a description rather than an explanation and, indeed, as a consequence rather than a cause. On these grounds, globalisation is best conceived as a *tendency* (to which there may be strong counter-tendencies) rather than as a causal *process* in its own right.[76]

In seeking to 'bring the subject back in' to the study of globalisation, authors such as Hay and Rosamond also emphasise the role of ideas in shaping economic and political outcomes.[77] After all, actors must interpret their environment in order to formulate and act upon decisions, and it is these interpretations – rather than the environment itself – that ultimately shape their behaviour.[78] This means that in one respect globalisation *can* be appealed to as a causal factor: when ideas about globalisation create material effects. In acting as if globalisation were real, policy-makers may serve to produce the very outcomes they attribute to globalisation itself.[79]

For the contingent theorists, these concepts can help explain current developments in the international political economy. For instance, Hay wholeheartedly agrees with the institutionalists that social expenditure can enhance economic performance (for instance by helping to provide social stability and a skilled labour force). However, he also concurs with the complex theorists that, despite the secular increase in welfare expenditure, some retrenchment has occurred once demand factors (such as demographic change) are accounted for. For Hay, the answer to this apparent paradox lies in the role played by ideas about globalisation. As he writes: 'the space for alternative welfare trajectories does indeed exist, but it is no longer perceived to exist'.[80] For instance, both the hyperglobalist and complex theorists assume that increased taxation in order to fund welfare spending is no longer viable due to the threat of capital exit. Hay dismisses this claim as false, for it may be more costly for capital to exit (and thus lose resources already invested in a plant) than it is to pay higher taxes. Yet if governments *believe* capital will exit, this may be enough to prevent taxes being raised. In this sense, the perceived threat of capital exit can be as powerful as actual exit.[81]

Indeed, Hay and Rosamond argue that discourses of globalisation are powerful not only if they are perceived to be *true* but also if they are perceived to be *useful*. In particular, policy-makers may appeal to globalisation as an external imperative in order to depoliticise strategies that could otherwise prove unpopular with their electorates. The 'logic of no alternative' often associated with globalisation thus provides politicians with the perfect alibi.[82] Yet, as Hay and Rosamond also note, there is no single unifying discourse of globalisation; rather, the concept is used in different ways within different contexts. For example, in some contexts it is appealed to as the threat of homogenisation, whereas in others it is presented as a desirable yet contingent outcome. Moreover, in some European states it is European integration rather than globalisation that is appealed to as an external economic imperative.[83]

Such discursive differences suggest that ideas about globalisation do not simply reflect its material reality, as is so often assumed. For, if (European) states were exposed to similar external challenges, there would be no need for this discursive variation.[84] Indeed, Hay argues that the empirical evidence for globalisation is, at best, highly suspect and, at worst, demonstrably false. For example, he uses gravity models to demonstrate that geographical proximity is becoming more rather than less important for EU-European economies in terms of their trade and investment flows. For Hay, this points to growing regionalisation (or, more specifically, EU-isation) rather than globalisation. Indeed, if anything, this EU-isation is promoting *de*globalisation over time.[85]

This relates to a further point, for the contingent theorists are not only interested in the role of discourses in explaining political outcomes. They point, for instance, to the significance of European integration (and particularly EMU) in shifting the terrain in which states operate.[86] Hay identifies 'powerful neoliberalising tendencies in the institutional architecture of EMU itself', which 'threaten the incremental dilution of all European social models'. In particular, he points to the deflationary bias 'enshrined at the heart of EMU' by the Maastricht convergence criteria and, now, the Stability and Growth Pact.[87] In turn, though, such developments cannot themselves be seen as inevitable and non-negotiable. Rather, they are 'contingent, contested and above all authored politically'.[88] For example, Verdun emphasises

THE GLOBALISATION DEBATE

the role of monetarist ideas in shaping the institutional architecture of EMU; indeed, without the strong convergence of these ideas 'it is unlikely that EMU would have happened'.[89]

In sum, the contingent theorists argue that the term 'globalisation' *can* be retained – but only if it is understood as a tendency rather than as a causal process in its own right. Moreover, it is the actions and ideas of human subjects that are crucial when understanding processes of social and political change.

Deconstructing 'globalisation'

Often couched in highly sophisticated terms, the globalisation literature has raised important questions about how to conceptualise social, political and economic change.[90] What is problematic about much of the literature, however, is that it attempts to *answer* these questions in terms of 'globalisation'. To suggest that significant developments in the international political economy are taking place is one thing; to characterise these processes in terms of 'globalisation' is quite another. As will now be discussed, the concept of globalisation can in fact tell us little about our contemporary experience. In this sense, it may be best to dispense with the term altogether for analytical purposes.

Perhaps the most obvious criticism of globalisation is that it is a vague and ambiguous concept. In fact, this argument has been made time and time again within the globalisation literature. However, most authors also tend to take the view that there is no smoke without fire. For example, Held et al. argue that globalisation is 'the cliché of our times' but then go on to suggest that clichés often contain elements of truth.[91] Indeed, it is now standard practice to begin with the claim that globalisation is vague and ambiguous – but then to put forward an alternative definition (which, of course, is presented as preferable to all the others). Yet the concept of globalisation is little more than an umbrella term used to lump together a number of actual processes of change. Indeed, the term is often used to signify processes that do not actually exist.

This highlights a fundamental problem with the umbrella term of globalisation – it is extremely difficult (if not impossible) to falsify. The 'complex' definition of globalisation in particular is so broad that it covers phenomena as diverse as the internet and EMU. This makes it extremely difficult to unpack and, in turn, to investigate empirically. Not only does the complex thesis cover processes that are far from global (such as the rise of regional trading blocs), but by defining globalisation as uneven and contradictory, any *counter*-tendencies can also conveniently be accounted for. This leaves us asking not so much what globalisation *is* but what it is *not*.[92] By defining globalisation so broadly, however, the complex globalisation thesis is unable to answer this question.

Surely, if the concept is to possess any meaning at all, it must refer to processes or tendencies that are (or at least are becoming) genuinely 'global'.[93] This means that globalisation cannot simply be conflated with such factors as trade openness, FDI or European integration. Rather, for these factors to be cited as evidence of globalisation, they must themselves be becoming truly global (rather than regionalised or triadised, for instance). This is in turn an open and empirical question. In fact, there is little evidence to suggest that truly 'global' tendencies are apparent. For instance, Chortareas and Pelagidis find that trade flows are becoming increasingly concentrated *within* specific regional trading blocs rather than between them, suggesting that a process of regionalisation is apparent that is not in turn translating into broader globalisation.[94] Similarly, Hay finds that both trade and investment flows within Europe are actually becoming 'deglobalised' in that geographical proximity has become more, rather than less, important.[95] Even access to the internet – often seen as the driver of globalisation – remains highly limited.[96] This book thus adopts a strict rather than broad definition of globalisation when examining processes of change. *If specific tendencies are not becoming truly 'global' in character then they cannot be cited as evidence of globalisation.*

This lack of empirical evidence is not the only reason to be sceptical of the term 'globalisation', however. Even if genuinely global tendencies *were* apparent, the term should still be resisted on theoretical (as opposed to empirical) grounds. As various authors have noted, there is a marked tendency to reify the concept of globalisation, ascribing causal properties to it.[97] But globalisation is not an actor and, as such, cannot act. This confusion of structure and agency – and of description and explanation – is misleading, for it underpins a tendency to see outcomes as predetermined rather than contingent.[98] Ultimately, it is the choices and actions of human agents that are responsible for existing social conditions.[99] The confusion of structure and agency is also dangerous. For, if outcomes are predetermined 'then we are all mere automata, passive dupes of structures beyond our comprehension and over which we exert no influence'.[100] How then can we ever hope to challenge the status quo?

For Hay, the dangers inherent in appealing to globalisation as a causal logic mean that it should be used only as a descriptor.[101] But the very nature of the term 'globalisation' seems to invite reification. After all, it does not simply refer to phenomena that are 'global' but actually suggests that they are being global*ised*. This clearly implies something that is active – something that is doing rather than being done. To avoid this potential for reification, why not simply dispense with the term altogether? For, as Hirst and Thompson note, even cautious arguments often provide evidence that is 'then used carelessly to bolster more extreme ones, to build a community of usage when there needs to be strict differentiation of meanings'. In turn, this community of usage serves to confuse public policy and debate, thus 'reinforcing the view that political actors can accomplish less than is actually possible in a global system'.[102] Rather than using globalisation as a descriptor, then, why not simply refer to (specific) 'global tendencies' instead?

This discussion may well raise the question: if globalisation has so little analytical utility, why devote considerable attention to it in the first place? Perhaps the most important reason to do so is that the concept remains extremely influential, not only in academic and journalistic discourse but also within policy-making circles. The competitive imperatives of globalisation are widely seen to set limits on what is possible in policy-making terms. As the contingent theorists rightly note, this discursive construction may in itself create material effects. This highlights the need to examine globalisation *critically* in order to puncture the conventional wisdom that it is driving social and political change. In other words, rather than assuming that particular outcomes are attributable to something called 'globalisation', we need to unpack and interrogate the specific mechanisms of change in contemporary political economies.[103]

This relates to a further point: if we are to understand these processes of change then we need actually to examine specific political economies in detail. The new institutionalists are quite right to point to the role of distinctive national environments in mediating external pressures – although they are misguided in their assumption that such pressures can be conflated with 'globalisation'. Indeed, it is not at all clear why the new institutionalists do not simply retain the concept of an 'international' economy rather than a 'globalised' one. Given their emphasis upon the role of specific national contexts, it would surely make more sense to explicitly embrace Hirst and Thompson's distinction between a 'global' economy and an 'international' one.[104] Despite their failure to do this, however, the new institutionalists' core claim still stands: that we need to examine specific national contexts in detail if we are to understand the dynamics of change in contemporary political economies.

In undertaking such analysis, moreover, it is vital that we do not simply replace one set of exogenous contextual factors (such as the rise in FDI) with a series of endogenous ones (such as pre-existing domestic institutions). This would run the risk of presenting a false dualism between structure and agency and, in turn, implying that social and political outcomes are somehow predestined by forces beyond the control of human agents. Thus, while it is certainly important to explore the international and domestic *context* in which policy decisions are made, it is also vital to consider the *conduct* of political decision-makers themselves.[105]

In turn, the role of ideas comes into play. For, as the contingent theorists correctly observe, the responses and strategies of political actors are crucially mediated by the ideas they hold about the context in which they find themselves. This context has increasingly come to be interpreted through the lens of 'globalisation'. Indeed, globalisation's real power may lie not in its material reality but in its discursive construction. This suggests that the political discourse of globalisation should be treated as an object of enquiry in its own right. Since globalisation is deployed in a variety of ways within different national contexts, this once again highlights the need to consider specific national contexts in order to explore how and why such discourses are articulated. The concept – or, more accurately, the different ways in which and reasons why the concept is *used* – thus remains crucial to our understanding of political outcomes.

Conclusion

This chapter has provided an overview of the globalisation debate. It has identified five competing conceptions of globalisation: the hyperglobalist thesis (which contends that a new global economic order has emerged in which nation-states are no longer important actors in social and economic affairs); the sceptical thesis (which dismisses globalisation as a 'myth' and reasserts the role of nation-states); the complex globalisation thesis (which conceives globalisation as an uneven, multifaceted and contradictory process that has redefined rather than eradicated the role of nation-states); the new institutionalist thesis (which argues that globalisation is both enabling and constraining and is, in turn, crucially mediated by existing national contexts); and the contingent globalisation thesis (which views globalisation as the contingent outcome of political agency rather than as a causal process in its own right). The chapter has then reconsidered what can be understood by the term 'globalisation'. It has argued that the concept can in fact offer very little, either empirically (for there is little evidence to suggest that genuinely global tendencies are apparent) or theoretically (for globalisation is little more than an umbrella term that cannot be falsified, and also invites reification). Yet globalisation's real power may lie not in its analytical utility but in its discursive construction.[106] This discursive power in itself highlights the need to examine globalisation critically in order to challenge the common perception that it is driving change across the world. This entails the analysis not only of *what* globalisation obscures (that is, by unpacking the actual processes of change often attributed to it) but also of *how* and *why* it does so (that is, by exploring the ways in which and reasons why globalisation discourse is used). With these aims and themes in mind, it is now appropriate to turn to the Irish case.

Notes

1 This is not least evident in the A. T. Kearney Globalisation Index – see, 'Measuring globalisation: economic reversals, forward momentum' *Foreign Policy* (March/April 2004).
2 K. Ohmae, *The Borderless Word: Power and Strategy in the Interlinked Economy* (London: Collins, 1990); J. Gray, *After Social Democracy* (London: Demos, 1996); R. O'Brien, *Global Financial Integration: The End of Geography* (New York: Council on Foreign Relations Press, 1992); R. B. Reich, *The Work of Nations: Preparing Ourselves for 21st-Century Capitalism* (New York: A. A. Knopf, 1991).
3 O'Brien, *Global Financial Integration*, p. 1.
4 D. Yergin and J. Stanislaw, 'The commanding heights: the battle between government and the marketplace that is remaking the modern world', in F. Lechner and J. Boli (eds), *The Globalisation Reader* (Oxford: Blackwell, 2000), p. 219.
5 UNCTAD, *World Investment Report 2003: FDI Policies for Development – National and International Perspectives* (New York: United Nations, 2003), p. 3.
6 K. Ohmae, *The End of the Nation State: The Rise of Regional Economies* (London: HarperCollins, 1996), p. 41.
7 See for instance J. Gray, *False Dawn: The Delusions of Global Capitalism* (New York: New Press, 1998), p. 88; W. Greider, *One World, Ready or Not: The Manic Logic of Global Capitalism* (New York: Simon &

Schuster, 1997), p. 360; J. Guéhenno, *The End of the Nation-State* (Minneapolis: University of Minnesota Press, 1995), pp. 10–11.
8   Ohmae, *The Borderless World*, p. 33.
9   Gray, *After Social Democracy*; Guéhenno, *The End of the Nation-State*; Ohmae, *The End of the Nation State*.
10 Reich, *The Work of Nations*, p. 8; see also Greider, *One World, Ready or Not*, p. 36; Ohmae, *The End of the Nation State*, p. 41; E. -S. Pang, 'The financial crisis of 1997–98 and the end of the East Asian developmental state', *Contemporary Southeast Asia*, 22: 3 (2000), p. 570; Yergin and Stanislaw, 'The commanding heights', p. 215.
11 M. Castells, *End of Millennium* (Oxford: Blackwell, 1998), p. 2.
12 Ohmae, *The Borderless World*, p. 215.
13 Gray, *False Dawn*; Greider, *One World, Ready or Not*.
14 K. R. Cox, *Spaces of Globalisation: Reasserting the Power of the Local* (New York: Guilford Press, 1997), pp. 2–3; A. McGrew, 'The globalisation debate: putting the advanced capitalist state in its place', *Global Society*, 12: 3 (1998), p. 303.
15 Greider, *One World, Ready or Not*, p. 11.
16 Ibid., p. 15.
17 P. Hirst and G. Thompson, *Globalisation in Question: The International Economy and the Possibilities of Governance* (Cambridge: Polity, 1999); A. Rugman, *The End of Globalisation* (London: Random House Business Books, 2000); R. Wade, 'Globalisation and its limits: reports of the death of the national economy are greatly exaggerated', in S. Berger and R. P. Dore (eds), *National Diversity and Global Capitalism* (London: Cornell University Press, 1996), pp. 60–88; J. Zysman, 'The myth of a "global economy": enduring national foundations and emerging regional realities', *New Political Economy*, 1: 2 (1996), pp. 157–84.
18 Hirst and Thompson, *Globalisation in Question*, pp. 5–6.
19 Ibid., p. 2.
20 Ibid., p. 74.
21 Wade, 'Globalisation and its limits', p. 67.
22 Calculated from WTO, *International Trade Statistics 2003* (Geneva: World Trade Organisation, 2003), p. 32.
23 UNCTAD, *World Investment Report 2003*, p. 23.
24 Hirst and Thompson, *Globalisation in Question*, p. 121; see also G. E. Chortareas and T. Pelagidis, 'Trade flows: a facet of regionalisation or globalisation?', *Cambridge Journal of Economics*, 28: 2 (2004), pp. 253–71; Rugman, *The End of Globalisation*, p. 2.
25 J. N. Bhagwati and A. Panagariya, 'Preface', in J. N. Bhagwati and A. Panagariya (eds), *The Economics of Preferential Trade Agreements* (Washington, DC: AIE Press, 1996), p. xiii; Rugman, *The End of Globalisation*, p. 4.
26 M. Gertler, 'Between the global and the local: the spatial limits of productive capital', in Cox, *Spaces of Globalisation*, p. 48.
27 W. Ruigrok and R. van Tulder, *The Logic of International Restructuring* (London: Routledge, 1995), p. 168.
28 Wade, 'Globalisation and its limits', p. 79

29 M. Feldstein and C. Horioka, 'Domestic saving and international capital flows', *Economic Journal*, 90 (1980), pp. 314–29.
30 Hirst and Thompson, *Globalisation in Question*, p. 7.
31 Gertler, 'Between the global and the local', p. 48.
32 D. Rodrik, *Has Globalisation Gone Too Far?* (Washington, DC: Institute of International Economics, 1997), p. 49.
33 V. Navarro, J. Schmitt and J. Astudillo, 'Is globalisation undermining the welfare state?', *Cambridge Journal of Economics*, 28 (2004), pp. 133–52.
34 Ibid., pp. 147–8.
35 Hirst and Thompson, *Globalisation in Question*, p. 3; Rugman, *The End of Globalisation*, p. 1; Zysman, 'The myth of a "global economy"', p. 157.
36 Hirst and Thompson, *Globalisation in Question*, p. xiii.
37 C. Hay and D. Marsh, 'Introduction: demystifying globalisation', in C. Hay and D. Marsh (eds), *Demystifying Globalisation* (London: Macmillan, 2000), p. 6.
38 Hirst and Thompson, *Globalisation in Question*, p. 4.
39 P. Dicken, *Global Shift: Reshaping the Global Economic Map in the 21st Century* (London: Sage, 2003), p. 12.
40 B. Axford, *The Global System: Politics, Economics, and Culture* (New York: St Martin's Press, 1995), pp. ix, 26; Dicken, *Global Shift*, p. 14; A. Giddens, 'Runaway world: The Reith Lectures revisited – lecture 1' (1999), www.lse.ac.uk/Giddens; D. Held, A. McGrew, D. Goldblatt and J. Perralon, *Global Transformations: Politics, Economics and Culture* (Stanford, CA: Stanford University Press, 1999), p. 27.
41 R. A. Falk, *Predatory Globalisation: A Critique* (Cambridge: Polity, 1999), p. 1.
42 Dicken, *Global Shift*, pp. 10–11; see also Held et al., *Global Transformations*, p. 17.
43 M. Rhodes, P. Heywood and V. Wright, *Developments in West European politics* (New York: St Martin's Press, 1997), p. 5.
44 A. Amin and N. Thrift, 'Living in the global', in A. Amin and N. Thrift (eds), *Globalisation, Institutions and Regional Development in Europe* (Oxford: Oxford University Press, 1994), p. 8; see also Dicken, *Global Shift*, p. 20; P. Dicken, M. Forsgren and A. Malmberg, 'The local embeddedness of transnational corporations', in Amin and Thrift, *Globalisation, Institutions and Regional Development in Europe*, p. 25.
45 Axford, *The Global System*, p. 98; see also A. Mair, 'Strategic localisation: the myth of the postnational enterprise', in Cox, *Spaces of Globalisation*, p. 67.
46 J. A. Scholte, *Globalisation: A Critical Introduction* (London: Macmillan, 2000), p. 16.
47 M. Bernard, 'Post-fordism and global restructuring', in R. Stubbs and G. Underhill (eds), *Political Economy and the Changing World Order* (Ontario: Oxford University Press, 2000), p. 153.
48 Held et al., *Global Transformations*, p. 16; S. Breslin and R. Higgott, 'Studying regions: learning from the old, constructing the new', *New Political Economy*, 5: 3 (2000), pp. 339–40; R. Cox, *Approaches to World*

Order (Cambridge: Cambridge University Press, 1996), p. 306; M. Rhodes, 'The welfare state: internal challenges, external constraints', in Rhodes, Heywood and Wright, *Developments in West European Politics*, p. 66.

49 P. G. Cerny, 'Paradoxes of the competition state: the dynamics of political globalisation', *Government and Opposition*, 32: 2 (1997), p. 269; R. Cox, 'Political economy and world order: problems of power and knowledge at the turn of the millennium', in Stubbs and Underhill, *Political Economy and the Changing Global Order*, p. 25; Falk, *Predatory Globalisation*, p. 39; Held et al., *Global Transformations*, p. 30; L. Panitch, 'Rethinking the role of the state', in J. H. Mittelman (ed.), *Globalisation Critical Reflections* (London: Lynne Reiner, 1997), p. 85; Scholte, *Globalisation*, p. 4.

50 Dicken, *Global Shift*; Falk, *Predatory Globalisation*, p. 35; B. Jessop, 'The transition to post-Fordism and the Schumpetarian workfare state', in R. Burrows and B. Loader (eds), *Towards a Post-Fordist Welfare State?* (London: Routledge, 1994), p. 240; Scholte, *Globalisation*, p. 4; S. Strange, *The Retreat of the State: The Diffusion of Power in the World Economy* (New York: Cambridge University Press, 1996), p. 4.

51 Cox, 'Political economy and world order', p. 33.

52 M. Rhodes and Y. Mény, 'Europe's social contract under stress', in M. Rhodes and Y. Mény (eds), *The Future of European Welfare: A New Social Contract?* (Basingstoke: Macmillan, 1998), pp. 9–11.

53 Cerny, 'Paradoxes of the competition state', p. 251; Jessop, 'The transition to post-Fordism', p. 24.

54 D. Coates, 'Capitalist models and social democracy: the case of New Labour', *British Journal of Politics and International Relations*, 3: 3 (2001), p. 303.

55 See for instance Held et al., *Global Transformations*, p. 12; Rhodes, Heywood and Wright, *Developments in West European Politics*, p. 5; M. Waters, *Globalisation* (London: Routledge, 2000), pp. 14–21.

56 Cerny, 'Paradoxes of the competition state', pp. 257–8; Cox, 'Political economy and world order', p. 28; B. Van Apeldoorn, 'The political economy of European integration: transnational social forces in the making of Europe's socio-economic order', in Stubbs and Underhill, *Political Economy and the Changing Global Order*, p. 241.

57 Cerny, 'Paradoxes of the competition state', p. 256; Cox, 'Political economy and world order', pp. 30–5; S. Gill, 'Knowledge, politics and neo-liberal political economy', in Stubbs and Underhill, *Political Economy and the Changing Global Order*, pp. 48–59.

58 P. A. Hall and D. Soskice, 'An introduction to varieties of capitalism', in P. A. Hall and D. Soskice (eds), *Varieties of Capitalism: The Institutional Foundations of Comparative Advantage* (Oxford: Oxford University Press, 2001), pp. 1–68; G. Garrett, *Partisan Politics in the Global Economy* (Cambridge: Cambridge University Press, 1998); L. Weiss, 'Introduction: bringing domestic institutions back in', in L. Weiss (ed.), *States in the Global Economy: Bringing Domestic Institutions Back In* (Cambridge: Cambridge University Press, 2003), p. 1; K. Thelen,

'Varieties of labour politics in the developed democracies', in Hall and Soskice, *Varieties of Capitalism*, pp. 71–103; F. W. Scharpf, 'The viability of advanced welfare states in the international economy: vulnerabilities and options', *Journal of European Public Policy*, 7: 2 (2000), pp. 190–228.

59 Weiss, 'Bringing domestic institutions back in', pp. 7–15.
60 Ibid., pp. 27–8.
61 For Weiss, previous approaches assume that globalisation acts primarily as a constraint on domestic institutions. While the hyperglobalists and complex theorists disagree about the extent to which globalisation limits national autonomy, they both deem it to restrict the freedom of manoeuvre for national authorities. Similarly, the sceptics' focus on measuring globalisation reflects their assumption that 'more globalisation' effectively means 'less government'. Weiss thus criticises the sceptics for their assumption that if they can demonstrate the extent of globalisation to be limited, then they can in turn show that there is greater scope for national governance – see ibid., pp. 7–14.
62 J. M. Hobson, 'Disappearing taxes or the "race to the middle"? Fiscal policy in the OECD', in Weiss, *States in the Global Economy*, p. 38.
63 Weiss, 'Bringing domestic institutions back in', p. 15.
64 Rodrik, *Has Globalisation Gone Too Far?*, p. 53; D. R. Cameron, 'The expansion of the public economy: a comparative analysis', *American Political Science Review*, 72: 4 (1978), p. 1250; P. J. Katzenstein, *Small States in World Markets: Industrial Policy in Europe* (Ithaca, NY: Cornell University Press, 1985), p. 192; Weiss, 'Bringing domestic institutions back in', p. 16.
65 Garrett, *Partisan Politics*, pp. 5, 26–7; G. Garrett, 'Shrinking states: globalisation and national autonomy', in N. Woods (ed.), *The Political Economy of Globalisation* (London: Macmillan, 2000), pp. 113–14.
66 S. Steinmo, 'Globalisation and taxation: challenges to the Swedish welfare state', *Comparative Political Studies*, 35: 7 (2002), p. 857.
67 Garrett, *Partisan Politics*, p. 18; Hall and Soskice, 'An introduction to varieties of capitalism', p. 58; D. Swank, 'Withering welfare? Globalisation, political economic institutions and contemporary welfare states', in Weiss, *States in the Global Economy*, p. 58; Thelen, 'Varieties of labour politics in the developed democracies', p. 72.
68 Hall and Soskice, 'An introduction to varieties of capitalism', p. 57.
69 C. Hay, 'Globalisation, social democracy and the persistence of partisan politics: a commentary on Garrett', *Review of International Political Economy*, 7: 1 (2000), p. 139.
70 V. A. Schmidt, *The Futures of European Capitalism* (Oxford: Oxford University Press, 2002), pp. 209–10.
71 Ibid., p. 210.
72 Ibid., p. 303.
73 Ibid., p. 211.
74 Navarro, Schmitt and Astudillo, 'Is globalisation undermining the welfare state?', pp. 133–52.
75 Hay and Marsh, 'Demystifying globalisation', p. 13.

76 Ibid., pp. 4–7; see also J. Rosenberg, *The Follies of Globalisation Theory: Polemical Essays* (London: Verso, 2000), pp. 2–3.
77 See for instance Hay and Marsh, 'Demystifying globalisation', pp. 1–17; B. Rosamond, 'Babylon and on? Globalisation and international political economy', *Review of International Political Economy*, 10: 4 (2003), pp. 661–7; M. Watson and C. Hay, 'The discourse of globalisation and the logic of no alternative: rendering the contingent necessary in the political economy of New Labour', *Policy & Politics*, 31: 3 (2003), pp. 289–305.
78 C. Hay and B. Rosamond, 'Globalisation, European integration and the discursive construction of economic imperatives', *Journal of European Public Policy*, 9: 2 (2002), p. 148.
79 Ibid.; Hay and Marsh, 'Demystifying globalisation', pp. 8–10; Rosamond, 'Globalisation and international political economy', p. 666.
80 C. Hay, 'Globalisation, welfare retrenchment and "the logic of no alternative": why second-best won't do', *Journal of Social Policy*, 27 (1998), p. 529.
81 C. Hay, 'Globalisation's impact on states', in J. Ravenhill (ed.), *Global Political Economy* (Oxford: Oxford University Press, 2004).
82 Hay and Rosamond, 'Globalisation and European integration', p. 148; see also C. Hay and M. Watson, 'The politics and discourse of globalisation: "sceptical" notes on the 1999 Reith Lectures', *Political Quarterly*, 70: 4 (1999), p. 423.
83 Hay and Rosamond, 'Globalisation and European integration', pp. 152–63; B. Rosamond, 'Discourses of globalisation and the social construction of European identities', *Journal of European Public Policy*, 6: 4 (1999), p. 667.
84 C. Hay and N. J. Smith, 'Horses for courses? The political discourse of globalisation and European integration in the UK and Ireland', *West European Politics*, 28: 1 pp. 150–2.
85 C. Hay, 'Common trajectories, variable paces, divergent outcomes? Models of European capitalism under conditions of complex economic interdependence', *Review of International Political Economy*, 11: 2 (2004), pp. 248–55.
86 See for instance B. Rosamond, *Globalisation and the European Union* (Basingstoke: Palgrave, 2005).
87 Hay, 'Common trajectories, variable paces, divergent outcomes?', pp. 256–7.
88 C. Hay, 'Contemporary capitalism, globalisation, regionalisation and the persistence of national variation', *Review of International Studies*, 26: 4 (2000), p. 525.
89 A. Verdun, 'Monetary integration in Europe: ideas and evolution', in M. G. Cowles and M. Smith (eds), *The State of the European Union* (Oxford: Oxford University Press, 2000), p. 108.
90 This is not least evident in the growth of the literature on 'spatial scales' – see for instance N. Hothi, *Globalisation and Manufacturing Decline* (London: Arena, 2005); L. McDowell, *Gender, Identity and Place: Understanding Feminist Geographies* (Cambridge: Polity, 1998);

E. Swyngedouw, 'Neither global nor local: "glocalisation" and the politics of scale', in Cox, *Spaces of Globalisation*, pp. 137–66.
91 Held et al., *Global Transformations*, p. 1.
92 I am grateful to Matthew Watson for making this distinction.
93 D. Wincott, 'Globalisation and European integration', in Hay and Marsh, *Demystifying Globalisation*, p. 175.
94 Chortareas and Pelagidis, 'Trade flows', pp. 253–71.
95 Hay, 'Common trajectories, variable paces, divergent outcomes?', pp. 248–55.
96 Indeed, this very point is acknowledged by Held et al., *Global Transformations*, p. 344.
97 Hay and Marsh, 'Demystifying globalisation', pp. 1–17; Rosenberg, *The Follies of Globalisation Theory*, pp. 1–5; Wincott, 'Globalisation and European integration', pp. 186–7.
98 C. Hay, 'Globalisation as a problem of political analysis: restoring agents to a "process without a subject" and politics to a logic of economic compulsion', *Cambridge Review of International Affairs*, 15: 3 (2002), pp. 379–92.
99 Ibid.; R. Sibeon, 'Anti-reductionist sociology', *Sociology*, 33: 2 (1999), p. 201.
100 C. Hay, 'Structure and agency', in D. Marsh and G. Stoker (eds), *Theory and Methods in Political Science* (London: Macmillan, 1995), p. 195.
101 Hay, 'Globalisation as a problem of political analysis', pp. 379–92.
102 Hirst and Thompson, *Globalisation in Question*, p. 4.
103 Hay, 'Globalisation as a problem of political analysis', pp. 379–92.
104 Whereas the former is 'autonomised and socially disembedded, as markets and production become truly global', outcomes in the latter 'emerge from the distinct and differential performance of the national economies'. Crucially, the antithesis of a global economy is 'not thus a truly nationally inward-looking one, but an open world market based on trading nations and regulated to a greater or lesser degree by both the public policies of nation-states and supra-national agencies' – see Hirst and Thompson, *Globalisation in Question*, pp. 10, 16.
105 C. Hay, *Political Analysis: A Critical Introduction* (Basingstoke: Palgrave, 2002), pp. 89–134.
106 M. Watson, 'International capital mobility in an era of globalisation: adding a political dimension to the "Feldstein–Horioka Puzzle"', *Politics*, 21: 2 (2001), p. 86.

2

Economic performance (1): Ireland the 'Celtic tiger'?

The Irish case is particularly pertinent to debates about globalisation. Once the 'sick man' of Europe, the Republic was hailed as a miracle economy in the 1990s due to its rapid economic growth rates. While this growth has since slowed considerably, Ireland remains famous for its dramatic transformation into Europe's 'tiger' economy. Journalists, scholars and policy-makers alike cite Ireland's supposedly dazzling success as evidence of how countries can prosper under conditions of globalisation. Ireland, it is argued, is a 'Celtic tiger in a global jungle'.[1] However, various critics have sought to question Ireland's 'tiger' status on such grounds as that growth is exaggerated by official statistics and is highly limited in sectoral terms. Indeed, some have argued that Ireland is best characterised as a 'Celtic kitten' or a 'paper tiger'.

This chapter documents the nature of Ireland's economic transformation in the 1990s in order to examine whether the Republic can indeed be considered a 'showpiece' economy. In so doing, it considers not only the extent of Ireland's economic growth but also the distribution of that growth, for critics such as Kirby argue that 'economic success goes hand in hand with glaring social failures'.[2] The dynamics behind Ireland's economic performance – and whether they can be understood in terms of 'globalisation' – will be discussed in the following chapter.

The 'Celtic tiger' thesis

Before turning to Ireland's economic performance in the 1990s, it is worth briefly placing this in historical perspective. After all, it is not just Ireland's rapid growth in the 1990s that is seen to have led to its 'Celtic tiger' status but also the fact that this represented such a dramatic turnaround in the Republic's fortunes. Ireland's experience prior to the 1990s has been described as 'a case study in failure'.[3] Having endured famine, mass emigration and deindustrialisation in the nineteenth century, Ireland continued to perform poorly relative to other European countries for most of the twentieth century. There was little growth in Irish output or living standards for the first three decades after independence in 1921, and while economic growth picked up in the 1960s (even slightly exceeding the European average in the 1970s), average income per head remained the lowest in the European Economic Community (EEC). The OECD reported at the time that 'Ireland must still rank as under-developed' and that 'the problems of Ireland are of a special and more grave character than in most OECD countries'.[4] In the 1980s Ireland continued to underperform, with 'stagnant' output, 'surging' unemployment, 'sliding' investment, high inflation and a government that was seriously in debt.[5] As Lee famously wrote: 'No other European country, east or west, north or south, for which remotely reliable evidence exists, has recorded so slow a rate of growth of national income in the twentieth century.'[6]

In the 1990s, however, perceptions about Ireland's economic performance changed dramatically. Rather than being simply dismissed as an economic basket case, Ireland became known as the 'Celtic tiger'. This term was coined in 1994 by Kevin Gardiner of the US investment bank Morgan Stanley, who suggested that Ireland's high growth rates were comparable to those of the East Asian 'tigers'. The Republic soon became known in the international press as the tiger economy of Europe. In one widely cited article, *The Economist* described Ireland as 'Europe's shining light', remarking that growth was at 'a positively East Asian pace'.[7] The *Financial Times*, too, congratulated Ireland on its 'exceptional growth' and argued 'Ireland fully deserves to be called the "Celtic tiger"'.[8] *The Times* labelled Ireland's economic performance as 'nothing short of remarkable'[9] and the *Wall Street Journal* described the Republic as the 'envy' of its European neighbours.[10] The research community, too, presented Irish performance as 'astonishing', 'phenomenal', 'remarkable' and 'spectacular'.[11] One economist with the Economic and Social Research Institute (ESRI) commented: 'We're living in a golden age ... Our economic progress in the past decade has been spectacular.'[12] The International Monetary Fund (IMF) described Ireland's economic expansion as 'remarkable', and the OECD argued: 'No other OECD country has been able to match its outstanding outcomes.'[13] Otmar Issing, chief economist with the European Central Bank, described Ireland's growth as 'almost without precedent' and argued that other European countries could 'take a leaf out of the Irish book'.[14] Indeed, Ireland has become something of a model economy for other states seeking to emulate its performance. For example, the Chinese premier Wen Jiabao spoke in 2004 of the lessons China can learn from Ireland's economic success.[15]

Certainly at first sight, the statistics do seem remarkable. In the 1990s Ireland's growth rate in terms of GDP was the highest in the OECD and three times that of the EU average (see also figure 2.1). In the latter half of the decade, its productivity (measured in terms of GDP growth per hour worked) rose by an average of 5.5 per cent per annum – the highest in the OECD area. By 2000 Ireland was being ranked as the fifth most competitive economy in the world by the World Economic Forum.[16] In terms of employment creation, too, Ireland topped the OECD league, with the total at work rising by a third and total unemployment falling from 15.7 per cent in 1993 to just 4.3 per cent by the end of the decade. In addition, Ireland's national debt was reduced from 99 to 41 per cent in the 1990s and, from 1998 onwards, the Republic enjoyed a series of budget surpluses (see table 2.1). Perhaps the most stunning statistic is that Ireland was reported in 2003 to be the fourth richest country in the world, with GDP per capita exceeded only by that of Luxembourg, the United States and Norway.[17] On these grounds, it is perhaps not surprising that Ireland became known as something of a miracle economy in the 1990s.

A 'paper tiger'?

However, this story of success has not been embraced by all. Increasingly, sceptics have sought to challenge Ireland's 'tiger' status, with suggestions that the Republic is better known as a 'paper tiger' or 'Celtic kitten'. One commentator in the *Irish Times* remarked that the term 'Celtic tiger' would have more utility if used to describe a 'franchised US baseball team'. Another urged that the term should get 'a bullet in the head' once and for all.[18]

One of the harshest critics of the 'Celtic tiger' thesis is Denis O'Hearn. Official statistics, he argues, grossly overstate the extent of the Republic's growth due to the phenomenon of transfer pricing. This practice is used by multinational corporations keen to raise their profits artificially by minimising the cost of imports and maximising the cost of exports. As O'Hearn notes, they have a particular incentive to do so in Ireland where there is a very low rate of corporation tax (at 10

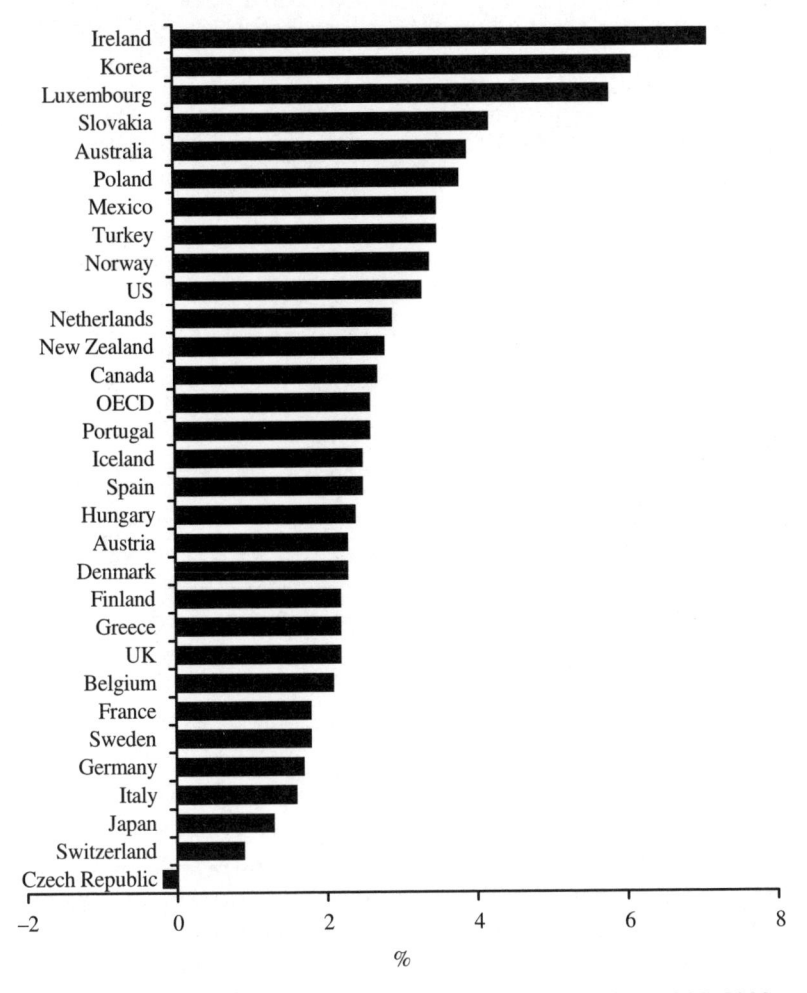

Figure 2.1 Irish GDP growth in international perspective, 1990–2000
Note: GDP growth refers to average annual volume change.
Source: OECD, *OECD in Figures 2001* (Paris: OECD, 2001), pp. 14–15.

per cent compared to the European standard of 30 to 40 per cent).[19] While it is difficult to specify the true extent of transfer pricing, other scholars agree that there can be 'little doubt' it is taking place.[20] For example, Ó Gráda and O'Rourke point to the very high profit rates achieved by some US firms: one company claimed to have pre-tax profits of £5.8 million on a turnover of £6 million.[21]

For critics such as O'Hearn, transfer pricing serves to inflate GDP figures, since import figures are underpriced and exports are overpriced.

Table 2.1 Irish economic performance (selected indicators), 1990s

	GDP growth (%)	Total employment (1,000s)	GDP growth per hour worked (%)	Unemployment (%)	Inflation (%)	National debt (% GNP)	Exchequer balance (€m)
1990	7.1	1,160	4.3	12.9	3.3	99.0	−620
1991	1.9	1,156	3.7	14.7	3.2	95.9	−655
1992	3.3	1,165	5.3	15.1	3.1	94.1	−915
1993	2.7	1,183	2.0	15.7	1.4	93.3	−880
1994	5.8	1,221	2.3	14.7	2.3	88.8	−854
1995	9.9	1,282	4.8	12.2	2.5	82.1	−796
1996	8.1	1,329	3.8	11.9	1.7	73.7	−554
1997	11.1	1,380	9.7	10.3	1.4	66.0	−298
1998	8.6	1,495	2.6	7.8	2.4	55.0	948
1999	11.3	1,591	6.5	5.7	1.6	52.0	1,512
2000	10.1	1,671	5.2	4.3	5.6	41.4	3,177

Source: adapted from Department of Finance, *Budgetary and Economic Statistics: March 2004* (Dublin: Department of Finance, 2004), pp. 7–8, 12, 60–6; OECD, 'Labour productivity – data: GDP per hour worked index and percentage change' (22 June 2004), www.oecd.org.dataoecd.

As evidence of this he points to the significant gap between the GDP and GNP (gross national product) in Ireland. Whereas the former measures a nation's overall output of goods and services, the latter measures the output accruing to a nation's residents. Since GNP does not include resources that leave the country (for example through transfer pricing), it is often seen as a better measure of national wellbeing than GDP. As O'Hearn notes, not only is Irish GNP considerably lower than GDP but this gap is widening over time.[22] For example, in 1980 GDP was just 3.8 per cent higher than GNP, but in 2000 this gap had risen to 14.3 per cent.[23] Seen in these terms, he argues, Irish economic growth is simply not in the same league as the East Asian 'tiger' economies.[24]

O'Hearn is certainly right to challenge some of the more enthusiastic claims regarding Ireland's 'tiger' status. For example, if Ireland's wealth is measured in terms of GNP rather than GDP per head, it ranks not as the fourth but as the sixteenth richest country in the world. As Cullen notes, Ireland is thus one of 'the poorest of the rich' rather than one of the richest *per se*.[25] Yet this (still highly impressive) statistic in itself highlights the need to temper O'Hearn's arguments. In fact, it is

IRELAND THE 'CELTIC TIGER'?

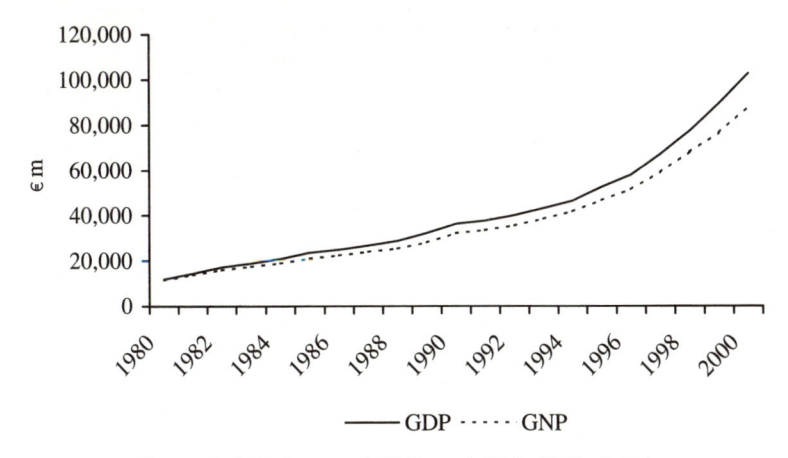

Figure 2.2 Volume of GNP and GDP, 1980–2000

Note: GNP and GDP refer to current market prices.
Source: Department of Finance, *Budgetary and Economic Statistics* (Dublin: Department of Finance, 2004), p. 12.

now widely recognised in Ireland that GDP figures provide a distorted image of the Republic's true wealth. Official bodies such as the Department of Finance, the Central Statistical Office (CSO) and the Central Bank and Financial Services Authority of Ireland (CBFSAI) now routinely use GNP figures to measure Irish growth rates. Moreover, while Ireland's GNP may not have risen as rapidly as GDP in the 1990s, it nevertheless *did* increase dramatically, reaching 10.2 per cent in 2000 and averaging at 8.8 per cent in the latter half of the decade (see also figure 2.2). This is clearly quite spectacular, not only in terms of Ireland's historical averages but also when spatial comparisons are made. If Irish GNP growth is compared to the GDP growth of other OECD countries in 1990–2000 (as shown earlier in figure 2.1), the Republic still comes out top (at 6.3 per cent), although Korea is a close second (at 6.1 per cent).

Even when compared to that of the four main East Asian tigers (Hong Kong, Singapore, South Korea and Taiwan), Ireland's growth in the 1990s is more impressive than O'Hearn admits. Certainly Irish growth rates prior to 1995 do not compare favourably with those of the Asian economies. But it was in the *latter* half of the 1990s that Ireland demonstrated 'peerless performance'.[26] In contrast, the East Asian tigers experienced negative growth rates after their collapse in 1997. Moreover, Irish growth in 1995–9 compares favourably to the East Asian tigers' growth *before* their economic collapse. This is not

Table 2.2 Irish and East Asian growth rates (annual average percentage change), 1960–99

	Ireland (GNP % change)	S. Korea (GDP % change)	Taiwan (GDP % change)	Singapore (GDP % change)	Hong Kong (GDP % change)
1960–70	4.0	8.5	9.2	8.8	10.0
1970–80	3.6	8.7	9.7	9.0	9.5
1980–90	2.0	9.2	9.0	6.9	8.9
1990–95	5.0	6.6	–	8.3	5.7
1995–99	8.5	3.3	5.0	4.2	2.1

Source: adapted from D. O'Hearn, *Inside the Celtic Tiger: The Irish Economy and the Asian Model* (London: Pluto Press, 1998), p. 61; P. Sweeney, *The Celtic Tiger: Ireland's Continuing Economic Miracle* (Dublin: Oak Tree Press, 1999), p. 14; Department of Finance, *Budgetary and Economic Statistics: March 2004*, p. 13.

only terms of GDP (at 9.8 per cent in 1995–9) but also, crucially, in terms of GNP (at 8.5 per cent in 1995–9 – see table 2.2). Certainly it is important not to overstate this – not least because of the sheer length of time the Asian 'tigers' achieved high growth rates (discussed later in this chapter). Nevertheless, Ireland's economic performance *is* more impressive than O'Hearn concedes – albeit less so than the GDP-based international league tables appear to suggest.

However, O'Hearn does not just question the *extent* of Ireland's growth but also expresses doubts as to whether the *nature* of Ireland's growth is comparable to that of the East Asian tigers. He identifies the key feature of East Asian growth to be very high rates of investment. The four main 'tigers' increased their average ratios from one fifth to one third in 1965–90. This was central to their rapid export growth, which, in turn, drove overall economic growth. In contrast, O'Hearn argues that Ireland's investment rates are 'stunningly low'.[27] While the output of foreign firms rose dramatically in the 1990s, the investment rate (that is, gross capital formation as a share of GDP) 'plummeted' in 1990–4 from 20 to 14 per cent.[28] Moreover, he notes, the fastest growing sectors in terms of output received the least investment: indeed, the reduction in investment for electronics and chemicals was greater than the average for total manufacturing. In total, he argues, multinational corporations invested a third less in the 1990s than in the 1980s, making Ireland's investment rate the lowest in Europe.

IRELAND THE 'CELTIC TIGER'?

For O'Hearn, this can be explained by the fact that Ireland's growth has largely been an illusion.[29]

Yet the picture is rather more complicated than this. In fact, the East Asian 'miracle' has itself been questioned precisely on the grounds that it was driven by inputs rather than gains in efficiency.[30] As Roubini argues, the 'cornerstone' of truly impressive growth is productivity.[31] For O'Hearn, this does not apply to the Irish case since productivity growth has largely been a phantom of accounting due to corporate profit shifting.[32] Honohan and Walsh question such claims, arguing that Ireland's productivity growth is not in fact a mirage. Adjusting Ireland's productivity figures to exclude all multinational profits, they find that Ireland converges with (but does not exceed) the EU and OECD averages. From this they conclude that Ireland's productivity is 'solid, rather than miraculous'.[33] In turn, Blanchard argues that Ireland's productivity has been even more impressive than Honohan and Walsh suggest. While he accepts that multinationals' profits may reveal little else than transfer pricing, the key issue, he argues, is the extent to which this affects the numbers for aggregate output and productivity growth. He finds that even if all profits repatriated by foreign firms are excluded, Ireland's productivity growth still averaged at 3.4 per cent annually in 1985–97. Combined with Ireland's rapid employment growth, he argues, this is impressive performance indeed.[34] Thus, even if Ireland's productivity growth is less impressive than the 'Celtic tiger' thesis suggests, it certainly does not appear to be a phantom of accounting.

Nor are Ireland's investment levels as low as O'Hearn suggests. As Ó Riain notes, while sales are 'certainly inflated' by transfer pricing, this may conceal significant resources produced by multinational firms within the Irish economy. In fact, while the *proportion* of manufacturing investments to GDP may have fallen, the fact that this occurred during a period of rapid GDP growth has meant that they have risen significantly in *absolute* terms. Between 1990 and 1996, absolute spending in the Irish economy by multinational corporations increased by 55.3 per cent.[35] Indeed, expenditure by foreign firms overtook that of Irish firms in 2000 (at €9.3 billion and €9.1 billion respectively) and was 23 per cent higher than in 1999 (compared to 6 per cent for Irish enterprises).[36] Again, it is important not to overstate this: for example, expenditure as a proportion of sales remains considerably lower for foreign firms than for indigenous ones;[37] and the rise in expenditure by foreign firms has almost exactly matched their growth in output.[38] Nevertheless, the absolute rise in expenditure by foreign companies cannot simply be dismissed as a mirage.

Finally, it is also worth noting that the increase in manufacturing investments has occurred at a time when the general orientation of the Irish economy has moved towards services. The greatest employment growth has occurred in the services sector, which rose from 57.4 to 63.9 per cent of civilian employment in 1991–2001 (compared to an increase from 28.8 to 29.1 per cent in industry and a fall from 13.8 to 7.0 per cent in agriculture, forestry and fishing).[39] O'Hearn acknowledges the growth in services, but points out that 'nearly a quarter of Irish employees are now "atypical" workers lacking either full-time work or job security'.[40] Yet the Irish economy has created many full-time jobs as well as part-time jobs, and the jobs created have not just been 'bad' jobs.[41] Indeed, O'Connell points to substantial upgrading in the occupational structure, with the largest increase in the professional occupations (from 14 to 18 per cent of total employment in 1987–95).[42] Kirby, by contrast, identifies an increase in both highly qualified white-collar jobs (by 16.6 per cent in 1993–7) and blue-collar jobs (by 17.2 per cent in 1993–7). He therefore points to a process of occupational polarisation rather than occupational upgrading.[43] Yet, while there has been some expansion in less privileged positions, the overall trend appears to be towards occupational upgrading and upward social mobility.[44] Layte and Whelan, for instance, find 'no evidence that barriers to mobility have risen for groups at the bottom of the class hierarchy. In fact the opposite is clearly the case.'[45] Thus, while the sceptics are right to qualify claims that Ireland's growth has been unambiguously positive, its performance is, on the whole, impressive.

Sustainability

A further criticism of the 'Celtic tiger' thesis is that Ireland's development is inherently unsustainable. In fact, O'Hearn identifies the key characteristic of the East Asian tigers to be their ability to sustain high growth rates over a period of several decades (see table 2.2). But the Irish economy, he argues, is highly vulnerable to changes in the global economy due to its dependence upon foreign investment.[46] This view is shared by other commentators such as Allen and Kirby, who identify serious structural weaknesses in the Irish economy due to the dominance of foreign capital. While foreign investment has certainly generated economic growth, they claim, it also leaves the Irish economy dangerously exposed to changes in global capital flows and thus to a sudden downturn.[47] For Allen, this is precisely what happened

IRELAND THE 'CELTIC TIGER'?

Table 2.3 Irish economic growth, 1997–2003

	GDP (%)	Value (€m)	GNP (%)	Value (€m)
1997	11.1	67,123	9.7	59,083
1998	8.6	77,543	7.9	68,161
1999	11.3	89,614	8.9	76,670,
2000	10.1	102,845	10.2	88,095
2001	6.2	114,743	3.8	96,448
2002	6.9	129,344	0.1	103,430
2003	1.4	131,922	3.3	109,221

Source: Department of Finance, *Monthly Economic Bulletin: May 2004* (Dublin: Department of Finance, 2004), p. 1.

at the start of this century, with the Irish economy sharply hit by the US economic slowdown.[48] Between 2000 and 2003 Irish growth rates in terms of both GDP and GNP declined significantly, accompanied by a rise in unemployment (from 4.2 to 4.7 per cent) and the end of Ireland's budget surplus.[49] This has prompted some commentators to declare that the era of the Celtic tiger is well and truly over.[50] For O'Hearn, the short-term nature of growth means that Ireland was never a 'tiger' in the first place.[51]

Yet, while Ireland has certainly experienced an economic downturn, this does not make the Republic a paper tiger. While Irish growth slowed to 1.4 per cent in terms of GDP and 3.3 per cent in terms of GNP by 2003, this was still higher than the EU average of 0.8 per cent in terms of GDP.[52] The Republic has also continued to attract impressive levels of foreign investment, with inflows in 2002 more than double the 2001 figure – making Ireland one of the few countries to experience such an increase.[53] Similarly, while unemployment rose to 4.7 per cent in 2003, the ESRI notes that this level is still remarkable given that labour force participation averaged over 60 per cent of the adult population for the first time.[54] Indeed, the total number at work rose by around 26,000 in 2003, whereas most other developed nations experienced a fall in employment at this time.[55] The ESRI, IMF, OECD and European Commission have therefore expressed considerable optimism about Ireland's long-term prospects, with the Commission, for instance, estimating that GDP growth will rise to 4.8 per cent in 2005 and 5.0 per cent in 2006.[56]

While only time will tell how Ireland fares in the long term, the future certainly does not look as bleak as the sceptics imply. In fact, as Barry, Bradley and O'Malley note, the 'dangers of instability due to having such a large foreign-owned sector may be overstated'. They point out that foreign firms tend to be 'stickers' rather than 'snatchers': in other words, they are more concerned with developing business in the long term than with quick profits.[57] For example, Görg and Strobl find in their survey of firms in Ireland that jobs created by multinationals tend to last longer than in the indigenous sector and that multinationals are more likely to recover lost jobs than indigenous firms.[58] The 'stickiness' of foreign firms also appears to be supported by the fact that new inward investment to Ireland is increasingly made up of reinvested earnings by foreign firms already located there. Reinvested earnings accounted for nearly two thirds of total inflows in 2002.[59] This trend seems set to continue, with Intel, for instance, announcing in 2004 that it would expand its operations in Ireland by investing €1.6 billion by 2006.[60]

Nor should the predominance of foreign-owned firms be allowed to conceal important developments that have taken place in the indigenous sector.[61] It is certainly the case that Irish-owned industry remains weak when compared to foreign-owned firms. For example, the level of gross value-added per employee is more than five times greater in the foreign-owned sector than for indigenous enterprises.[62] Yet indigenous performance has improved significantly in recent years, with export growth rising more than sixfold in 1993–2000, profit levels (as a percentage of sales) increasing from 3.3 to 6.1 per cent in 1987–97,[63] and employment in indigenous manufacturing rising by 10 per cent in 1987–97. This is not only impressive by international standards but is 'without historical precedent in twentieth century Ireland'.[64] Moreover, while Ireland's share of outward investment to total investment is the lowest in the EU, this masks an absolute rise in outward investment in the 1990s. Outward flows increased from an estimated IR£1.0 billion in 1990 to IR£4.0 billion in 1999: higher than many larger EU economies such as those of Italy, Austria, Portugal and Denmark.[65] A further encouraging development is the dramatic rise in expenditure on research and development (R&D) by indigenous firms (from 0.6 to 1.1 per cent of gross output in 1993–7).[66] As will be discussed in chapter 3, it is important not to overstate the extent and impact of this indigenous revival. This is not least because growth has not taken place 'across the board' but has instead been concentrated in more highly traded and internationally competitive sectors that are themselves sensitive to changes in the international economy. Nevertheless, as O'Sullivan concludes: 'we should not ... ignore the signs of favourable developments in the indigenous sector. It is true that they are as yet tentative, narrowly concentrated in most sectors, and of relatively minor significance in influencing national aggregates for the industrial sector, with the exception of employment, but they are nevertheless evident.'[67]

Finally, it is worth noting that cries of 'unsustainability' were also a common feature of the East Asian experience.[68] Indeed, after the East Asian crash a common point of debate was whether Ireland would follow a similar path. By the late 1990s there were significant fears that the Irish economy would overheat, fuelled by rising inflation, generalised wage shortages, soaring property prices and infrastructural bottlenecks. Commentators such as Sweeney argued that Ireland was 'straining at the seams', just like the East Asian economies before their collapse.[69] Given this risk of overheating, the OECD has described Ireland's economic slowdown as 'inevitable and even desirable'.[70] It may be that Ireland's full integration into wider EU structures will serve to cushion the economy from a 'boom to bust' scenario, whereas the Asian 'tigers' had no similar regional safety-net. This in turn suggests that the Irish and East Asian experiences are not easily comparable. In fact, the term 'Celtic tiger' was originally used only to claim that Ireland's growth rates were similar to those of the East Asian tigers, not that the *conditions* of growth were comparable. It 'takes no economist' to acknowledge the substantial differences between the economic, political and cultural conditions in Ireland and the East Asian economies.[71] The East Asian tigers tend to be authoritarian and have only become democratic in recent years. In stark contrast to Ireland's social partnership approach (see chapter 3), they also have harsh labour regimes (with trade unions banned in Korea until 1993, for example).[72] Indeed, O'Hearn himself notes that the conditions of growth differ greatly between the Asian economies themselves. For example, in Singapore industrial development has largely depended upon foreign investment, but in South Korea and Taiwan the emphasis has been upon the establishment of a strong industrial base.[73] Hence, Ireland is hardly an East Asian-style 'tiger' economy, but should not be expected to be so in the first place.

Delayed convergence?

So far, this chapter has examined the 'Celtic tiger' and 'paper tiger' theses and suggested that Ireland's growth is neither a miracle nor a mirage. Before moving forward, it is worth outlining a further perspective on Ireland's growth: that the Republic has simply caught up with other developed countries.[74] As Ó Gráda writes, the 'Celtic tiger' era will 'be remembered mainly as the interlude when Ireland made up all the ground it had lost and became a "normal" European economy'.[75] Examining Irish incomes in the period 1950–98, he finds that while they lagged behind the OECD average prior to the 1990s, by 1998 they were 'on track'.[76] Similarly, Fitz Gerald finds that Ireland's productivity has been moving towards the EU average since the 1970s – albeit at an accelerated rate in the 1990s.[77] For these authors, Ireland has not experienced an economic 'miracle' but instead has undergone a process of (belated) convergence.

Seen in these terms, the real question for these scholars is not why Ireland did so well in the 1990s but why it failed to catch up with other European states earlier on. In fact, they argue, the Republic already had the preconditions for economic growth (such as an educated workforce) prior to the 1990s. However, it failed to realise its potential due to inappropriate policies pursued by successive Irish governments: from the continued commitment to protectionism in the immediate post-war years to the failure to achieve a stable fiscal environment in the 1980s (see also chapter 4). With the removal of these obstacles (for example, through trade liberalisation in the 1960s and fiscal stabilisation in the late 1980s), Ireland's delayed structural transformation could finally take place. In turn, this meant that convergence 'was telescoped into a short period'.[78]

Yet can Ireland's economic growth really be understood in these terms? In fact, as Barry observes, authors such as Ó Gráda imply that convergence was essentially automatic: all that was needed was the removal of the various obstacles identified by the convergence theorists and Ireland's success was guaranteed. By this token, Ireland would have experienced convergence in earlier decades if only these barriers had been removed.[79] But as Barry notes, the dynamics behind Ireland's growth have relied upon a number of timing-specific factors – not least the establishment of the Single European Market (SEM) in 1992, which stimulated the acceleration of inward investment into the EU (see also chapter 3).[80] Moreover, the delayed convergence thesis assumes that 'we can now rest on our laurels': convergence can be maintained as long as governments continue to adopt appropriate policies. This in turn *under*estimates Ireland's economic vulnerabilities (in contrast to critics such as O'Hearn who *over*estimate them).[81] For example, the Republic's membership of EMU leaves policy-makers less scope to use fiscal policy measures to adjust to external economic shocks (see chapter 6). Thus, while Ireland has certainly caught up with other developed economies, its ability to achieve (and in turn sustain) economic growth has by no means been inevitable. Rather, as will be discussed in chapter 3, the dynamics behind Ireland's growth have been both highly complex and highly contingent.

Poverty and inequality

So far, this chapter has examined Ireland's performance solely in terms of economic growth. Yet, as authors from a variety of perspectives have noted, this is not the only measure of Ireland's performance. Rather, the issue is not so much whether Ireland has experienced a boom or not as whether the Irish people have benefited from this.[82] Thus, while it is possible to accept that Irish growth rates have improved, this does not necessarily make Ireland an economic success. Progress, it is argued, cannot simply be gauged in terms of GDP (or even GNP), for 'high rates of economic growth are valuable only if they deliver improvements in the community's material standard of living'.[83] Thus, indicators such as income distribution and poverty are also crucial.

For many critics, when viewed in terms of these indicators, Ireland's performance is far from spectacular. Indeed, the Combat Poverty Agency's head of research and policy, Jim Walsh, has described Ireland as in 'the top half of the EU poverty league'.[84] As table 2.4 shows, Ireland continues to score poorly in the United Nations' human poverty index, coming second only to the US of the developed countries in terms of poverty levels. This is largely due to the Republic's low literacy figures, with 22.6 per cent of the population lacking functional literacy skills in the UN index. Ireland also ranks fifth highest of the developed countries in terms of long-term unemployment, which accounted for 3.2 per cent of the labour force in 2001. On these grounds, the critics argue, Ireland's economic growth has not been accompanied by success in social terms.

Yet the picture is not as clear cut as this. As the Irish government has been quick to point out, the UN's human poverty index is based upon out-of-date figures (in some cases up to five years old) and significant progress has since been made.[85] For example, long-term unemployment in Ireland has fallen from 10.0 per cent in 1993 to just 1.5 per cent in 2003 – considerably lower than the EU15 average of 3.3 per cent (and the EU25 average of 4.0 per cent).[86] Similarly, 'consistent poverty' (defined as the lack of certain basic necessities such as

Table 2.4 Human and income poverty (developed countries), 1990–2001

Overall score on human poverty index	Country	Population below 50% median income, 1990–2000	Income/consumption share ratio of richest 20% to poorest 20% (latest available year)	People lacking functional literacy skills (% age 16–65), 1994–8	Long-term unemployment (% labour force), 2001
1	Sweden	6.6	3.8	7.5	1.1
2	Norway	6.9	3.7	8.5	0.2
3	Finland	5.4	3.5	10.4	2.4
4	Netherlands	8.1	5.5	10.5	1.6
5	Denmark	9.2	4.3	9.6	0.9
6	Germany	7.5	7.9	14.4	4.2
7	Luxembourg	3.9	4.9	–	0.5
8	France	8.0	5.6	–	3.3
9	Spain	10.1	5.4	–	4.6
10	Japan	11.8	3.4	–	1.4
11	Italy	14.2	7.1	–	6.1
12	Canada	12.8	5.4	16.6	0.7
13	Belgium	8.0	4.5	18.4	3.2
14	Australia	14.3	7.0	17.0	1.4
15	UK	12.5	7.1	21.8	0.3
16	*Ireland*	*12.3*	*6.4*	*22.6*	*3.2*
17	US	17.0	9.0	20.7	0.3

Source: adapted from United Nations, *Human Development Report 2003: Millennium Development Goals: A Compact Among Nations to End Human Poverty* (New York: Oxford University Press, 2003), pp. 248, 282.

heating in addition to a low income) has fallen rapidly (from 15 per cent in 1994 to 5 per cent in 2001 – see also table 2.5).[87] Consistent poverty among children has been reduced from 25 per cent in 1987 to just 6.5 per cent in 2001.[88]

However, there is significant debate in Ireland as to whether poverty should be defined in absolute or relative terms.[89] Whereas absolute poverty refers to access to basic utilities, relative poverty is 'built around the economic resources that a person has in relation to the resources of others'.[90] Although absolute poverty has fallen, critics argue that the gap between rich and poor is becoming wider in Ireland. Indeed, Allen argues that instead of a trickle-down effect there has been a 'trickle up'.[91] Taking into account a variety of factors, Whelan et al. identify a 'clear trend' towards rising poverty in the 1990s, with the income gap between the incomes of the poor and the poverty line

Table 2.5 Percentage of persons lacking basic deprivation items in Ireland, 1994–2001

Item lacked	Percentage of persons lacking item		
	1994	1997	2001
Meal with meat, chicken or fish	5.0	1.9	0.9
New not second-hand clothes	9.6	7.7	2.6
Adequate heating	9.7	6.2	2.8
Arrears relating to mortgage payments or utility bills	19.5	11.7	6.1
Having friends or family for a meal or drink once a month	21.8	12.7	6.6
Replacing worn-out furniture	33.4	20.8	14.0
A week's annual holiday away from home	45.5	35.0	22.9

Source: C. T. Whelan et al., *Monitoring Poverty Trends in Ireland: Results from the 2001 Living in Ireland Survey* (Dublin: Economic and Social Research Institute, 2003), p. 62.

Table 2.6 Percentage of persons below relative income poverty lines in Ireland, 1994–2001

Type of measure	Poverty line	Percentage of persons below line				
		1994	1997	1998	2000	2001
Mean relative income poverty line	50% mean income line	5.2	6.3	8.2	8.5	8.1
	60% mean income line	17.4	18.1	19.3	18.0	18.4
	70% mean income line	30.4	30.1	27.8	27.1	27.5
Median relative income poverty line	50% mean income line	6.0	8.6	9.9	12.0	12.9
	60% mean income line	15.6	18.2	19.8	20.9	21.9
	70% mean income line	26.7	29.0	26.9	28.1	29.3

Source: Whelan et al., *Monitoring Poverty Trends*, p. 12.

widening between 1994 and 2001 'irrespective of the measure used' (see for instance table 2.6).[92] Critics also point to significant disparities *across* Ireland in terms of regional inequalities.[93] According to CSO figures, disposable income per person was 3.4 per cent above the state average in the Southern and Eastern regions but 9.6 per cent below the state average in the Border, Midland and Western regions in 2001.[94]

Yet, while the fruits of economic growth have not been distributed equally, it would be wrong to suggest that economic growth has spelt social disaster, as authors such as Allen and Kirby claim. In fact, as Whelan et al. find, there has been an absolute increase in real incomes for all groups, accompanied by a large reduction in the proportion of

Table 2.7 Percentage of persons below 1994 relative income standards in Ireland, 1994–2001

Type of measure	Poverty line	Percentage of persons below line				
		1994	1997	1998	2000	2001
Real income standard	50% mean income line	5.2	2.3	1.2	1.1	1.0
	60% mean income line	17.4	7.8	5.5	3.1	2.4
	70% mean income line	30.4	17.3	12.2	8.6	6.3

Source: Whelan et al., *Monitoring Poverty Trends*, p. 12.

the population under a 'real income' poverty line (see table 2.7).[95] It is difficult to conclude, then, that Ireland's performance – including in terms of its social impact – is either dazzling or disappointing. On the one hand, many significant gains have been made (not the least of these being the fall in consistent poverty and the rise in real incomes). On the other hand, the widening gap between rich and poor suggests that Ireland is hardly a model of social inclusion. Once again, this undermines the binary distinction between the Celtic and the paper tiger, for Ireland's performance has been impressive in some respects but less so in others.

Discourses of the Celtic tiger

The ambiguity surrounding Ireland's status as a Celtic or a paper tiger is in itself interesting, for it points to the role of interpretation and ideas. An analogy can be made with the debate about globalisation. Much of the literature tends to focus upon globalisation as a material reality, whether to affirm or reject it. In so doing, it neglects the role that *ideas* about globalisation may play in shaping policy outcomes. Similarly, the 'Celtic tiger' literature – whether it affirms or rejects Ireland's 'tiger' status – tends to focus upon 'success' in material terms.[96] Yet the concept may also have significant discursive power, irrespective of its analytical utility.

The 'Celtic tiger' discourse

Policy-makers in Ireland have indeed embraced the concept of the 'Celtic tiger'. The term itself appears regularly in Dáil debates, ministerial speeches, press releases and policy documents. Ireland's economic performance is also frequently described in such terms as 'outstanding', 'staggering', 'exceptional', 'enviable', 'unprecedented' and 'world-beating'.[97] While Irish policy-makers seem genuinely to believe in Ireland's 'tiger' status and 'enormous' economic transformation,[98] there may also be important strategic reasons for them to do so. As a number of scholars have noted, perhaps the key electoral issue in contemporary Irish politics is not a party's ideological stance but its record in terms of economic performance.[99] Opinion polls show economic issues to be the most important for voters, with low priority given to 'social' issues such as abortion, divorce and contraception.[100] It is perhaps not surprising, then, that Irish politicians are keen to promote the image of Ireland's 'spectacular' economic performance. As Fianna Fáil's 2002 election manifesto stated: 'Under Fianna Fáil Ireland has become the world's most dynamic economy ... Fianna Fáil has led Ireland through a period of unprecedented prosperity and growth ... we consolidated an economy that is still the envy of the world.'[101] By the same token, the main opposition party (Fine Gael) has been keen to exploit the 'paper tiger' discourse in order to discredit the government's record, pointing for example to Ireland's low rating in the UN's Human Development Index.[102]

On the international stage, too, Irish policy-makers have been keen to promote Ireland's image as the 'Celtic tiger'. As the taoiseach told the EU heads of mission in 1998: 'We have carved out a presence in Europe and in the world, which far exceeds the normal expectations of a country of our size.'[103] In interviews, senior policy-makers and opinion formers argued that this has important political benefits by helping to enhance the Republic's status and bargaining position within and outside the EU.[104] In addition, Ireland's 'tiger' status may yield important economic benefits. In particular, it may in itself contribute to the Republic's success in attracting FDI (see also chapter 3). As one chief executive remarked: 'There is almost no business publication in the United States that hasn't talked about the Celtic tiger.'[105] The Industrial Development Agency (IDA) thus urges foreign firms to 'Invest in Ireland', claiming: 'Over 1,200 companies have chosen Ireland as their base to serve the European market and beyond ... choose Ireland, you'll be in good company.'[106] In this sense, the 'Celtic tiger' discourse may in itself yield material effects, as a kind of self-fulfilling prophecy. As one senior policy-maker stated: 'success breeds success and success writes history, really'.[107]

The 'paper tiger' discourse

Yet, on occasion, the government has tried to downplay the extent of Ireland's economic success. One particular incentive for them to do so has been to postpone the withdrawal of EU funding. As *The Economist* noted, Irish politicians have been: 'Modest fellows, no doubt; shrewd as well.'[108] Since payments of structural funds are based on GDP figures, policy-makers have claimed that they do not accurately reflect the real wealth of the Irish economy. Policy-makers were successfully able to exploit Ireland's ambiguous status in the Agenda 2000 negotiations. Along with Greece, Portugal and Spain, the Republic remained eligible for funding under Agenda 2000 on the grounds that per capita GNP was less than 90 per cent of the EU average. While the Southern and Eastern regions were classed as Objective One in transition, the Midlands, Western and Border regions remained eligible for full Objective One funding. Ireland is therefore set to receive some €3.35 billion from the structural funds between 2000 and 2006.[109]

In the domestic context, too, politicians may seek to exploit the ambiguity surrounding Ireland's economic performance. In interviews, it was felt that the very success of the Celtic tiger discourse has in itself become a source of pressure on the government. As one senior civil servant stated: 'people's expectations have gone up, people are keen on hearing about the Celtic tiger and everyone says I want my share of the Celtic tiger'.[110] Policy-makers may attempt to downplay Ireland's success in order to moderate public expectations. For example, at the height of Ireland's economic boom the minister for finance argued that the East Asian economies had also been hailed as 'glittering success stories' but then turned into 'economic chaos'. He therefore emphasised the need for fiscal discipline in Ireland.[111] This also relates to the social partnership negotiations, with significant pressure from unions to increase wages. According to one business representative: 'people talk about the famous Celtic tiger and all that, and in those circumstances it's probably not surprising that the unions react by saying let's try to get as much out of this as we can'.[112] As will be discussed in chapter 7, the Irish government has sought to temper these expectations not least through appeals to Ireland's vulnerability as a 'globalised' economy. Thus, there may be strategic advantages not only in articulating the 'Celtic tiger' discourse but also in exploiting its ambiguity.

Conclusion

This chapter has assessed the nature of Ireland's economic transformation in the 1990s. It has outlined the conventional wisdom that Ireland became the miracle of Europe in the 1990s and has then examined sceptical claims that official figures distort the true nature of growth, that the Irish model is unsustainable and that the fruits of growth have not been equally shared. The chapter has argued that while Ireland's performance is certainly not as spectacular as the 'Celtic tiger' label suggests, the Republic is no 'paper tiger', either. Rather, a middle-ground position – acknowledging that Ireland's growth has been impressive but not miraculous – is preferable. For, while Ireland's performance has improved in some respects – not only in terms of economic growth itself but also in terms of its social impact – it has been less impressive in others. Yet the chapter has also argued that this ambiguity is in itself interesting, for it points to the role of interpretation and ideas. In particular, Irish policy-makers have embraced and exploited discourses of the 'Celtic tiger' in order to attract foreign investment and to appeal to the electorate. They may also have utilised the ambiguity surrounding Ireland's success, for example in order to justify fiscal restraint and to postpone the withdrawal of EU funding. Thus, while the Celtic and paper tiger labels may have limited utility in analytical terms, they nevertheless possess significant discursive power.

Having discussed the extent of Ireland's economic growth, it is now possible to turn to the reasons for economic growth and, in particular, to examine whether this can in turn be attributed to 'globalisation'.

Notes

1 R. Quinn, 'Celtic tiger in a global jungle – address by the minister for finance', IBEC Annual Business Conference, Dublin Castle (29 May 1997).
2 P. Kirby, *The Celtic Tiger in Distress: Growth and Inequality in Ireland* (Basingstoke: Palgrave, 2002), p. 3.
3 J. Fitz Gerald, 'Ireland's failure – and belated convergence', ESRI Working Paper No. 133, Dublin (2000), p. 2.
4 OECD, *Regional Problems and Policies in OECD Countries: France, Italy, Ireland, Denmark, Sweden, Japan* (Paris: OECD, 1976), pp. 60, 68.
5 OECD, *Economic Surveys: Ireland 1999* (Paris: OECD, 1999), p. 10.

6 J. Lee, *Ireland, 1912–85: Politics and Society* (Cambridge and New York: Cambridge University Press, 1989), p. 515.
7 'Ireland shines', *The Economist* (17 May 1997).
8 M. Wolf, 'Ireland's miracle', *Financial Times* (19 August 1999).
9 J. Bush, 'A Celtic tiger for Europe', *The Times* (25 June 1996).
10 T. Raphael, 'Ireland's European rivals are green with envy', *Wall Street Journal* (18 December 1998).
11 See for instance F. Barry, 'Introduction', in F. Barry (ed.), *Understanding Ireland's Economic Growth* (Basingstoke: Macmillan, 1999), p. 1; A. Leddin and B. Walsh, *The Macro-Economy of Ireland* (Dublin: Gill & Macmillan, 1998), p. i; F. Ruane and H. Görg, 'Ireland's economic growth', *Economic Review*, 18: 1 (2000), p. 15; J. J. Sexton and P. O'Connell, *Labour Market Studies: Ireland* (Brussels: European Commission, 1996), p. xxvi; D. Schmitt, 'Conclusion: continuity, change and challenge', in W. J. Crotty and D. E. Schmitt (eds), *Ireland and the Politics of Change* (London: Longman, 1998), p. 217; P. Sweeney, *The Celtic Tiger: Ireland's Continuing Economic Miracle* (Dublin: Oak Tree Press, 1999), p. 1.
12 C. Whelan, cited C. Holmquist, 'Drowning in the rising tide', *Irish Times* (7 September 1998).
13 IMF, *Ireland – Staff Report for the 2001 Article IV Consultation* (Washington, DC: International Monetary Fund, 2001), p. 4; OECD, *Economic Surveys: Ireland 1999*, p. 9.
14 Cited in J. Brown, 'Ireland: catch up phase runs its course', *Financial Times* (4 November 1999).
15 M. Donohoe, 'China appreciates Irish growth and learning', *Irish Times* (29 April 2004).
16 World Economic Forum, *Global Competitiveness Report 2001–2* (Geneva: World Economic Forum, 2002).
17 OECD, *OECD in Figures 2003* (Paris: OECD, 2003), pp. 12–13.
18 A. Murphy, 'Beneath Celtic tiger mask is US high-tech face', *Irish Times* (30 January 1998); O. O'Conner, 'Time for the Celtic tiger to be slain', *Irish Times* (9 January 1998).
19 D. O'Hearn, *The Atlantic Economy: Britain, the US and Ireland* (Manchester: Manchester University Press, 2001), pp. 176–7; D. O'Hearn, 'Macroeconomic policy in the Celtic tiger: a critical reassessment', in C. Coulter and S. Coleman (eds), *The End of Irish History? Critical Reflections on the Celtic Tiger* (Manchester: Manchester University Press, 2003), pp. 37–8.
20 A. Murphy, 'The "Celtic tiger" – an analysis of Ireland's economic growth performance', European University Institute Working Paper, San Domenico (2000), p. 18.
21 Ó Gráda and O'Rourke also point to a huge fall in the share of wages and salaries in net output of the industrial sector as a whole, from over half in the 1950s and 1960s to less than a third today. They contend that this 'can hardly be explained by technological change or composition effects' (although they do not specify what these might be). See C. Ó Gráda and K. O'Rourke, 'Economic growth: performance and explanations', in J.

O'Hagen (ed.), *The Economy of Ireland: Policy and Performance of a Small European Country* (Dublin: Gill & Macmillan, 1995), p. 214.
22 O'Hearn, 'Macroeconomic policy in the Celtic tiger', p. 40.
23 Department of Finance, *Budgetary and Economic Statistics: March 2004* (Dublin: Department of Finance, 2004), p. 12.
24 D. O'Hearn, 'Globalisation, "new tigers," and the end of the developmental state? The case of the Celtic tiger', *Politics & Society*, 28: 1 (2000), pp. 74–5.
25 'There's lies, damned lies, and wealth statistics', *Irish Times* (11 May 2004).
26 OECD, *Economic Surveys: Ireland 1999*, p. 29.
27 D. O'Hearn, *Inside the Celtic Tiger: The Irish Economy and the Asian Model* (London: Pluto Press, 1998), p. 84.
28 O'Hearn, 'Macroeconomic policy in the Celtic tiger', pp. 43–6.
29 O'Hearn, 'Globalisation, "new tigers," and the end of the developmental state?', p. 77; O'Hearn, *Inside the Celtic Tiger*, p. 83.
30 See for instance P. R. Krugman, *Pop Internationalism* (Cambridge, MA: MIT Press, 1996), p. 175.
31 N. Roubini, 'What causes long run growth? The debate on the Asian miracle' (1998), www.stern.nyu.edu/globalmacro.
32 O'Hearn, *Inside the Celtic Tiger*, pp. 84–6.
33 P. Honohan and B. Walsh, 'Catching up with the leaders: the Irish hare', Brookings Panel on Economic Activity, Washington, DC (4–5 April 2002), pp. 5, 21–2.
34 O. Blanchard, 'Comments on "catching up with the leaders: the Irish hare", by Patrick Honohan and Brendan Walsh', *Brookings Papers on Economic Activity*, 1 (2002). Similarly, Barry compares Ireland's productivity to that of the UK and finds that even if productivity is adjusted to exclude all profit repatriation, then Ireland's levels are still 110 per cent higher than the UK's – see F. Barry, 'Irish growth in historical and theoretical perspective', in Barry, *Understanding Ireland's Economic Growth*, p. 36.
35 S. Ó Riain, 'The flexible developmental state: globalisation, information technology and the "Celtic tiger"', *Politics & Society*, 28: 2 (2000), pp. 160–1.
36 Forfás, *International Trade and Investment Report 2001* (Dublin: Forfás, 2002), p. 12.
37 M. O'Sullivan, 'Industrial development: a new beginning?', in J. W. O'Hagen (ed.), *The Economy of Ireland: Policy and Performance of a European Region* (Dublin: Gill & Macmillan, 2000), p. 270. Forfás finds that expenditure by (agency-supported) indigenous enterprises in the Irish economy accounted for 71 per cent of their sales in 2003, compared to just 23 per cent by (agency-supported) foreign-owned enterprises – see Forfás, *International Trade and Investment Report 2003* (Dublin: Forfás, 2004), p. 20.
38 As Forfás states: 'it is difficult to conclude that there is growing embeddedness of [foreign firms] in the domestic economy' – see Forfás, *International Trade and Investment Report 2001*, p. 12.

39 OECD, *OECD in Figures 2003*, p. 16.
40 O'Hearn, 'Globalisation, "new tigers," and the end of the developmental state?', pp. 79–80.
41 Ó Riain, 'The flexible developmental state', p. 162.
42 P. O'Connell, 'The dynamics of the Irish labour market in comparative perspective', in B. Nolan, P. O'Connell and C. T. Whelan (eds), *Bust to Boom? The Irish Experience of Growth and Inequality* (Dublin: Institute of Public Administration, 2000), p. 86.
43 P. Kirby, *Macroeconomic Success and Social Vulnerability: Lessons for Latin America from the Celtic Tiger* (Santiago de Chile: United Nations, 2003), p. 39.
44 O'Connell, 'The dynamics of the Irish labour market', p. 86.
45 C. T. Whelan and R. Layte, 'Economic boom and social mobility: the Irish experience', ESRI Working Paper No. 154, Dublin (2004), p. 15.
46 O'Hearn, *Inside the Celtic Tiger*, pp. 5, 61; O'Hearn, 'Globalisation, "new tigers," and the end of the developmental state?', p. 87.
47 K. Allen, 'Neither Boston nor Berlin: class polarisation and neo-liberalism in the Irish Republic', in Coulter and Coleman, *The End of Irish History*, p. 58; Kirby, *The Celtic Tiger in Distress*, p. 4.
48 Allen, 'Neither Boston nor Berlin', pp. 56–9; see also P. Clinch, F. Convery and B. Walsh, *After the Celtic Tiger: Challenges Ahead* (Dublin: O'Brien Press, 2002).
49 Department of Finance, *Budgetary and Economic Statistics, 2004*, pp. 5, 63.
50 See for instance Allen, 'Neither Boston nor Berlin', p. 56; Clinch, Convery and Walsh, *After the Celtic Tiger*, cover materials; OECD, *Economic Surveys: Ireland 2003* (Paris: OECD, 2003), p. 6.
51 See for instance O'Hearn, *Inside the Celtic Tiger*, p. 61.
52 European Commission, *Economic Forecasts Spring 2004* (Luxembourg: Eurostat, 2004), p. 1.
53 UNCTAD, *WID Country Profile: Ireland* (Geneva: United Nations, 2004), p. 1.
54 ESRI, 'Quarterly economic commentary, summer 2004: executive summary' (2004), www.esri.ie.
55 Forfás, *End of Year Statement 2003* (Dublin: Forfás, 2004), p. 2.
56 A. Bergin, J. Cullen, D. Duffy, J. Fity Gerald, I. Kearney and D. McCoy, 'Introduction', in A. Bergin, J. Cullen, D. Duffy, J. Fity Gerald, I. Kearney and D. McCoy (eds), *Medium-Term Review 2003–10* (Dublin: Economic and Social Research Institute, 2002), p. 1; IMF, *Ireland – Staff Report for the 2002 Article IV Consultation* (Washington, DC: International Monetary Fund, 2002), p. 3; OECD, *Economic Surveys: Ireland 2003*, p. 21; European Commission, *Economic Forecasts Autumn 2004* (Luxembourg: Eurostat, 2004), p.59.
57 F. Barry, J. Bradley and E. O'Malley, 'Indigenous and foreign industry: characteristics and performance', in Barry, *Understanding Ireland's Economic Growth*, p. 70.
58 H. Görg and E. Strobl, 'Footloose multinationals?', Leverhulme Centre for Research on Globalisation and Economic Policy Research Paper 2001/07 (2001), p. 12.

59 CSO, *Foreign Direct Investment 2001 and 2002* (Cork: Central Statistical Office, 2003), p. 2.
60 J. Smyth, '€1.6 billion investment by Intel will create 400 jobs', *Irish Times* (20 May 2004).
61 Ó Riain, 'The flexible developmental state', p. 161.
62 Forfás, *International Trade and Investment Report 2002* (Dublin: Forfás, 2003), p. 15.
63 NESC, *An Investment in Quality: Services, Inclusion and Enterprise* (Dublin: National Economic and Social Council, 2003), p. 33; K. Allen, *The Celtic Tiger: The Myth of Social Partnership in Ireland* (Manchester: Manchester University Press, 2000), p. 61.
64 E. O'Malley, 'The revival of Irish indigenous industry 1987–97', in T. J. Baker, D. Duffy and F. Shortall (eds), *Quarterly Economic Commentary, April 1998* (Dublin: Economic and Social Research Institute, 1998), p. 35.
65 Forfás, *International Trade and Investment Report, 2000* (Dublin: Forfás, 2001), pp. 38–40.
66 O'Sullivan, 'Industrial development', p. 273.
67 Ibid., p. 275.
68 See for instance P. R. Krugman, 'The myth of Asia's miracle', *Foreign Affairs* (November/December 1994).
69 A. Sweeney, *Irrational Exuberance: The Myth of the Celtic Tiger* (Dublin: Blackhall, 1999), pp. 35, 77.
70 OECD, *Economic Surveys: Ireland 2003*, p. 6.
71 O'Conner, 'Time for the Celtic tiger to be slain'.
72 Sweeney, *The Celtic Tiger*, p. 14.
73 O'Hearn, *Inside the Celtic Tiger*, p. 31.
74 See for instance Bergin et al., 'Introduction', p. 3; C. Ó Gráda, 'Is the Celtic tiger a paper tiger?', in D. McCoy, D. Duffy, J. Hore and C. Maccoille (eds), *Quarterly Economic Commentary, Spring 2002* (Dublin: Economic and Social Research Institute, 2002), p. 5; Honohan and Walsh, 'Catching up with the leaders: the Irish hare', pp. 2–3; J. Fitz Gerald, 'Ireland – a multicultural economy', in W. Crotty and D. E. Schmitt (eds), *Ireland on the World Stage* (Manchester: Manchester University Press, 2002), p. 67.
75 Ó Gráda, 'Is the Celtic tiger a paper tiger?', p. 9.
76 Ibid., pp. 1–2.
77 In turn, he attributes this to a shift in Ireland's dependency ratio (that is, the ratio of the population not in paid employment to those who are at work), which was very high prior to the 1990s but has since fallen rapidly – see Fitz Gerald, 'Ireland – a multicultural economy', pp. 70–1.
78 Honohan and Walsh, 'Catching up with the leaders: the Irish hare', p. 2; see also Bergin et al., 'Introduction', p. 3; Fitz Gerald, 'Ireland – a multicultural economy', p. 66; Ó Gráda, 'Is the Celtic tiger a paper tiger?', pp. 2–5.
79 F. Barry, 'The Celtic tiger era: delayed convergence or regional boom?' in McCoy et al., *Quarterly Economic Commentary, Summer 2002*, p. 3.

80 F. Barry, 'Economic policy, income convergence and structural change in the EU periphery' (2002), www.ucd.ie?~economy/staff/barry/fdi.html.
81 Barry, 'The Celtic tiger era: delayed convergence or regional boom?', p. 6.
82 See for instance P. Tansey, *Ireland at Work: Economic Growth and the Labour Market, 1987–97* (Dublin: Oak Tree Press, 1998), p. 1; S. Healy and B. Reynolds, *Social Policy in Ireland: Principles, Practice and Problems* (Dublin: Oak Tree Press, 1998), pp. 4–17; Kirby, *The Celtic Tiger in Distress*, pp. 169–81; O'Hearn, *Inside the Celtic Tiger*, pp. 117–46.
83 Tansey, *Ireland at Work*, p. 1.
84 Cited in M.-A. Wren, 'No fall in numbers living in poverty despite boom years', *Irish Times* (17 April 2002).
85 *Irish Times*, 'Human development' (24 July 2002).
86 Eurostat, 'Total long-term unemployment rate' (2004), europa.eu.int/comm/eurostat.
87 C. T. Whelan, R. Layte, B. Maitre, B. Gannon, B. Nolan, D. Watson and J. Williams, *Monitoring Poverty Trends in Ireland: Results from the 2001 Living in Ireland Survey* (Dublin: Economic and Social Research Institute, 2003), p. 71.
88 Combat Poverty Agency, 'Factsheet: child poverty in Ireland' (2004), www.cpa.ie/facts_factsheet_children.html.
89 For example, Mac Cárthaig contends that relative definitions can yield some 'perverse results', noting that if the income of every person in Ireland quadrupled overnight, no increase in relative poverty would be recorded. Callan et al. reject this notion, arguing that there are 'enormous difficulties in deriving any standard which could be taken to represent "absolute" needs'. Often, they argue, this is taken to be a poverty line, which is held constant in real terms and does not increase with incomes. They write: 'What this misses is that the *meaning* of poverty changes over time: poverty in 1990 is simply not the same as poverty in 1960, but it does violence to the common understanding of the concept to therefore conclude that there is no poverty in 1990.' See S. Mac Cárthaig, 'Measuring poverty in Ireland: a comment', *Economic and Social Review*, 21: 2 (1990), pp. 228–9; T. Callan, D. F. Hanna, B. Nolan and B. J. Whelan, 'Measuring poverty in Ireland – reply', *Economic and Social Review*, 21: 2 (1990), pp. 232–3.
90 P. A. O'Hara, *Encyclopedia of Political Economy* (London and New York: Routledge, 1999), p. 890.
91 Cited in 'Partnership masks surge in inequality,' *Irish Times* (19 October 1999).
92 C. T. Whelan, R. Layte, B. Maitre, B. Gannon, B. Nolan, D. Watson and J. Williams, 'Executive summary', in Whelan et al., *Monitoring Poverty Trends in Ireland: Results from the 2001 Living in Ireland Survey*, p. i.
93 See for instance P. Breathnach, 'Exploring the "Celtic tiger" phenomenon: causes and consequences of Ireland's economic miracle', *European Urban and Regional Studies*, 5: 4 (1998), p. 314.

94 CSO, *County Incomes and Regional GDP 2001* (Cork: Central Statistical Office, 2004), p. 1.
95 Whelan et al., 'Executive summary', p. i.
96 Although see for instance P. Kirby, L. Gibbons and M. Cronin (eds), *Reinventing Ireland: Culture, Society and the Global Economy* (London: Pluto Press, 2002); G. Taylor, *Negotiated Governance and Public Policy in Ireland* (Manchester: Manchester University Press, 2005), pp. 2–3.
97 See for instance B. Ahern, 'Ireland and Europe: embracing change', Thomas Davis Lecture (27 January 2003); B. Ahern, 'Speech by the taoiseach', Meeting of the Fianna Fáil Parliamentary Party (27 September 2000); M. Harney, 'Foreword', *Enterprise 2010* (Dublin: Forfás, 2000), p. i; C. McCreevy, 'Introductory statement', Meeting of the Dail Select Committee on Finance and the Public Service (16 June 1999); M. Tutty, 'Presentation to the social partners on economic and budgetary performance and outlook' (16 November 1999).
98 Interviews.
99 See for instance N. Collins and T. Cradden, *Irish Politics Today* (Manchester: Manchester University Press, 1997), p. 23; M. Laver and M. Marsh, 'Parties and voters', in J. Coakley and M. Gallagher (eds), *Politics in the Republic of Ireland* (London: Routledge, 1999), p. 167; M. Marsh and R. Sinnott, 'The voters: stability and change', in M. Gallagher and M. Laver (eds), *How Ireland Voted 1992* (Folens: PSAI Press, 1993), p. 100; see also chapter 8.
100 Laver and Marsh cite as one notable example that only 4 per cent of voters rated abortion as a key issue in the election of 1992, despite the referendums being held at the time on this issue. In the election of 1997 only 13 per cent of voters gave priority to the Northern Ireland issue, despite the significance of the peace process at the time. See Laver and Marsh, 'Parties and voters', p. 167. Similarly, a 1992 IMS poll found that voters were much more likely to vote for Fianna Fáil if they believed the economy would improve than if they thought it would get worse. See Marsh and Sinnott, 'The voters', p. 100.
101 Fianna Fáil, *A Lot Done: More to Do – Fianna Fáil Manifesto 2002–7* (Dublin: Fianna Fáil, 2002), pp. 4–6.
102 Fine Gael, 'A plan for the nation: Fine Gael's vision of Ireland in 2010 – summary' (1999), www.finegael.ie/policydocs/summaryanation.htm.
103 B. Ahern, 'Address to EU heads of mission' (30 April 1998). Similarly, he told the World Economic Forum in 2004 that Ireland is 'perhaps the best example' of how member states can achieve economic convergence – B. Ahern, 'Speech by the taoiseach', World Economic Forum, Davos, Switzerland (24 January 2004).
104 In the words of one interviewee: 'because we've done so well at the European level we have not been afraid to take on people on the world stage as well'.
105 Cited in O'Clery, 'Irish tech start-ups still a hot item for US VCs' (2001), www.xacp.com/news.html.

106 IDA Ireland, 'Invest in Ireland' (2001), www.idaireland.com.
107 Interviews.
108 'Europe's tiger economy', *The Economist* (17 May 1997).
109 National Development Plan/Community Support Framework Information Office, 'Overview' (2000), www.csfinfo.com/overview.
110 Interviews.
111 C. McCreevy, 'Discipline needed for health of Celtic Tiger, 24 November 1997' (1997), www.gov.ie/finance/news/archives/1997/Bcp.htm.
112 Interviews.

3

Economic performance (2): a 'showpiece of globalisation'?

Just as there has been significant debate about the nature of Ireland's economic transformation in the 1990s, so too there has been considerable controversy about the dynamics behind it. Yet, despite this disagreement, many commentators nevertheless agree that globalisation has played an important role in shaping Ireland's rapid growth in the 1990s. In particular, commentators point to Ireland's openness in terms of trade, its success in attracting foreign direct investment, and its membership of the EU. In turn, the Irish state is perceived to have embraced the globalisation process enthusiastically through a number of measures such as low corporate taxation and fiscal rectitude. This chapter assesses such claims through analysis of a range of factors behind Ireland's growth, both exogenous and endogenous. In so doing, it examines whether Ireland can really be considered a 'showpiece of globalisation' and, indeed, whether the Republic's growth can be understood in terms of globalisation at all.

Showcasing globalisation?

The significance of globalisation in Ireland's economic turnaround is widely cited by commentators from a variety of political perspectives.[1] To take just a few examples, Sweeney argues that Ireland has been a 'particular beneficiary' of globalisation, Crotty identifies Ireland as 'the prototype of a country' to have gained from globalisation, Murphy claims that '[g]lobalisation enabled Ireland to move from the periphery towards the centre of the new global economy', and Fitz Gerald emphasises 'the major economic benefits that have derived from the enthusiastic embrace of [the] process of globalisation'.[2] In the national and international press, too, Ireland has become known as globalisation's success story. As the *Irish Times* has argued: 'By successfully hitching its wagon to the locomotive of globalisation, the Republic has become a model for states everywhere seeking a fast track to prosperity.'[3] Similarly, *The Economist* has declared: 'If any country lends substance to the cliché that the global economy is an opportunity not a threat, it is Ireland.'[4] Perhaps more importantly, this view has also been wholeheartedly embraced within policy-making circles (see chapter 7). As the Irish minister for finance has stated: 'As regards globalisation and economic integration, Ireland's track record shows that we can exploit the opportunities and manage the undoubted challenges that they bring.'[5] Even international institutions such as the IMF have argued that Ireland has reaped the benefits of globalisation.[6]

While it is sometimes unclear what is actually meant by 'globalisation' with respect to the Irish case, three factors in particular are often seen to stand out as *prima facie* evidence that Ireland has been globalised: the fact that it is a small and open economy; its remarkable success in attracting FDI; and its membership of the EU. Each of these exogenous factors will now be discussed. The role of a number of endogenous factors will then be considered.

Trade openness

A particularly striking feature of the Irish economy is widely seen to be its extreme openness. Ireland has been described as having 'one of the greatest exposures to international trade of any country of the world'.[7] In the 1990s alone Ireland's ratio of trade to GDP increased by over 50 per cent, whereas the degree of openness in trade for the EU average fell. Ireland now comes second only to Luxembourg of all the OECD countries in terms of trade openness (see also figure 3.1). Moreover, its surplus in merchandise trade as a proportion of national income has been described as 'unparalleled in the industrial world'.[8] Despite being one of the smallest countries in the EU, Ireland ranked as the nineteenth leading exporter in the world for merchandise trade in 2002.[9]

This exposure to external trade is often cited as evidence of Ireland's globalisation. For example, Forfás argues that as 'one of the most open economies in the world', Ireland has been a 'major participant in the accelerating "globalisation" of economic activity in the 1990s.'[10] Similarly, Sweeney points to the growth in international trade and argues: 'It is precisely this change that provides a small open economy like Ireland with the opportunity to exploit its advantages in the globalising economy.'[11] Indeed, the A. T. Kearney

A 'SHOWPIECE OF GLOBALISATION'?

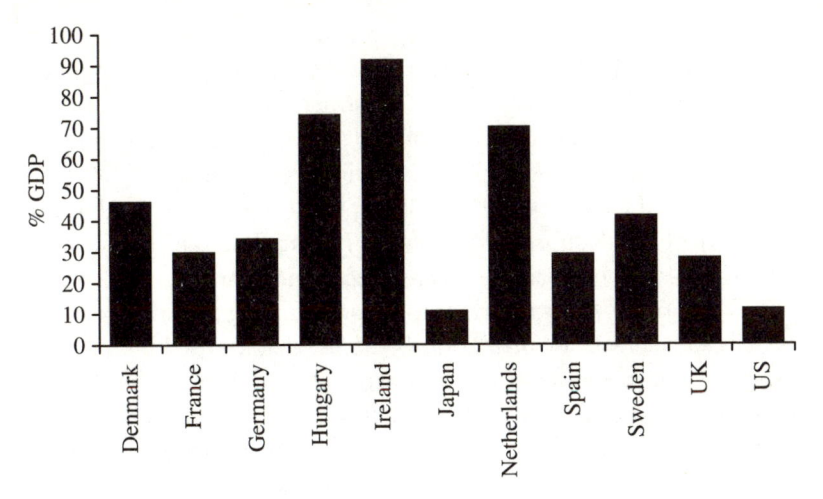

Figure 3.1 Trade openness in selected OECD countries, 2001

Note: Trade openness refers to exports + imports of goods + services to GDP.
Source: National Competitiveness Council (NCC), *Annual Competitiveness Report 2003* (Dublin: Forfás, 2003), p. 67.

Globalisation Index of 2004 ranked Ireland as the third most globalised country in the world in terms of trade.[12]

Yet several qualifications should be noted. First, while Ireland's openness has clearly been important to growth, it cannot in itself explain the Republic's impressive performance in the 1990s. While Ireland's export-market share grew by 50 per cent in 1987–97, other highly open economies such as Luxembourg and Belgium experienced an increase of only 10 per cent during this period.[13]

Second, the fact that the Irish economy is small and open does not mean that it is 'globalised'. As suggested in chapter 1, trade openness is by no means synonymous with globalisation. Rather, for trade flows to be cited as evidence of globalisation they must be (or be becoming) truly 'global' in scope. Nor, for that matter, does openness imply a process of deterritorialisation (as 'complex' theorists imply). For this would imply that territorial space is becoming less and less important in the flows of trade. In the Irish case, while the economy is certainly highly *open*, it is neither 'global' nor 'deterritorialised'. Rather, the Republic's external trade is highly concentrated in geographical terms. In fact, it is much more accurate to refer to a process of integration into the triad – or, more specifically, the *diad* – of Europe and the US. In 2005, trade with other EU states accounted for a massive two thirds of total exports, with the US taking up a further fifth of the total.[14] In contrast, Ireland's trade with the rest of the world has actually *fallen* slightly (from 20 per cent in 1980 to 18 per cent in 2005).[15]

Moreover, Ireland's patterns of trade are not only regionally concentrated but also highly nationally specific. For example, in 2005 the UK accounted for nearly half of Irish imports from the EU (and nearly a quarter of total exports), followed by Belgium (accounting for over a fifth of EU exports) and Germany (accounting for over 10 per cent of EU exports).[16] This suggests that Ireland's trading patterns are much better characterised as *inter*national (that is, characterised by relations *between* distinct nations) than *trans*national (that is, characterised by flows *across* national borders). Nor is this a new development: rather, as will be discussed in chapter 6, the importance of external transactions (albeit largely with the UK for many decades) has long been a feature of Irish economic development, even during the period of protectionism in the 1930s to 1950s. Ireland's economy is thus small and open but not globalised.

Foreign direct investment

It is not just Ireland's openness in terms of trade that is seen to signify globalisation. Commentators also point to the Republic's considerable success in attracting FDI in the 1990s – particularly from the US.[17] According to the OECD, the amount of FDI flows to Ireland, when compared to its actual GDP share, is 'out of all proportion'.[18] Despite its small size, Ireland accounted for 1.7 per cent of total world FDI inflows (and 3.9 per cent of total EU FDI inflows) in 1991–2002.[19] Indeed, Ireland ranked fourth in the UNCTAD FDI performance index for 1999–2001 (compared to a ranking of just 59 in 1988–90).[20] In terms of FDI per capita, Ireland is the EU's largest recipient, with almost three times as much FDI per capita as the Netherlands (which ranks second).[21] For many commentators, FDI is by far the most significant factor in Ireland's growth. O'Hearn, for instance, declares that 'the Irish tiger economy boils down to a few US corporations in IT and pharmaceuticals'. Murphy, too, contends that Ireland's success can be attributed to a 'small group' of US multinationals.[22]

The significance of FDI to the Irish economy is often cited as evidence of Ireland's globalisation (see also chapter 6). For example, Forfás describes FDI and trade as 'the two main pillars of globalisation'.[23] Similarly, Sweeney writes: 'One vital aspect of globalisation is the rate of growth of FDI, which has been phenomenal. Ireland has

A 'SHOWPIECE OF GLOBALISATION'?

been a particular beneficiary of this.'[24] In the A.T. Kearney Globalisation Index of 2004 the Republic ranked first in the world in terms of FDI, portfolio investment and investment income.[25]

It is indeed the case that foreign investment has had an enormous impact on the Irish economy. By the year 2000, over 500 industrial foreign affiliates had located in Ireland, employing more than 120,000 workers and producing an overall turnover of $57 billion. This investment has been concentrated in the dynamic, export-oriented sectors (electrical equipment and chemicals), with the foreign-owned sector accounting for about 90 per cent of total exports in 1999. Overall, Ireland's FDI stock rose from $32 billion in 1980 to $157 billion in 2002,[26] accounting for 129 per cent of GDP in 2002 (see figure 3.2). Yet, as Ó Riain notes, the 'disproportionate impact' on growth of multinational corporations such as Intel 'should not blind us to their relative lack of contribution to the very real transformation of production and innovation capabilities within parts of the Irish economy'.[27] As noted in chapter 2, important developments have taken place in the indigenous sector. Having performed poorly for several decades, indigenous industry experienced a revival after 1988 – if initially a slow and hesitant one. O'Malley notes that in 1988–96 employment by indigenous firms grew by 0.8 per cent in Ireland, compared

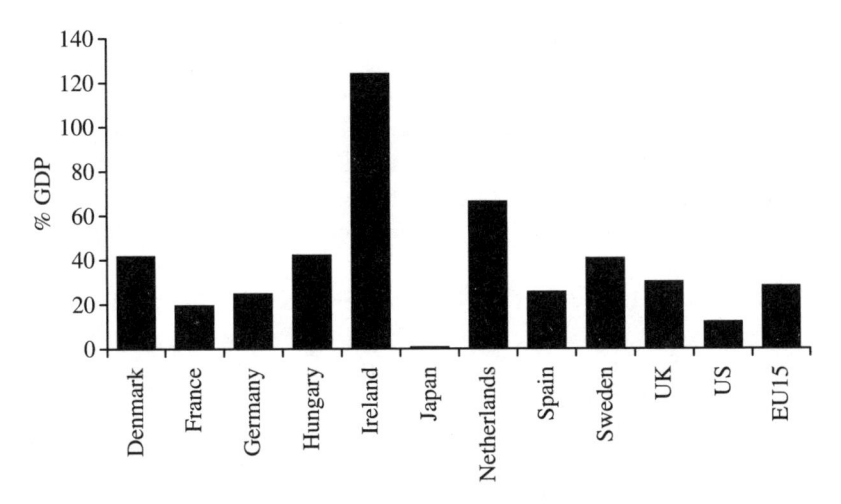

Figure 3.2 Inward foreign direct investment stocks as a share of GDP, 2002

Source: UNCTAD, *World Investment Report 2003: FDI Policies for Development – National and International Perspectives* (New York: United Nations, 2003), pp. 278–88.

to −1.9 per cent in the EU, −0.6 per cent in the US and 0.0 per cent in Japan. While employment in all Irish manufacturing grew at the higher rate of 1.5 per cent during this time, 'this is really the only comparison that makes the recent trend in Irish industry look relatively poor'. Employment in indigenous industry has been particularly impressive in the high technology sectors such as electrical engineering and data processing, suggesting that indigenous industry has been 'showing signs of developing new areas of competence'.[28] In the indigenous software industry, for example, employment rose by 142 per cent, the number of companies grew by 93 per cent, sales revenue increased by 252 per cent and exports rose by 498 per cent between 1991 and 1997.[29]

Nor can this growth in indigenous industry simply be dismissed as a spin-off of foreign investment. While there is some evidence of backward linkages from foreign firms,[30] this is 'insufficient to explain current success'.[31] As Ó Riain notes, while few firms have no connection at all with other companies, foreign multinationals are weakly networked with other firms in Ireland, both foreign and indigenous. Contact tends to be in low-end activities such as the contracting of labour to achieve flexibility in staffing. Instead, Ó Riain argues, the dynamics behind the growing indigenous software sector have primarily been local. In contrast to the multinational corporations, there is significant local networking between indigenous firms, not only in terms of the contract of labour and programming services but also in more advanced relationships such as joint ventures. Indigenous firms tend to produce goods for international niche markets such as systems software and thus do not have to 'directly challenge the dominance of the major US firms'. Ó Riain therefore concludes that indigenous companies have 'generally emerged relatively autonomously' of the multinational corporations.[32]

This is not to overstate the extent and impact of indigenous growth – not least because it remains concentrated in specific sectors and, indeed, specific firms. In fact, most Irish-owned companies remain small in terms of both employment and revenue.[33] In software, for example, while 8 per cent of companies are now in the 'over €10 million' revenue bracket, two thirds remain in the 'sub-€1 million' revenue bracket.[34] Moreover, foreign-owned firms remain much more important than Irish ones in generating industrial output and exports.[35] Yet, despite these limitations, significant developments have nevertheless taken place in the indigenous sector that cannot simply be attributed to the rise in FDI.

Nor can the rise of foreign investment into Ireland be assumed to represent a process of 'globalisation'. As with the Republic's trade flows, it is vital to consider the geographies of Ireland's investment patterns rather than simply assuming that an economy which is highly open to foreign investment is inevitably more 'global' or 'deterritorialised'. For, as noted earlier, if openness (here in terms of FDI) is indeed leading to a broader process of globalisation then it is not unreasonable to expect FDI flows to be becoming increasingly 'global' in scope.

What then is the case in Ireland? While the data on FDI into Ireland is rather limited, it is nevertheless possible to gain some insight into the Republic's investment patterns (which are discussed in further detail in chapter 6). The US was by far the biggest source of investment to Ireland in the 1990s, accounting for over two thirds of total inflows in 1990–7.[36] However, in 2001 there was significant disinvestment (of € 8,088 million) by US firms, although US investment rose again in 2002 (by € 7,859 million). But, rather than spelling disaster for the Irish economy, the disinvestment by US firms was offset by significant inflows from Europe (of € 17,579 million in 2001). Indeed, in 2001–2 the Netherlands was the single most important source of foreign direct investment to Ireland, accounting for around half of total FDI inflows (the bulk of which consisted of reinvested earnings) and just over a third of total FDI stocks.[37] While this might at first sight point to a story of European integration rather than globalisation, it is important to note that a significant proportion of the inflows of Dutch investment themselves originated in the US (see also chapter 6). But, as with Ireland's trade flows, this in turn points to a process not of 'globalisation' but of integration into the diad of the US and EU: indeed, in 2002 the EU and the US accounted for a massive 87 per cent of Ireland's FDI stocks.[38]

Moreover, as the above figures also reveal, Ireland's investment patterns are not only regionally concentrated but also highly nationally specific. In terms of FDI inflows, the Netherlands and the US combined accounted for 72 per cent of total FDI into Ireland. In terms of FDI stocks, they accounted for a more modest 55 per cent. But if the UK is included, nearly two thirds of *all* Ireland's inward investment stocks came from just three countries. Thus, if we embrace Hirst's and Thompson's distinction between a 'global' and an 'international' economy (discussed in chapter 1), then the Republic clearly falls into the latter category.

Membership of the European Union

Nevertheless, Ireland's integration into the EU is itself often cited as evidence of its globalisation (see also chapter 6). For example, Murphy writes: 'Ireland's transformation, one primarily caused by multinationals, was facilitated by the phenomenon of globalisation and in particular the shifting together of two economic tectonic plates, that of the United States and the European Union.'[39] In particular, Ireland's EU membership is seen as a crucial reason for its ability to attract foreign investors in search of a platform to export into Europe.[40]

As noted earlier, the bulk of Irish exports do indeed go to other EU states. Ireland's export market share of trade in the EU rose by 50 per cent in 1987–97 and, if the UK is excluded, it rose by an even more impressive 70 per cent during this period.[41] More specifically, it is access to the SEM since 1992 that is seen to have had a crucial impact on the Republic's ability to attract FDI. Ireland's FDI accelerated dramatically in the early 1990s – just as the SEM was being implemented.[42] FDI into Ireland rose from an annual average of $368 million in 1986–91 to an annual average of $1.2 billion in 1992–5.[43] The significance of the SEM is also confirmed by the fact that US investment has been concentrated in 'exactly those sectors where there were significant reductions in trade barriers'. For example, Ireland's share of US capital expenditures in the EU in the electronic equipment sector rose from an average of 5.5 per cent in 1989–91 to 28.6 per cent in 1992–4 and 19.3 per cent in 1995–6.[44]

Once again, though, while Ireland has certainly become more integrated into the EU, this cannot be taken as *a priori* evidence that it has been 'globalised'. As outlined in chapter 1, there is considerable debate as to whether the rise of regional trade blocs such as the EU can indeed be seen as part of a broader process of globalisation. Whereas the sceptics emphasise the trade-diverting character of regional trade blocs (in part due to the preferential nature of trade agreements), the complex theorists highlight their trade-creating qualities (since new member-states must open up their economies to the world as a whole). Yet, if regional integration were indeed simply part of a wider process of globalisation, then we would expect the trade and investment patterns of member-states to be increasingly dispersed in geographical terms. Instead, as outlined in chapter 1, gravity models reveal that geographical distance is becoming more rather than less important in the trade and investment flows of EU-European economies.[45] In the case of Ireland, as we have already seen, the Repub-

A 'SHOWPIECE OF GLOBALISATION'?

lic's trade and investment flows have not become more geographically dispersed over time but instead remain highly concentrated within the diad of the EU and US.[46] Hence, while the Irish economy has certainly become more open over time (not least due to EU membership), this does not appear to be translating into a broader process of globalisation – that is, if globalisation refers to tendencies that are becoming more global in their reach.

It should also be noted that while Ireland's integration into the EU has clearly contributed to growth, this cannot in itself account for Ireland's success. The Republic joined in 1973 but by 1987 its per capita GDP was just 63 per cent of the overall EU average, 'much the same proportion' as when it first became a member.[47] While access to the single market undoubtedly made Ireland more attractive to inward investors in the 1990s, this, too, is insufficient to explain its success.[48] Not only did Ireland's FDI inflows rise in *absolute* terms (reflecting the overall rise in investment to the EU at this time), but its *share* of FDI flows into the EU rose from an annual average of just 0.2 per cent in 1984–9 to an annual average of 1.4 per cent in 1992–5.[49] In contrast, US investment did not rise significantly in other peripheral countries such as Greece, Portugal and Spain after 1992.[50] As will be discussed later on, this suggests that other factors have been at work in boosting Ireland's growth.

Finally, it worth pointing out that Ireland has not only benefited from EU membership in terms of trade and FDI, but has also received considerable subsidies since joining in 1973, particularly after 1988 in preparation for the single market (see figure 3.3). The funds have been spent on infrastructure (including roads, railways, airports and telecommunications), on human capital (particularly training programmes) and on encouraging local initiatives. Barry estimates that in 1994–9 about 35 per cent of the funds went on physical infrastructure, 30 per cent on human resources, 25 per cent on the private sector and 10 per cent on income support.[51] While the relative contribution of the EU funds declined in the 1990s (from 6.5 to 1.1 per cent of GDP in 1991–2001),[52] this was not least due to Ireland's rapid growth during this time.[53] In particular, the timing of the funds was particularly beneficial; indeed, for Sweeney, they were comparable to a Keynesian boost.[54] The EU subsidies helped shield Ireland from the effects of the world recession in the early 1990s and also came during a period of fiscal retrenchment. Without them, Ireland might not have able to invest in infrastructure, industry and education at this time, in turn placing it in a less favourable position to attract foreign investment.[55]

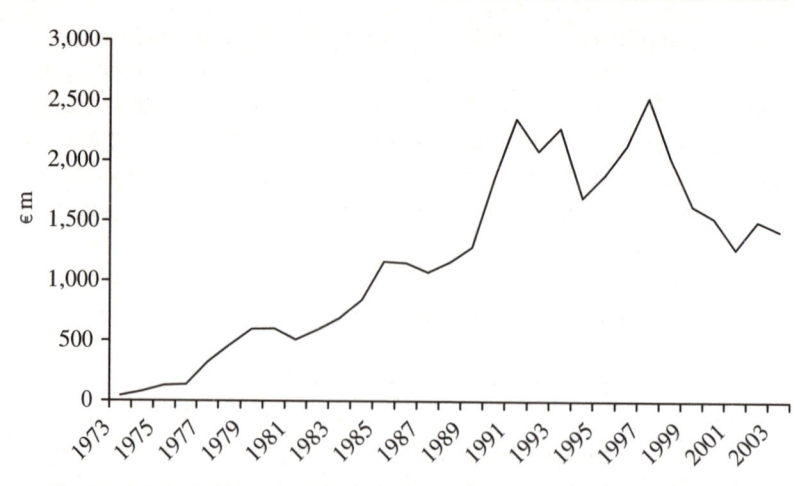

Figure 3.3 Ireland's net receipts from the EU budget, 1973–2003

Source: Department of Finance, *Budgetary and Economic Statistics: March 2004* (Dublin: Department of Finance, 2004), p. 10.

Yet, as helpful as the structural funds have been, they cannot explain why other poor countries in receipt of EU subsidies have come 'nowhere near' Ireland's record.[56] Overall, it has been estimated that the structural funds have boosted GNP growth by about half a percentage point per annum throughout the 1990s,[57] a figure that can be described as 'useful, but not decisive'.[58]

Hence, Ireland's economic growth in the 1990s can in part be attributed to a number of exogenous processes: most notably the rise in international trade, increased inflows of FDI and accelerating European integration. Yet these factors can neither be cited as evidence of Ireland's 'globalisation' nor in themselves explain the Republic's success. This highlights the need to examine more closely the endogenous reasons for Ireland's growth. For, as authors such as Weiss note, countries may experience common pressures, but the existence of distinctive institutional environments means that states may respond quite differently and, in turn, achieve different outcomes (see chapter 1).[59]

Common pressures, different outcomes

Low corporate taxation

For some commentators, the single most important reason for Ireland's ability to attract such high levels of FDI relative to many of its

A 'SHOWPIECE OF GLOBALISATION'?

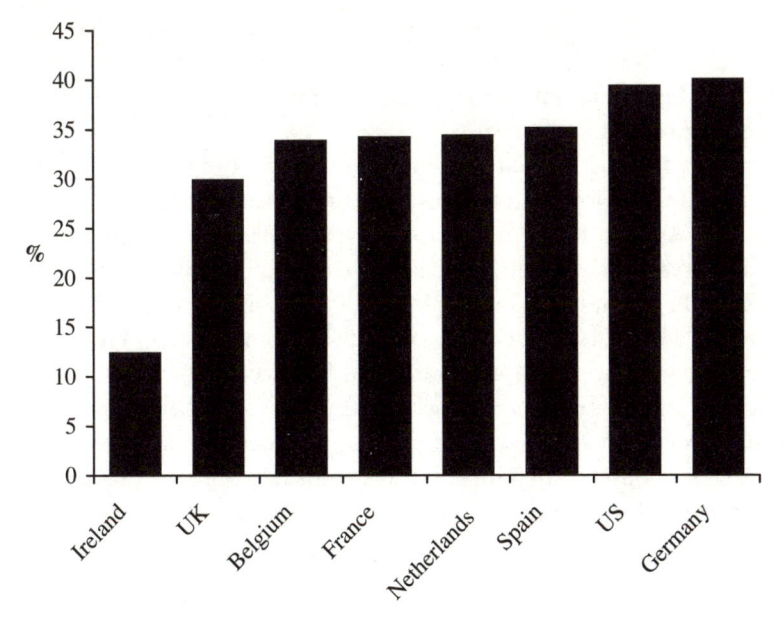

Figure 3.4 Corporate tax rates for selected countries, 2003
Source: IDA Ireland, *Ireland: Vital Statistics* (Dublin: Industrial Development Agency, 2004), p. 8.

European neighbours is the low corporate taxation regime. For example, the managing director of the IDA in 1981–90, Padriac White, argues that low corporate taxation 'remains to this day, the unique and essential foundation stone of Ireland's investment boom'.[60] By contrast with the European standard of 30 to 40 per cent, Ireland's corporate taxation stands at just 12.5 per cent (see figure 3.4). It is seen as particularly attractive to foreign firms due to the transfer pricing opportunities it presents. As noted in chapter 2, the exceptionally high profit rates achieved by foreign firms are cited as evidence that they use Ireland as a tax haven.

In fact, such claims have much in common with the hyperglobalist thesis (and, to a lesser extent, the complex globalisation thesis). According to this logic, states must engage in a 'race to the bottom' in order to attract and retain foreign capital, in turn placing downward pressure on government expenditure and social protectionism. As O'Hearn writes, the Republic's dependence on foreign capital has required it to 'follow the prescriptions of radical globalisation' by pursuing deregulated free-market capitalism – not least evident in the low corporate taxation regime.[61] While Kirby takes a more mediated approach, he too argues that the attraction of FDI through low corporate taxation is the 'central feature of Ireland's industrialisation', in turn enabling economic growth but undermining the state's ability to address issues of social justice.[62]

Yet while the low corporate taxation regime can certainly be seen as attractive to foreign investors, it cannot in itself explain Ireland's success. As Breathnach notes, foreign investment to Ireland has not only increased in quantity but has also changed in quality. Prior to the late 1980s, it tended to involve low-skill assembly and packaging work across a wide range of sectors, with few local linkages and high profit repatriation. Since then, however, it has been concentrated in technologically sophisticated sectors such as electronics and pharmaceuticals.[63] Ireland's low tax regime cannot explain these developments – particularly if one considers that these taxes have actually *risen* over time (from zero in 1958 to 10 per cent in 1981 and 12.5 per cent in 2003).[64] As the deputy managing director of Xerox in Europe has commented, Ireland's low corporate tax rate is 'the cream on the cake rather than the cake itself'.[65]

The claim that Ireland's economic growth rests upon the low taxation regime is underpinned by the assumption that investors are primarily attracted to low-cost locations. Yet there is little evidence to support this. In fact, one study of US manufacturers found that inward flows to low-cost locations have *fallen* dramatically (by 83 per cent in 1999–2002), with higher-cost countries receiving an ever-greater share of FDI (rising from 61 to 84 per cent of the total in 2000–2).[66] This suggests (as discussed in chapter 1) that higher-cost locations may yield significant benefits to foreign investors that are more attractive to them than low costs.

Education and skills

One such factor is the role of education and skills. This has been treated as a key priority by Irish governments since the 1960s. For example, the introduction of free secondary-level education in 1966 reflected 'an explicit acknowledgement of the importance of investment in education for economic growth and development'.[67] Overall, the proportion of government spending on education has risen from 16 to 20 per cent between 1965 and 1993.[68] As a result, Ireland has experienced a dramatic increase in terms of both educational participation and educational attainment. For example, the rate of retention at secondary level rose by a massive 70 percentage points (from 20 to 90 per cent)

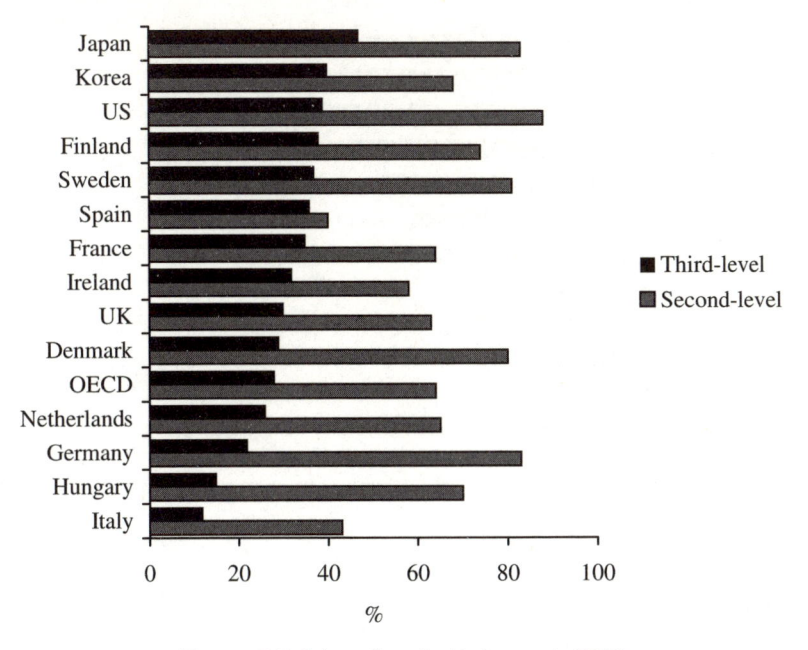

Figure 3.5 Educational attainment, 2001

Notes: Second-level refers to proportion of population (aged 25–64) with at least upper-secondary-level education; third-level refers to proportion of population (aged 25–34) with at least third-level education.
Source: NCC, *Annual Competitiveness Report 2003*, pp. 73–4.

between 1960 and 2000. At tertiary level, the number of students increased more than sixfold between 1964 and 1994. Indeed, the proportion of the population aged 25–34 with at least third-level education now exceeds the OECD average (at 32 per cent compared to 28 per cent).[69] However, a number of commentators have noted that while the quality of Ireland's workforce has improved dramatically, it still trails behind that of other developed countries.[70] As figure 3.5 illustrates, although Ireland's performance for third-level education is above average, it is rather less impressive with respect to second-level education. Nevertheless, it is in specific *sectors* that Ireland scores particularly highly. Of all degrees awarded in Ireland, nearly a third are in the area of science and engineering, with the number of science and engineering graduates per 1,000 of the population aged 20–34 more than double the OECD average (see also figure 3.6).[71] Ireland also ranks first in the European Innovation Scoreboard's Innovation Index in terms of the output of science and engineering graduates.[72]

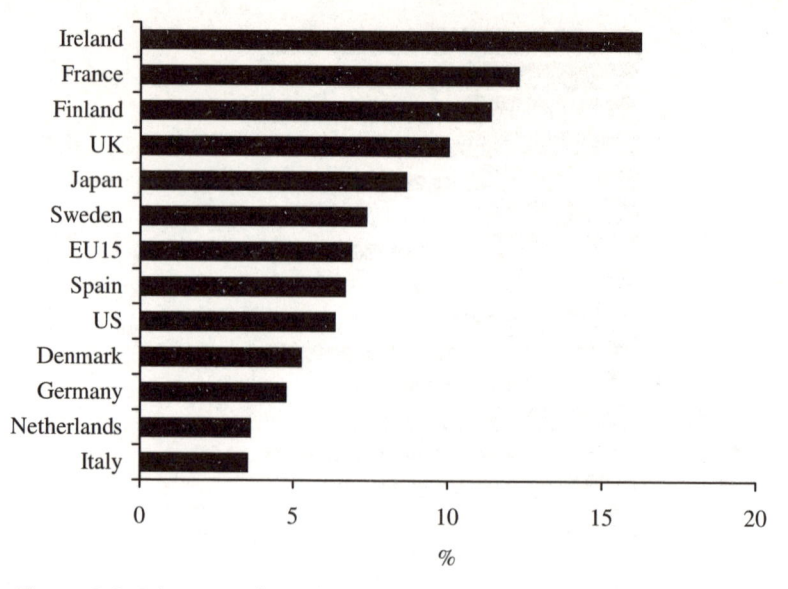

Figure 3.6 Science and engineering graduates per 1,000 population (aged 20–34), 2000

Source: NCC, *Annual Competitiveness Report 2003*, p. 74.

In turn, the availability of a highly skilled workforce can be seen as a significant reason for Ireland's ability to attract foreign investment in technologically sophisticated sectors such as electronics and pharmaceuticals.[73] In one survey appropriate skills levels were ranked as the most important advantage by 57 per cent of foreign enterprises. In another international survey of businesspeople, Ireland ranked first in terms of the relevance of its educational system to the needs of business.[74] In turn, Ireland's strong skills base has not arisen by accident but instead reflects the strong emphasis placed on education in the dynamic sectors of the economy such as electronics and pharmaceuticals. Measures have included the establishment of a Scientific and Technological (Investment) Fund in order to expand third-level participation and increase the resources for students at all levels.[75] This supports the claims of authors such as Weiss and Hay that state intervention (here in terms of educational expenditure) can enhance rather than hinder economic performance.[76] It stands quite at odds with the common assumption that the 'competitive imperatives of globalisation' require governments to reduce their expenditure in order to attract and maintain foreign capital.

A 'SHOWPIECE OF GLOBALISATION'?

Increased labour supply

Ireland's stock of human capital has increased not only in qualitative terms but also in quantitative terms with a rise in the labour supply. As noted in chapter 2, Ireland had the best job-creation record in OECD in the 1990s, with employment levels rising by a third. This can in part be seen as an outcome of economic growth itself. For, as Breathnach notes, increases in the labour supply have traditionally led to emigration rather than employment growth (which continued throughout the 1980s despite increases in educational attainment). In the 1990s, however, Ireland experienced a reversal in the tradition of emigration to net inward migration (see figure 3.7), suggesting that other factors have been at work in generating the demand for labour – not least in terms of the attraction of FDI.[77]

Nevertheless, while the demand for labour has increased in Ireland, a number of endogenous factors have also helped to boost its supply. One of the Republic's distinctive features is its 'unusually favourable demographics', in part due to the late baby boom (which did not reach its peak until 1980).[78] The Irish population has been described as the 'most youthful in the industrial world',[79] with 39 per cent of the population under the age of 25 (compared to the EU15 average of 17 per cent) and just 15 per cent over the age of 60 (compared to the EU15 average of 22 per cent).[80] The Republic's increased labour supply can

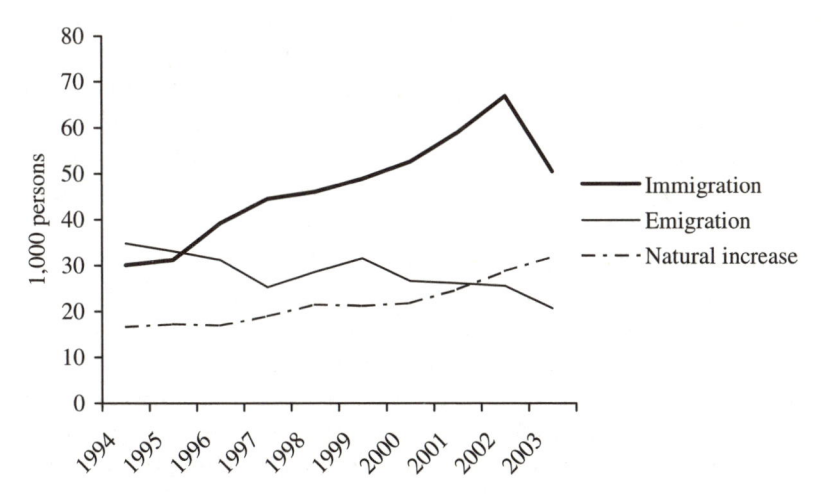

Figure 3.7 Migration and natural increase in population in Ireland, 1994–2003

Source: CSO, *Measuring Ireland's Progress* (Cork: Central Stastistical Office, 2003), p. 49.

also be attributed to the rising participation rate. This has traditionally been low in Ireland, in part due to the low numbers of women in the workforce. Since the 1970s, though, there has been a steady rise in the number of women at work due to such factors as the decline in the fertility rate, the rise in part-time and service sector jobs, developments in the education system and attitudinal changes. Between 1971 and 1996 the number of women participating in the labour force rose by nearly 90 per cent.[81]

This abundance of labour can be seen as an important incentive for foreign investors to locate in Ireland. For example, the Republic has been ranked second in terms of the availability of skilled labour in one international survey of businesspeople.[82] Rather than emphasising Ireland's low corporate tax rate, posters in the IDA's head office declare: 'We're the young Europeans' and 'People are to Ireland what champagne is to France.' The fact that the Irish labour force is English-speaking may also make it particularly attractive to foreign investors – not only from English-speaking nations but also from other countries, since English is used by business worldwide.[83] Given that English is *the* language of information technology, it may also have contributed to Ireland's ability to attract investors in this field.[84]

Yet, while a number of pre-existing factors such as the late baby boom and the English-speaking environment have helped to enhance Ireland's workforce, it should be noted that the Irish government has also sought to boost Ireland's labour supply through a number of active measures. These have included a variety of policies to reduce work disincentives, such as the cutting of personal tax rates, the raising of allowances, the widening of standard rate bands and the lowering of social security contribution rates. In fact, Ireland has become one of the leading nations in active labour market policy expenditure (see figure 3.8).[85] As Auer notes, unemployment might have been considerably higher without this active labour market growth; indeed, he argues that state activism lies at the heart of Ireland's employment revival.[86]

A favourable labour supply has thus been an important factor in Ireland's economic growth. This is not explained by 'globalising' forces: rather, the interventionist policies of the state have assisted demographic trends. Indeed, the state could do even more to boost Ireland's performance in these terms. For example, a number of studies have identified a lack of coherence and coordination by state agencies in relation to active labour market policy in Ireland, with the emphasis being more on quantity than quality. O'Connell therefore calls for the much greater allocation of resources in promoting active labour market measures.[87] Much more could also be done to encourage female

A 'SHOWPIECE OF GLOBALISATION'?

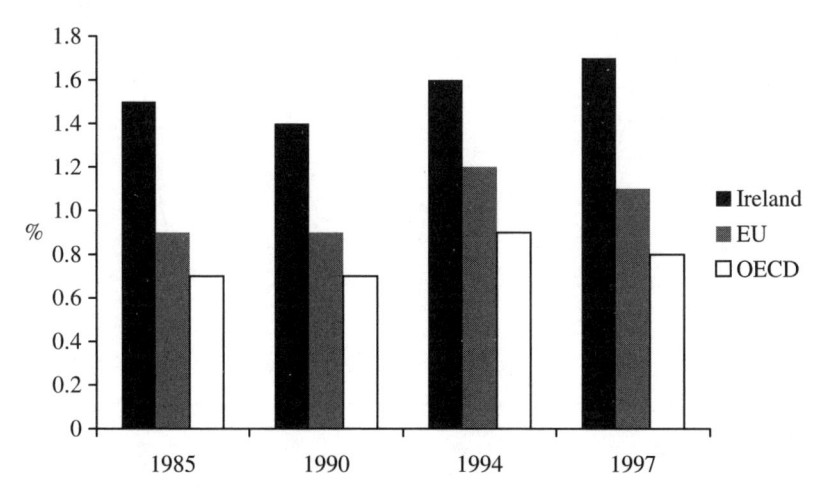

Figure 3.8 Spending as a percentage of GDP on active labour market policies, 1985–97

Source: Martin, J. P., 'What works among active labour market policies: evidence from OECD countries' experiences, *OECD Economic Studies*, 30: 1 (2000), p. 85.

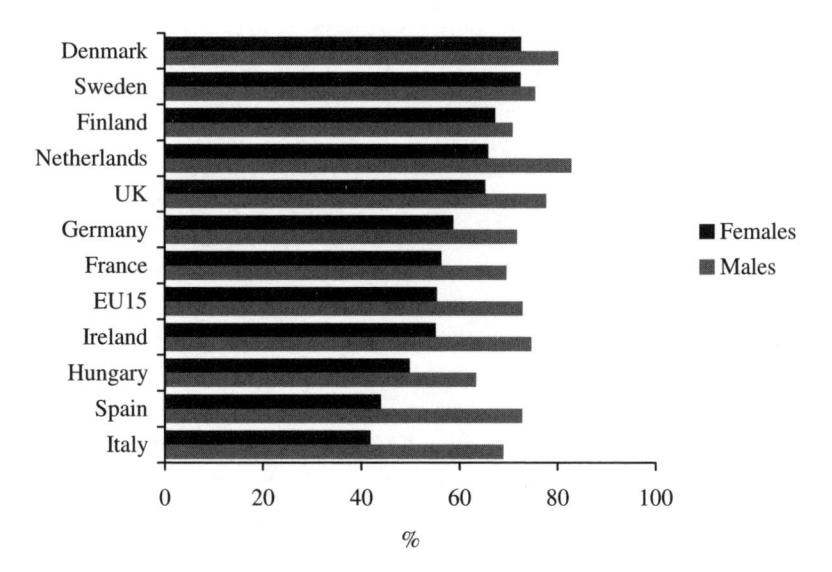

Figure 3.9 Participation rates, 2002

Source: CSO, *Measuring Ireland's Progress*, p. 30.

participation, not least in terms of providing affordable childcare.[88] While Ireland's female participation rate has risen dramatically, the Republic still lags far behind other countries such as Sweden, Denmark and the UK (see figure 3.9).[89] Thus, it appears that Ireland's

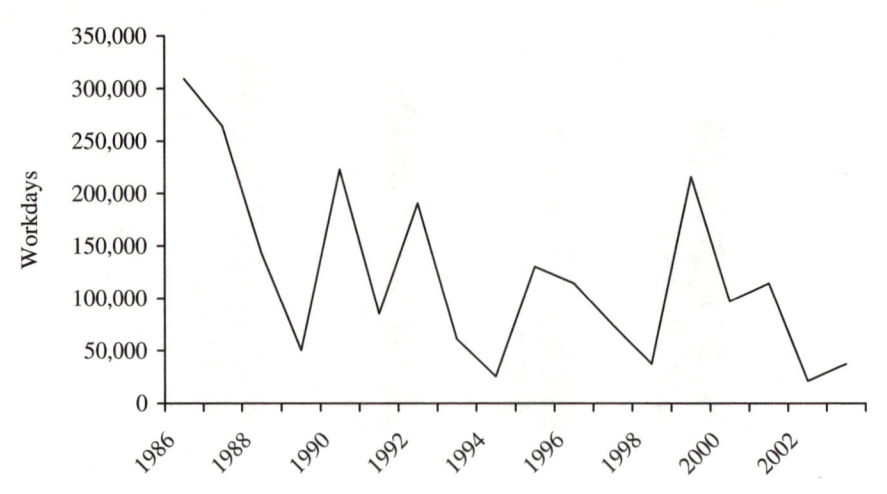

Figure 3.10 Workdays lost to industrial disputes in Ireland, 1986–2003
Source: Labour Relations Commission, 'Industrial dispute statistics' www.lrc.ie (2004).

labour market performance would benefit from enhanced, not reduced, government intervention.

Social partnership

The Irish government has also played a highly active role in terms of macro-political bargaining. Since 1987, it has negotiated a series of national agreements with key economic and social interests (see also chapter 5). This 'social partnership' approach is widely cited as having played a central role in revitalising the Irish economy. In particular, wage bargaining is seen to have boosted growth by creating a virtuous circle in which competitiveness is enhanced by wage restraint, thus generating employment, boosting tax revenues, allowing tax reduction and in turn underpinning wage moderation.[90] Yet the impact of social partnership does not just relate to the issue of pay. Rather, macro-political bargaining has also helped to reduce industrial strife in Ireland (see figure 3.10), in turn helping to provide a stable and co-operative environment for both workers and management.[91] In turn, the agreements may have facilitated management in the implementation of workplace change such as the introduction of flexible working practices and new technology.[92] More broadly, the centralised agreements have also helped to promote macro-economic stability and credibility, in turn enhancing Ireland's attractiveness to foreign investors.

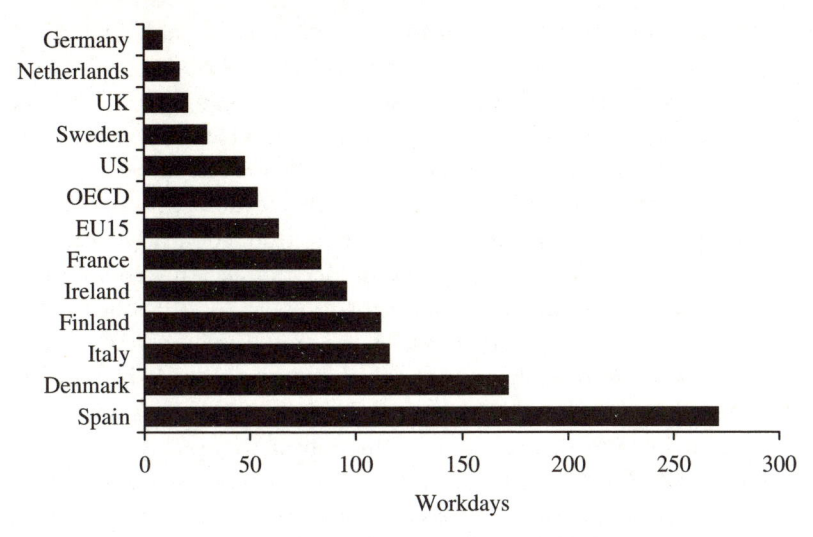

Figure 3.11 Workdays lost due to industrial disputes per 1,000 employees (annual averages), 1992–2001

Source: Monger, J., 'International comparisons of labour workdays disputes in 2001', *Labour Market Trends*, April (2003), p. 182.

Yet one should not overplay the impact of social partnership on Ireland's growth. For example, while Ireland's levels of industrial strife have fallen, the Republic still scores poorly relative to the EU and OECD averages in terms of strike action (see figure 3.11). Nor can wage restraint be seen as a particularly important concern for foreign investors, who tend to pay 'well above' the terms agreed in the social partnership agreements.[93] In fact, most transnational corporations are non-union employers and many have systems of human resource management that entail direct involvement from employees.[94] Similarly, while the social partnership agreements may have facilitated workplace change in some firms, such developments have also taken place in non-unionised workplaces. For example, Roche and Geary find that the instances of workplace change in Ireland in the 1990s were broadly comparable for unionised and non-unionised workplaces.[95]

Nevertheless, while the role of social partnership should not be exaggerated, it should not be dismissed either. The national agreements have been criticised by liberal economists on the grounds that they create labour market rigidities because trade unions are able to exercise excessive influence on economic policy. Yet, as Taylor notes, one cannot assume *a priori* that market responses are more flexible than corporatist ones;[96] indeed, the National Economic and Social Council

(NESC) argues that 'it is through a coordinated and consensual approach that flexibility measures are likely to have most success'.[97] This is supported by the World Economic Forum's findings that the Irish labour market is actually *more* responsive to labour market conditions than that in other EU countries.[98] Rather than constraining management, centralised bargaining may actually create opportunities for them.[99] For example, Taylor points to the introduction of a local bargaining clause, which retained wage moderation at a macro-level but also enabled management to 'tie negotiations to local labour market conditions'. Successful negotiations on the local bargaining clause were achieved in more than three quarters of firms monitored. The unions have taken an active role in this process, willingly collaborating in the search for investment and the introduction of technology.[100] In their survey of 402 employees in nine unionised manufacturing plants, D'Art and Turner found that the 'presence of a strong and cohesive union organisation is associated with relatively lower levels of a "them and us" divide'. They point out that unions can be more effective than individual employees at voicing workers' preferences, thus helping to increase worker morale and to reduce labour turnover, training costs and accidents.[101] In this sense, the social partnership approach can be seen to have played a broadly positive role in Ireland's growth. This in turn supports arguments put forward by authors such as Weiss and Garrett that state intervention can enhance rather than hamper economic performance.[102]

Fiscal adjustment

That having been said, a number of authors have questioned the extent to which Irish social partnership represents genuine state activism (see chapter 5). Teague, for instance, argues that the adoption of centralised bargaining in 1987 represented little more than an 'institutional adjunct to a harsh and uncompromising disinflation strategy'.[103] For, as will be discussed later in this volume, the social partnership approach was born out of a sense of economic crisis – a sense that was shared by government, employers and unions alike. With Ireland's finances widely perceived to be spiralling out of control by the mid-1980s, the government, employers and unions agreed upon a programme of significant fiscal adjustment (embodied in the first corporatist agreement of 1987). For example, the current account deficit was reduced from over 6 per cent of GNP in 1987 to just 0.6 per cent in 1990 and became a surplus in 1996. Similarly, the national debt was cut dra-

Table 3.1 Exchequer balance and debt in Ireland, 1987–2002

	Exchequer balance		Current account		National (exchequer) debt	
	€m	% GNP	€m	% GNP	€m	% GNP
1987	−2,268	−9.4	−1,498	−6.2	30,085	125.0
1988	−786	−3.1	−403	−1.6	31,250	122.7
1989	−608	−2.2	−334	−1.2	31,525	111.9
1990	−620	−2.0	−193	−0.6	31,849	99.0
1991	−655	−1.9	−379	−1.1	32,223	95.9
1992	−915	−2.6	−566	−1.6	33,450	94.1
1993	−880	−2.3	−481	−1.2	36,006	93.3
1994	−845	−2.0	19	0.0	37,111	88.8
1995	−796	−1.7	−459	−1.0	38,358	82.1
1996	−554	−1.1	371	0.7	37,980	73.7
1997	−298	−0.5	767	1.3	38,967	66.0
1998	948	1.4	2,654	3.9	37,509	55.0
1999	1,512	2.0	4,365	5.7	39,848	52.0
2000	3,177	3.6	6,971	7.9	36,511	41.4
2001	653	0.7	4,729	4.9	36,183	37.4
2002	93	0.1	5,400	5.2	36,361	35.2
2003	−980	−0.9	4,410	4.0	37,611	34.3

Source: Department of Finance, *Budgetary and Economic Statistics: March 2004* (Dublin: Department of Finance, 2004), pp. 5–7.

matically: from 125 per cent of GNP in 1987 to just over 34 per cent in 2003 (see table 3.1).

For some commentators, it was this fiscal correction (rather than social partnership *per se*) that was the decisive factor in Ireland's economic turnaround. For example, Ó Gráda writes that without the harsh programme of fiscal adjustment, the Celtic tiger simply 'would not have roared'.[104] According to this view, Ireland's failure to achieve convergence with other OECD countries prior to the 1990s was precisely due to the lack of fiscal stability. With the removal of this obstacle – and with the preconditions for growth such as an educated workforce already in place – Ireland's economic transformation could finally occur. Giavazzi and Pagano also attribute Ireland's growth primarily to the role of fiscal retrenchment. In contrast to Keynesian predictions that this would suppress economic growth, they argue, the subsequent performance of the Irish economy demonstrates how fiscal contraction can actually be expansionary.[105]

However, a number of authors have questioned such claims with respect to the Irish case. For example, Barry and Devereux note that although Ireland's growth after 1987 appears to contradict Keynesian analysis, fiscal contraction was actually counter-cyclical.[106] Hogan also points out that Ireland experienced a large devaluation prior to fiscal adjustment, so that expansion may in fact have been due to rising net exports.[107] Factors such as declining foreign interest rates and buoyant growth in export markets also offset the recessionary impact of spending cuts, as did the increase in EU funds (which helped to prevent infrastructural deficiencies that would, in turn, have deterred foreign investment).[108] In this sense, Ireland was 'merely fortunate in undertaking much of its fiscal correction at a propitious moment'.[109]

Moreover, if authors such as Ó Gráda are correct that Ireland's economic growth represents little more than delayed convergence due to the removal of fiscal obstacles, then we can assume that such convergence could have been achieved much earlier on if only fiscal stabilisation had been secured (see chapter 2). Yet, as Barry notes, other small European economies, such as Greece, Portugal, and Spain, all converged with the European average in terms of living standards in the 1960s, despite having policy environments that were 'no more benign than Ireland's'.[110] In fact, timing has played a crucial role in Ireland's economic growth: not least in terms of the rapid influx of FDI into the EU in the 1990s due to the establishment of the SEM in 1992.

But can Ireland's programme of fiscal adjustment explain its ability to attract FDI? Certainly it can be seen to have enhanced the Republic's attractiveness to foreign investors, by helping to provide macro-economic stability and credibility. Yet, this cannot in itself account for Ireland's disproportionate share of FDI in the EU, for other countries have also undergone a process of consolidating their public finances in order to adhere to the Maastricht convergence criteria.[111] Rather, as will be discussed in the next section, Irish governments have not only sought to attract foreign investment through macro-economic policy but also pursued a highly proactive industrial policy that has, in turn, played a vital role in the Republic's ability to secure such high levels of FDI.

Before turning to Irish industrial policy, however, it is also worth emphasising that while Ireland engaged in fiscal *adjustment* from 1987, this has not turned into a process of sustained fiscal *retrenchment*. For example, while real government expenditure did fall slightly in 1987, it rose again in 1988 and from then on the 'cuts' were 'really reductions in the rate of increase in borrowing, rather than cuts in spending'.[112] In fact, absolute public expenditure (as opposed to spending as a proportion of GDP) has risen 'especially strongly in Ireland' due to its high growth rates.[113] While Irish politicians certainly emphasise the need for fiscal and wage restraint in order to maintain Ireland's attractiveness to foreign investors, this has by no means translated into the adoption of stark neo-liberalism. Rather, as will be discussed in chapter 5, the trajectory of Irish economic policy (including both fiscal policy and the broader social partnership approach) simply cannot be characterised in terms of a shift towards neo-liberalism, but is much more complex (and, at times, contradictory) than this.

Industrial policy

As noted above, Ireland's success in attracting foreign investment has not least been due to the state's active industrial policy. In fact, Irish governments had pursued foreign investment since the 1950s, making the Republic one of the first nations to adopt this strategy. Since the late 1980s, though, Ireland's industrial policy has shifted considerably. While it had traditionally been characterised by a 'scatter-gun' approach to FDI (in that it emphasised the attraction of FDI in the most labour-intensive industries across a range of sectors), it has increasingly moved towards a 'rifle-shot' approach.[114] In particular, the IDA has sought to target leading international firms in the high technology sectors such as electronics and pharmaceuticals. This highly aggressive and proactive approach has played a vital role in Ireland's ability to attract major international corporations such as Motorola and Intel.[115] Indeed, the IDA is now widely regarded as a prototype for state intervention in the attraction of foreign investment.

But Irish industrial policy has not been confined to the attraction of foreign investment. While priority tended to be given to this issue prior to the late 1980s, industrial policy has since been reoriented to give much greater attention to the need to nurture indigenous industry. Measures have included the introduction of programmes in order to develop indigenous industry, the decision to increase resources allocated to indigenous industry from 40 to 50 per cent, the phasing out of export sales relief and the removal of accelerated depreciation allowances. These developments can be seen to have played a significant role in the revival of indigenous industry. While firms had previously failed to overcome barriers to entry such as the lack of specialised skills and experience, changes in industrial policy have helped counter this. In particular, the government has adopted a more selective approach in order to develop larger and stronger indigenous firms. This has included the selective allocation of grants to firms with the greatest potential of export growth and an increased focus on specific areas of weakness such as export marketing and management skills. The success of this more targeted approach can be seen in the fact that the employment record of indigenous firms assisted by industrial grants has improved more than that of grant-assisted foreign industry.[116] Hence, the Irish state has played a central role not only in Ireland's ability to attract FDI but also in the revival of indigenous industry.

Discursive factors

So far in this chapter we have considered the 'material' factors behind Ireland's success, both exogenous (the role of external trade, foreign investment and European integration) and endogenous (the low corporate tax rate, human capital, social partnership, fiscal policy and industrial policy). Yet there is also an important discursive element in Ireland's success. As noted in chapter 2, the very *image* of Ireland as the 'Celtic tiger' may have itself contributed to growth. For Krugman, this has been absolutely vital to Ireland's ability to attract FDI. In particular, he points to the tendency of firms to agglomerate in specific locations. He writes: 'investors may, entirely rationally, end up "following the herd"' so that 'early decisions about the location of investment can produce a cascade of followers'.[117] Surveys of executives of new foreign firms in sectors such as pharmaceuticals have found that the decision to locate in Ireland has been 'strongly influenced by the fact that other key market players are already located in Ireland'.[118] As one chief executive has remarked, the 1990s saw an 'amazing' change in US investors' perceptions of Ireland, in turn due to 'the amount of favourable press you have gotten'.[119] Another commented: 'The first question for any company looking to put an operation in Europe is why not Ireland? Because most senior executives have heard such good stories about Ireland, you almost have to get over the Irish hump if you want to go somewhere else.'[120]

This is not to contend that the 'Celtic tiger' discourse has no material base. The very fact that Irish policy has concentrated upon specific sectors can help explain why agglomerations have formed in these sectors rather than in other areas.[121] Nevertheless, it suggests that the 'Celtic tiger' discourse in itself yields material effects.

Explaining Ireland's economic growth

In sum, it is clear that developments in the international political economy have played a decisive role in boosting Ireland's economic growth. In particular, the Republic benefited from the rapid rise of FDI to Europe in the 1990s, due in large part to the establishment of the SEM and then EMU. Crucially, though, such developments *cannot be cited as evidence of 'globalisation'*: that is, if we resist the temptation to use 'globalisation' as an umbrella term but instead employ a strict definition to refer to tendencies that are becoming truly global in scope. Seen in these terms, the Irish economy is certainly open in terms of both trade and FDI, but it has not become more global.

As important as international economic developments have been, however, one cannot understand Ireland's growth by looking at the external picture alone. It simply cannot explain why the Republic has experienced such high levels of FDI relative to other small and open EU economies. Crucially, this highlights the role of endogenous factors in Ireland's growth such as its low corporate taxation regime, its highly skilled and English-speaking workforce and its unusually favourable demographics. Ireland's domestic context has thus played an important role in mediating external challenges and opportunities, as authors such as Weiss would note.[122]

Just as it is important to consider the role of pre-existing institutional environments in explaining economic outcomes, so too it is vital to reinsert the role of human agency. Otherwise, we run the risk of replacing one set of *ex*ogenous contextual factors with another set of *en*dogenous ones, thus posing a false dualism between structure and agency (and, indeed, the economic and political). It is no accident that Ireland has been able to attract such high levels of FDI in technologically sophisticated sectors such as electronics and pharmaceuticals. Rather, this has reflected the highly targeted and aggressive industrial strategy adopted by Irish governments since the late 1980s.[123] Similarly, the existence of a highly skilled and technologically adept workforce has arisen precisely because human capital has been treated as a major priority by successive Irish governments. Thus, the Irish state has been 'deeply implicated in the entire process',[124] at times adopting a highly interventionist and proactive role in economic development.

Hence, Ireland's growth has not been inevitable but has – at least in part – been contingent upon the strategies pursued by Irish policy-makers themselves. This at least raises the possibility that other countries to can similarly enhance their economic performance through a proactive and interventionist approach. But this does not mean that the Irish case should be seen as a model economy for other countries to emulate. This is not only because economic growth has been accompanied by growing inequality (see chapter 2) but also because factors such as the late baby boom make the Republic's experience difficult to replicate. Thus, while the Irish case can certainly offer lessons (both positive and negative) for other countries, it should not be regarded as a blueprint for other nations to follow. Ultimately, Ireland is no 'showpiece' economy – and it is certainly not a showpiece of globalisation.

Conclusion

This chapter has examined the dynamics behind the Republic's economic transformation in the 1990s. First, it has considered the exogenous reasons for Ireland's rapid growth (most notably the role of external trade, the rapid influx of FDI and, finally, European integration). It has argued that while these elements have certainly played an important role in Ireland's economic growth, they do not represent a broader process of 'globalisation'. Nor can such factors in themselves explain Ireland's success in the 1990s. Rather, a number of endogenous factors have played a vital role, both in creating the preconditions for growth (for example in providing foreign investors with highly skilled and English-speaking workers) and in the Irish state's highly proactive approach to economic development (for example in terms of social partnership and industrial policy). The chapter has highlighted the need to restore the role of human agency in shaping economic outcomes. Both the globalisation and Irish literatures tend to confuse structure and agency questions, presenting globalisation itself as an agent of change. But Ireland's economic growth can neither be described in terms of globalisation nor explained by it. Ultimately, economic outcomes – as in the social and political spheres – are contingent upon the choices and actions of human agents rather than upon an exogenous and inexorable logic called 'globalisation'.

Notes

1 S. Ó Riain, 'The flexible developmental state: globalisation, information technology and the "Celtic tiger"', *Politics & Society*, 28: 2 (2000), p. 159. A review of the Irish literature with respect to globalisation will be provided in chapter 6.

2 P. Sweeney, *The Celtic tiger: Ireland's Continuing Economic Miracle* (Dublin: Oak Tree Press, 1999), p. 128; W. J. Crotty, 'Democratisation and political development in Ireland', in W. J. Crotty and D. E. Schmitt (eds), *Ireland and the Politics of Change* (London: Longman, 1998), p. 17; A. Murphy, 'The "Celtic tiger" – an analysis of Ireland's economic growth performance', European University Institute Working Paper, San Domenico (2000), p. 4; J. Fitz Gerald, 'Ireland – a multicultural economy', in W. Crotty and D. E. Schmitt (eds), *Ireland on the World Stage* (Manchester: Manchester University Press, 2002), p. 80.
3 D. O'Brien, 'The economy is still on course but the fruits of globalisation could yet turn sour', *Irish Times* (22 April 2003).
4 'Ireland shines', *The Economist* (17 May 1997).
5 C. McCreevy, 'Speech by the minister for finance', Institute of Directors luncheon (9 February 2000).
6 Cited in Department of Finance, 'IMF review of the Irish economy' (1997), www.irlgov.ie/finance.
7 US Department of State, 'Economic policy and trade practices report – Ireland' (1997), http://state.gov/www/issues/economic/trade_reports/europe-canada97/ireland97.html.
8 Forfás, *International Trade and Investment Report, 2000* (Dublin: Forfás, 2001), p. 3.
9 World Trade Organisation, *International Trade Statistics 2003* (Geneva: World Trade Organisation, 2003), p. 21.
10 Forfás, *International Trade and Investment Report, 2000*, p. 9.
11 Sweeney, *The Celtic Tiger*, p. 130.
12 *Foreign Policy* (March/April 2004).
13 Forfás, *Enterprise 2010: A New Strategy for the Promotion of Enterprise in Ireland in the 21st Century* (Dublin: Forfás, 2000), p. 17; Forfás, *International Trade and Investment Report, 2000*, pp. 10–12.
14 CSO, *External Trade, March 2005* (Cork: Central Statistical Office, 2005), p. 6.
15 OECD, *Economic Surveys: Ireland 2000–2001* (Paris: OECD, 2001), p. 30; CSO, *External Trade, March 2005* (Cork: Central Statistical Office, 2005), p. 6. Figures for 2005 refer to the period January to March.
16 CSO, *External Trade, November 2003*, p. 6. This will be discussed further in chapter 6.
17 See for instance P. Kirby, *The Celtic Tiger in Distress: Growth and Inequality in Ireland* (Basingstoke: Palgrave, 2002); Murphy, 'The "Celtic tiger"', p. 4; D. O'Hearn, 'Globalisation, "new tigers," and the end of the developmental state? The case of the Celtic tiger', *Politics & Society*, 28: 1 (2000), p. 73; S. Ó Riain, 'A tale of two globalisations: the Irish software industry and the global economy', Working Paper, University of California (1998).
18 OECD, *Economic Surveys: Ireland 1999* (Paris: OECD, 1999), p. 12.
19 Calculated from UNCTAD, *World Investment Report 2003: FDI Policies for Development – National and International Perspectives* (New York: United Nations, 2003), pp. 257–9.

20 Ibid., p. 10.
21 M. A. Miles, E. J. Feulner, M. A. O'Grady and A. I. Eiras, *2004 Index of Economic Freedom* (Washington, DC: Heritage Foundation, 2004), p. 231.
22 O'Hearn, 'Globalisation, "new tigers," and the end of the developmental state?', pp. 75, 87; Murphy, 'The "Celtic tiger"', p. 16.
23 Forfás, *International Trade and Investment Report, 2000*, p. 9.
24 Sweeney, *The Celtic Tiger*, p. 128.
25 *Foreign Policy* (March/April 2004).
26 UNCTAD, *WID Country Profile: Ireland* (Geneva: United Nations, 2004), p. 1.
27 Ó Riain, 'The flexible developmental state', p. 161.
28 E. O'Malley, 'The revival of Irish indigenous industry 1987–1997', in T. J. Baker, D. Duffy and F. Shortall (eds), *Quarterly Economic Commentary, April 1998* (Dublin: Economic and Social Research Institute, 1998), pp. 39–43.
29 M. O'Sullivan, 'Industrial development: a new beginning?', in J. W. O'Hagen (ed.), *The Economy of Ireland: Policy and Performance of a European Region* (Dublin: Gill & Macmillan, 2000), p. 274.
30 For example, O'Malley estimates that the number of people employed in Irish manufacturing in producing industrial products as inputs for overseas industry rose from about 10,200 to 14,000 between 1983 and 1991. In turn, he estimates that for every 100 direct jobs in overseas manufacturing, the number of jobs in indirect manufacturing rose from 12 to 16 between 1983 and 1991. As Barrios, Görg and Holger note, 'FDI can be positive for local firms' expansion'; indeed, they find that 'positive externalities are more likely to occur the larger is the amount of capital transferred through FDI and the greater is the efficiency of local firms'. For example, there is evidence that foreign firms benefit new entrepreneurs by acting as 'incubators', with two thirds of entrepreneurs in the indigenous software sector having worked for foreign companies at some point in their careers. Foreign firms also appear to be an important source of demand, requiring high standards in the early stages of new company start-ups. In turn, this may help indigenous suppliers to meet the standards demanded in international sectors. See E. O'Malley, *An Analysis of Secondary Employment Associated with Manufacturing Industry* (Dublin: Economic and Social Research Institute, 1995), p. 4; O'Malley, 'The revival of Irish indigenous industry', p. 55; S. Barrios, H. Görg and E. Strobl, 'Foreign direct investment, competition and industrial development in the host country', Leverhulme Centre for Research on Globalisation and Economic Policy Research Paper 2004/06, (2004), p. 19; F. Barry, J. Bradley and E. O'Malley, 'Indigenous and foreign industry: characteristics and performance', in F. Barry (ed.), *Understanding Ireland's Economic Growth* (Basingstoke: Macmillan, 1999), pp. 64–5.
31 Barry et al., 'Indigenous and foreign industry', pp. 64–5.
32 S. Ó Riain, 'An offshore silicon valley? The emerging Irish software industry', *Competition and Change*, 2 (1997), p. 198; see also Ó Riain, 'The flexible developmental state', pp. 170, 199.

33 This is discussed in detail in O'Sullivan, 'Industrial development', pp. 273–4.
34 HotOrigin, *Ireland's Software Cluster: Preparing for Consolidation* (Dublin: HotOrigin, 2004), p. 2.
35 O'Sullivan, 'Industrial development', p. 283.
36 Calculated from UNCTAD, *Country Profile: Ireland*, p. 8.
37 Although some of this can be assumed to be related to the International Financial Services Centre (IFSC). CSO, *Foreign Direct Investment 2001 and 2002* (Cork: Central Statistical Office, 2003), p. 4; UNCTAD, *Country Profile: Ireland*, p. 11.
38 Calculated from UNCTAD, *Country Profile: Ireland*, p. 11.
39 Murphy, 'The "Celtic tiger"', p. 4.
40 See for instance D. O'Hearn, 'Macroeconomic policy in the Celtic tiger: a critical reassessment', in C. Coulter and S. Coleman (eds), *The End of Irish History? Critical Reflections on the Celtic Tiger* (Manchester: Manchester University Press, 2003), pp. 51–2.
41 Forfás, *Enterprise 2010*, pp. 17–18.
42 Murphy, 'The "Celtic tiger"', p. 14.
43 UNCTAD, *World Investment Report 1998: Trends and Determinants* (Geneva: United Nations, 1998), p. 361.
44 H. Görg and F. Ruane, 'European integration and peripherality: lessons from the Irish experience', *World Economy*, 23: 3 (2000), pp. 413–15.
45 C. Hay, 'Common trajectories, variable paces, divergent outcomes? Models of European capitalism under conditions of complex economic interdependence', *Review of International Political Economy*, 11: 2 (2004), pp. 248–55.
46 Forfás, *International Trade and Investment Report 2003* (Dublin: Forfás, 2004), p. 35.
47 P. Breathnach, 'Exploring the "Celtic tiger" phenomenon: causes and consequences of Ireland's economic miracle', *European Urban and Regional Studies*, 5: 4 (1998), p. 305.
48 F. Barry, J. Bradley and A. Hannan, 'The European dimension: the single market and the structural funds', in Barry, *Understanding Ireland's Economic Growth*, pp. 106–7; Breathnach, 'Exploring the "Celtic tiger" phenomenon', p. 309; Görg and Ruane, 'European integration and peripherality', pp. 415–16.
49 UNCTAD, *World Investment Report 1998*, p. 361.
50 Görg and Ruane, 'European integration and peripherality', pp. 415–16.
51 F. Barry, 'Convergence is not automatic: lessons from Ireland for Central and Eastern Europe', *World Economy*, 23: 10 (2000), p. 1390.
52 Department of Finance, *Budgetary and Economic Statistics: March 2004* (Dublin: Department of Finance, 2004), p. 10.
53 Barry et al., 'The European dimension', p. 107; Barry, 'Convergence is not automatic', p. 1390.
54 Sweeney, *The Celtic Tiger*, p. 86.
55 See for instance Barry et al., 'The European dimension', p. 115; R. Mac Sharry and P. White, *The Making of the Celtic Tiger: The Inside Story of*

Ireland's Boom Economy (Cork: Mercier Press, 2000), p. 373; F. Ruane and H. Görg, 'Ireland's economic growth', *Economic Review*, 18: 1 (2000), p. 14; Sweeney, *The Celtic Tiger*, p. 87.
56 'Europe's tiger economy', *The Economist* (17 May 1997).
57 Barry et al., 'The European dimension', p. 114.
58 M. Wolf, 'Ireland's miracle', *Financial Times* (19 August 1999).
59 L. Weiss, 'Introduction: bringing domestic institutions back in', in L. Weiss (ed.), *States in the Global Economy: Bringing Domestic Institutions Back In* (Cambridge: Cambridge University Press, 2003), p. 1.
60 Mac Sharry and White, *The Making of the Celtic Tiger*, p. 250.
61 O'Hearn, 'Macroeconomic policy in the Celtic tiger', pp. 51–2.
62 P. Kirby, *Poverty Amid Plenty: World and Irish Development Reconsidered* (Dublin: Gill & Macmillan, 1997), pp. 140–3.
63 Breathnach, 'Exploring the "Celtic tiger" phenomenon', pp. 305–9.
64 For a chronology of Irish industrial policy, see Mac Sharry and White, *The Making of the Celtic Tiger*, pp. 227–8.
65 Cited in 'People still trump card in attracting US companies', *Irish Times* (29 March 2001).
66 Deloitte, *Globalisation Divided? Global Investment Trends of US Manufacturers* (New York: Deloitte Research, 2004), pp. 1–2.
67 P. O'Connell, *Astonishing Success: Economic Growth and the Labour Market in Ireland* (Geneva: International Labour Office, 1999), p. 66; see also OECD, *Economic Surveys: Ireland 1995* (Paris: OECD, 1995), p. 70.
68 OECD, *Economic Surveys: Ireland 1995*, p. 70; J. J. Sexton and P. O'Connell, *Labour Market Studies: Ireland* (Brussels: European Commission, 1996), p. 125.
69 IDA Ireland, *Ireland: Vital Statistics* (Dublin: Industrial Development Agency, 2004); P. Tansey, *Ireland at Work: Economic Growth and the Labour Market, 1987–1997* (Dublin: Oak Tree Press, 1998), p. 114; National Competitiveness Council (NCC), *Annual Competitiveness Report 2003* (Dublin: Forfás, 2003), p. 74.
70 See for instance J. Durkan, D. Fitz Gerald and C. Harmon, 'Education and growth in the Irish economy', in Barry, *Understanding Ireland's Economic Growth*, p. 135; Tansey, *Ireland at Work*, p. 116; NCC, *Annual Competitiveness Report 2000* (Dublin: Forfás, 2000), p. 29.
71 NCC, *Annual Competitiveness Report 2003*, p. 74.
72 European Commission, *Commission Staff Working Paper: European Innovation Scoreboard* (Brussels: European Commission, 2003), p. 13.
73 Tansey, *Ireland at Work*, p. 105; J. Considine and E. O'Leary, 'The growth performance of Northern Ireland and the Republic of Ireland: 1960 to 1995', in N. Collins and T. Cradden (eds), *Political Issues in Ireland Today* (Manchester: Manchester University Press, 1999), p. 121.
74 Forfás, *International Trade and Investment Report 2001* (Dublin: Forfás, 2002), p. 34; OECD, *Economic Surveys: Ireland 1996–1997* (Paris: OECD, 1997), p. 16. As one business executive has remarked, the calibre of Irish employees is the 'critical issue' in the decision to locate in Ireland,

with the Republic 'ahead of the pack' in terms of education – cited in *Irish Times*, 'People still trump card in attracting US companies'.
75 Irish Council for Science, Technology and Innovation, '£250 million Scientific and Technological Education (Investment) Fund' (2004), www.forfas.ie/icsti/statements/250inv/intro.htm.
76 Weiss, 'Introduction: bringing domestic institutions back in', pp. 1–36; C. Hay, 'Globalisation's impact on states', in J. Ravenhill (ed.), *Global Political Economy* (Oxford: Oxford University Press, 2005).
77 Breathnach, 'Exploring the "Celtic tiger" phenomenon', pp. 307–8.
78 OECD, *Economic Surveys: Ireland 1999*, p. 34.
79 D. Coleman, 'Demography and migration in Ireland, North and South', in A. F. Heath, R. Breen and C. T. Whelan (eds), *Ireland North and South: Perspectives from Social Science* (Oxford: Oxford University Press, 1999), p. 71.
80 Ireland also has the lowest old age dependency ratio out of the EU15 countries, at just 17 per cent compared to the EU15 average of 25 per cent. European Commission, *50 Years of Figures on Europe* (Luxembourg: European Commission, 2003), pp. 26, 29, 37.
81 T. Fahey and J. Fitz Gerald, 'The educational revolution and demographic change', in D. Duffy, J. Fitz Gerald, I. Kearney and F. Shortall (eds), *The Medium-Term Review: 1997–2003* (Dublin: Economic and Social Research Institute, 1997), pp. 22–3; P. O'Connell, 'Sick man or tigress? The labour market in the Republic of Ireland', in Heath et al., *Ireland North and South*, p. 225.
82 OECD, *Economic Surveys: Ireland 1996–1997*, p. 16.
83 Görg and Ruane, 'European integration and peripherality', p. 416. For example, a survey of the linguistic skills of EU citizens found that over half of respondents spoke English as their first or second language and 69 per cent agreed that 'everyone should speak English'. See 'English is still on the march', *The Economist* (24 February 2001).
84 K. Allen, *The Celtic Tiger: The Myth of Social Partnership in Ireland* (Manchester: Manchester University Press, 2000), p. 25.
85 In terms of expenditure on total labour market measures, Ireland ranked fourth out of 26 OECD countries, spending just over 4 per cent of GDP in 1996 compared to the OECD average of 2.25 per cent in 1997. Of this, the share of expenditure on active measures was 41 per cent compared to the OECD average of 35 per cent. See J. P. Martin, 'What works among active labour market policies: evidence from OECD countries', *OECD Economic Studies*, 30: 1 (2000), p. 83.
86 P. Auer, *Employment Revival in Europe: Labour Market Success in Austria, Denmark, Ireland and the Netherlands* (Geneva: International Labour Office, 2000), p. 2.
87 Empirical research suggests that programmes with weak labour market linkages, with general training and direct employment schemes are much less effective than those with strong labour market linkages, such as specific skills training and employment subsidies. One study found that, of 3,200 people interviewed in 1994 who left active labour market pro-

grammes in 1992, only one third of those in general training and one fifth from direct employment schemes were employed at any time in the 20 months post-programme. In contrast, nearly two thirds of those involved with employment subsidies were at work at any time during this period. See O'Connell, 'Sick man or tigress?', pp. 241–4; Sexton and O'Connell, *Labour Market Studies: Ireland*, pp. 156–7.

88 The CSO estimates that nearly a third of working mothers have children under the age of 5. CSO, *Quarterly National Household Survey: First Quarter 2002* (Cork: Central Statistical Office, 2002), p. 3.

89 The Irish government could also do more to attract workers from abroad. For example, it has been criticised for failing to establish greater links with the Irish diaspora, with little right of political participation afforded to Irish citizens abroad and no established structures for representing their interests in relation to the Irish state. Indeed, 1.2 million who were born in Ireland live abroad, but the total of people living outside Ireland who are classed as Irish citizens is about 3 million. It has also been estimated that there are 70 million people living abroad who can be classed as identifying with Ireland. See P. Gillespie, 'Diaspora a resource to the Celtic tiger', *Irish Times* (22 January 2000).

90 See for instance N. Hardiman, 'The political economy of growth', in Crotty and Schmitt, *Ireland on the World Stage*, pp. 170–1; IMF, *Ireland – Recent Economic Developments* (Washington, DC: International Monetary Fund, 1996), p. 11; R. O'Donnell and C. O'Reardon, 'Social partnership in Ireland's economic transformation', in G. Fajertag and P. Pochet (eds), *Social Pacts in Europe* (Brussels: European Trade Union Institute, 2000), p. 241.

91 Nor can pay be identified as the primary reason for industrial strife in Ireland. Rather, the Labour Relations Commission has found other issues such as poor human relations to be the most important. See G. Taylor, *Negotiated Governance and Public Policy in Ireland* (Manchester: Manchester University Press, 2005), p. 39.

92 Ibid.

93 Ó Riain, 'The flexible developmental state', p. 161. Barry, Bradley and O'Malley find that the average wage in foreign industry was approximately 25 per cent higher than in indigenous industry in 1995. Barry et al., 'Indigenous and foreign industry', p. 54.

94 Indeed, just one third of workers (many of whom are in the public sector) were formally covered by the wage agreements in 2000. It may be that wage moderation has been more important to the growth in indigenous industry, by countering upward pressure on wages created by the ability of foreign firms to pay higher wages than domestic firms. See Barry et al., 'Indigenous and foreign industry', p. 61.

95 They find that 72 per cent of non-union workplaces introduced new plant and technology in the 1990s (compared to 78 per cent in unionised workplaces). Similarly, 61 per cent of non-union workplaces implemented changes in working practice (compared to 67 per cent in unionised workplaces). Moreover, in some instances workplace change was *greater* for non-union workplaces. For instance, Roche and Geary find that 70 per

cent of non-union firms introduced initiatives to involve employees, compared to 58 per cent of unionised firms. See W. K. Roche and J. F. Geary, '"Collaborative production" and the Irish boom: work organisation, partnership and direct involvement in Irish workplaces', *Economic and Social Review*, 31: 1 (2000), pp. 1–36.

96 Taylor, *Negotiated Governance and Public Policy in Ireland*, pp. 23–52; G. Taylor, 'Labour market rigidities, institutional impediments and managerial constraints: Some reflections on the recent experience of macro-political bargaining in Ireland', *Economic and Social Review*, 27: 3 (1996), pp. 253–77.

97 NESC, *Opportunities, Challenges and Capacities for Choice* (Dublin: National Economic and Social Council, 1999), p. 115.

98 Cited in J. Sachs, 'Ireland's growth strategy: lessons for economic development', in A. Gray (ed.), *International Perspectives on the Irish Economy* (Dublin: Indecon Economic Consultants, 1997), p. 61. In any event, surveys of employers have found that inflexibility arising from labour market regulation was not a significant concern. See Sexton and O'Connell, *Labour Market Studies: Ireland*, p. 111.

99 Taylor, *Negotiated Governance and Public Policy in Ireland*, pp. 25–33; Taylor, 'Labour market rigidities', pp. 253–77.

100 Taylor, 'Labour market rigidities', pp. 268–9.

101 D. D'Art and T. Turner, 'An attitudinal revolution in Irish industrial relations: the end of "them and us"?', *British Journal of Industrial Relations*, 37: 1 (1999), pp. 112–13.

102 Weiss, 'Introduction: bringing domestic institutions back in', pp. 1–36; G. Garrett, 'Shrinking states: globalisation and national autonomy; in N. Woods (ed.), *The Political Economy of Globalisation* (London: Macmillan, 2000), pp. 113–14.

103 P. Teague, 'Pay determination in the Republic of Ireland – towards social corporatism', *British Journal of Industrial Relations*, 33: 2 (1995), p. 263.

104 C. Ó Gráda, 'Is the Celtic tiger a paper tiger?', in D. McCoy, D. Duffy, J. Hore and C. Maccoille (eds), *Quarterly Economic Commentary, Spring 2002* (Dublin: Economic and Social Research Institute, 2002), p. 5.

105 F. Giavazzi and M. Pagano, 'Can severe fiscal contractions be expansionary? Tales of two small European countries', in O. Blanchard and S. Fischer (eds), *NBER Macroeconomics Annual* (London: MIT Press, 1990), p. 87.

106 F. Barry and M. B. Devereux, 'The expansionary fiscal contraction hypothesis – a neo-Keynesian analysis', *Oxford Economic Papers: New Series*, 47: 2 (1995), pp. 249–64.

107 V. Hogan, 'Expansionary fiscal contractions?', Working Paper, University College Dublin (2001), p. 2.

108 Barry, 'Convergence is not automatic', p. 1391.

109 OECD, *Economic Surveys: Ireland 1999*, p. 47.

110 F. Barry, 'The Celtic tiger era: delayed convergence or regional boom?', in McCoy et al., *Quarterly Economic Commentary, Summer 2002*, p. 6.

111 Auer, *Employment Revival in Europe*, p. 42.
112 Sweeney, *The Celtic Tiger*, p. 93.
113 Auer, *Employment Revival in Europe*, p. 44.
114 Mac Sharry and White, *The Making of the Celtic Tiger*, p. 368; Breathnach, 'Exploring the "Celtic tiger" phenomenon', p. 309.
115 Breathnach, 'Exploring the "Celtic tiger" phenomenon', p. 309; Görg and Ruane, 'European integration and peripherality', p. 418.
116 C. Ó Gráda, *A Rocky Road: The Irish Economy Since the 1920s* (Manchester: Manchester University Press, 1997), p. 119; E. O'Malley, 'The problem of late industrialisation and the experience of the Republic of Ireland', *Cambridge Journal of Economics*, 9 (1985), p. 148; E. O'Malley, 'Problems of industrialisation in Ireland', in J. H. Goldthorpe and C. T. Whelan (eds), *The Development of Industrial Society in Ireland* (Oxford: Oxford University Press, 1992), p. 45; O'Malley, 'The revival of Irish indigenous industry', pp. 55–7.
117 P. R. Krugman, 'Good news from Ireland: a geographical perspective', in Gray, *International Perspectives on the Irish Economy*, pp. 49–50.
118 Barry et al., 'Indigenous and foreign industry', p. 65.
119 O'Clery, 'Irish tech start-ups still a hot item for US VCs' (2001), www.xacp.com/news.html.
120 Cited in 'People still trump card in attracting US companies'.
121 Görg and Ruane, 'European integration and peripherality', p. 418.
122 Weiss, 'Introduction: bringing domestic institutions back in', pp. 27–8.
123 Breathnach, 'Exploring the "Celtic tiger" phenomenon', p. 309; Görg and Ruane, 'European integration and peripherality', p. 418.
124 B. Nolan, P. O'Connell and C. T. Whelan, 'Introduction', in B. Nolan, P. O'Connell and C. T. Whelan (eds), *Bust to Boom? The Irish Experience of Growth and Inequality* (Dublin: Institute of Public Administration, 2000), p. 2; see also Barry et al., 'Indigenous and foreign industry', p. 59.

4

The trajectory of the Irish state (1): 1921 to 1987

As discussed in chapter 3, Ireland's economic turnaround can only be understood if consideration is given to the Republic's specific national context. This not only points to the importance of spatial factors but also suggests that the temporal dimension is crucial. While Ireland experienced rapid growth in the 1990s, the reasons for this success have been influenced by policy decisions taken years earlier. For example, the strategy of attracting foreign investment, the decision to join Europe and the decision to invest in education can all be traced back to a shift in policy approach from 1958 towards an export-oriented and interventionist strategy. Similarly, social partnership was not an entirely new strategy for Ireland but had already been developed (if weakly) in the 1970s. While these earlier policies cannot in themselves explain why Ireland's success occurred when it did, they can be seen to have shaped (though certainly not determined) the trajectory of the Irish state in the 1990s. It therefore seems crucial to consider the historical context when attempting to understand contemporary developments in Ireland. This temporal dimension is particularly important within the context of the globalisation debate, for it is often assumed not only that state trajectories have shifted markedly but that this is in itself a response to globalisation (see chapter 1).

This chapter places the trajectory of Irish economic policy in historical perspective, outlining the period from 1921 (when the Irish Republic was established) to 1987 (which is widely seen to mark the beginning of the current political project). The period 1987 to 2004 is considered in the following chapter. It should be noted that both chapters confine themselves to describing policy change rather than explaining it. While it is no easy task to disentangle description from explanation, it is vital that we do so in order to resist the common tendency to conflate the two (which is not least evident in the globalisation literature). The dynamics *of* policy change (that is, how it has occurred) are thus considered in chapters 4 and 5, whereas the dynamics *behind* that change (that is, why it has occurred) are explored in chapters 6 and 7.

Conceptualising change

Before turning to the Irish case, it is worth spending some time considering how we might conceptualise change. For, if politics is ultimately about power – the ability to shape or transform our context – then it is also essentially about change.[1] Yet surprisingly few accounts in political analysis study change in a reflexive and systematic way. Rather, as Hay notes, many adopt either a synchronic approach (equivalent to taking a 'snapshot' of a moving object) or a comparative statics approach (equivalent to taking two photographs and comparing them). The latter approach, involving the posing of such binary oppositions as 'social democracy' and 'neo-liberalism' or 'closed national economies' and 'open global economies',[2] is pervasive in the globalisation literature (see chapter 1).

Such conceptions of change are inherently problematic for several reasons. First, they reveal very little about the character of change. Like a photograph, the synchronic approach may produce a very sharp image but reveals nothing about the nature and extent of change. Similarly, the comparative statics approach may tell us something about the extent and direction of change but reveals little about its actual process and pace.[3] Second, there is the real danger of reification in the use of ideal types such as 'Fordism' and 'post-Fordism'. While these labels may possess some limited utility in heuristic terms, the tendency is most often to treat them as 'real things'. In turn, this runs the risk of functionalism: the state exhibits Fordist or post-Fordist tendencies because it is a Fordist or post-Fordist state. Description therefore very quickly presents itself as explanation. Third, while authors may indeed point to the diversity and complexity of specific models, their use of ideal types can only serve to mask rather than highlight this complexity. Thus, even if the state exhibits strong tendencies towards a particular model, this does not mean that it is ultimately defined by those tendencies. Rather, there are likely to be at least some counter-tendencies to the dominant tendencies at any one point in time. Finally, it is important to note that these labels can and do possess discursive power, serving to constrain perceptions of the political alternatives available to a state at any given point in time. This is revealed by such claims as:

'Two models of capitalism, Anglo-Saxon and European, are on offer – and we've made the wrong choice.'[4]

How then might we conceptualise change? In contrast to synchronic or comparative static accounts, a number of authors have advocated a processual or 'diachronic' approach to change.[5] This focuses upon the dynamic of change itself and is equivalent to a video 'panning' shot following the movement of an object.[6] By treating the actual process of change as an open and empirical question, the diachronic approach 'often tends to dispel or at least qualify significantly the sharp and dualistic periodisations which tend to be associated with comparative static methodologies'.[7] This allows us to explore the pattern of change over time. Change is often characterised as revolutionary (where periods of stasis are interrupted by moments of rapid and profound transformation) or evolutionary (where change is slower, longer-term, cumulative and directional).[8] Yet, as various authors have noted, periods of relative stability and continuity may be interrupted be moments of sudden and intense change.[9] As Hodgson writes: 'even gradual change can eventually put such a strain on a system that there can be sudden outbreaks of conflict or crisis, leading to a significant change in attitudes, conventions, and social practices'.[10] Conversely, even moments of sudden and dramatic change are unlikely to represent a complete break with the past.[11] Paradoxically, then, periods of relative stability may lead to significant (if gradual and incremental) change over time, and moments of apparent transformation may exhibit certain elements of continuity. This highlights the need to conceptualise change as essentially fluid and dynamic: that is, in terms of the ebb and flow of particular tendencies and counter-tendencies that may shift considerably – whether gradually or rapidly – over time.

That having been said, we cannot understand the process(es) of change through conceptualisation alone. For, as we have seen, the shape and direction of change should above all be treated as an open and empirical question. Thus, while the above discussion can provide a theoretical lens through which to examine state trajectories, we need also to engage in detailed empirical analysis. With this aim in mind, we shall now turn to the Irish case.

Periodising the Irish state, 1921–87

Various authors have sought to trace the path of Irish economic policy over time. In so doing, they have deployed a number of periodisations in order to characterise different 'phases' of Ireland's development.[12] While the length of the periods specified varies (not least depending upon whether a broader or more detailed account is given), most authors accept that, prior to 1987, the year 1958 marked a key moment of transformation for the Irish state.[13] As Breen et al. note, the Irish state adopted an essentially 'auxiliary' role (that is, supplementary to other institutions such as the church) until 1958, when the state became much more active and outward looking. These authors therefore label the Irish state before 1958 the 'auxiliary state' and post-1958 the 'active state'.[14]

As will be outlined, 1958 did indeed mark a decisive turning point in the trajectory of the Irish state. From then on, the Irish state adopted a much more interventionist and outward-looking role than before. Yet this does not mean that Ireland shifted from one state form ('the auxiliary state') to another ('the active state'). For, while Irish economic policy was characterised by strong 'auxiliary' tendencies prior to 1958 and strong 'activist' tendencies thereafter, it was not ultimately *defined* by those tendencies. Rather, counter-tendencies were also apparent during both periods (indeed, Breen et al. are themselves at pains to note the limits of state activism after 1958). By conceptualising the trajectory of the Irish state in terms of tendencies and counter-tendencies, we can remain sensitive to the fluid, dynamic and multidimensional nature of change. By using such an approach, moreover, we can avoid implying that this change occurs in a similar way and for similar reasons to that of other states. For, as we shall see in the chapters that follow, both the dynamics *of* change and the dynamics *behind* change are, at least in part, distinctive to Ireland's specific national context.

The Irish state prior to 1958

Laissez-faire

Born in 1921 with the signing of the Anglo-Irish Treaty, the new Irish state 'seemed destined to mark out a new course'.[15] Yet, as Meenan notes, Ireland was 'essentially an old country setting up for itself as a new state'.[16] The Irish economy had developed within the framework of the British capitalist system and was closely tied to the UK in terms of trade. In addition, the state structures (including the main administrative departments) were largely inherited from the British system, as indeed were the personnel of the state.[17] The institutions inherited by the Irish government also included a toned-down version of the British welfare state, including the poor relief system, basic social insurance, subsidised education and limited health and housing services.[18]

Just as the basic state structures were retained after 1921, so too there was little change in economic policy-making. The Irish state played an auxiliary (though not necessarily subordinate) role to other institutions such as the church. While limited tariffs were introduced to raise revenue, the Cumann na nGaedheal administration interfered very little in economic and social affairs. Agriculture continued to be a main priority, with policy geared towards exports and the needs of larger farmers. The new government left the banking system alone and retained the link with sterling. Irish industrial policy, too, continued to follow the British model of free collective bargaining.[19]

Yet, while the overall tendency was towards non-interventionism, the economy after 1921 was 'not unplanned'.[20] In particular, the state appeared willing to adopt a more active role in the pursuit of major obstacles such as electrification. In 1927 the Electricity Supply Board was established, along with the Dairy Disposal Company and the Agricultural Credit Corporation. While it is important not to overstate the significance of these developments,[21] they nevertheless represent counter-tendencies to the broad trend of non-interventionism.

The adoption of economic nationalism

In 1932 a shift in governmental power occurred when the anti-treaty party, Fianna Fáil, took office. A key aim of the new administration was for Ireland to become self-sufficient through the expansion of industry. This entailed a radical change in policy from laissez-faire to protectionism through such measures as the Control of Manufactures Act in 1932, which was designed to keep industry under Irish control.[22] The Irish market was soon one of the most protected in the world, with tariffs of up to 75 per cent imposed on more than 4,000 categories of imports by 1936.[23] Protectionism also extended to agriculture, with duties imposed on various imports and bounties offered to encourage tillage.

Striking though this sea-change may seem, continuity remained the 'hallmark' of Irish economic policy-making.[24] Fianna Fáil did 'little to alter the structural dispositions of the economy'.[25] Despite the introduction of tariffs, the export of livestock to Britain remained vital to the economy. The link with sterling was kept and industrial relations continued to follow the British model. The state also retained strong auxiliary tendencies, offering only limited supervision in major areas of activity such as education and health. With the government (and most notably the Department of Finance) regarding state borrowing as a 'cardinal sin',[26] by the end of the 1930s Ireland's national debt remained modest by European standards. Even the tariffs and subsidies imposed by the state did not involve direct state involvement in production, but instead aimed to encourage private activity. Policy also proceeded on an essentially *ad hoc* basis, with little attention given to longer-term considerations such as what to do when the new industries matured.[27]

Yet, despite the state's strong auxiliary tendencies, there were some moves towards a more active approach. This included the extension of the state-sponsored sector in both industry and commerce. A range of new bodies was established, including the Industrial Credit Corporation, the Turf Development Board, the Irish Life Assurance Company and the Irish Tourist Board.[28] The new government's agenda also entailed a degree of social radicalism, including the raising of unemployment assistance, old age pensions, widows' and orphans' pensions and the introduction of income-maintenance schemes. Key initiatives included an ambitious housing scheme and a major programme to build schools.[29] Fianna Fáil also adopted a more conciliatory and consultative approach towards the trade unions. In an attempt to ensure parliamentary representation of major interest groups, the 1937 constitution provided for most Seanad members to be elected on 'vocational panels'. In practice, however, the elections rapidly became party political rather than vocational in character.[30] Nevertheless, while the Irish state exhibited strong auxiliary tendencies in the 1930s, some counter-tendencies were clearly evident.

War and recovery

The advent of World War II did not mark a change in Ireland's inward-looking stance. Indeed, the government immediately declared the Republic to be neutral. During the so-called 'Emergency', Ireland was almost entirely closed off from world markets, with the ratio of imports to national income falling by over half.[31] After the war, the absence of policy change is quite striking. Other European countries attempted to restructure their economies in accordance with the main tenets of modernisation and internationalisation.[32] In Ireland, by contrast, protectionism was restored and some new tariffs were imposed. When Fine Gael (previously Cumann na nGaedheal) formed a coalition government with the leftist Clann na Poblachta in 1948, they too were committed to protectionism.

However, although the Irish state continued to exhibit strong protectionist tendencies, counter-tendencies were also apparent. Ireland did make some tentative steps towards a more outward-looking approach after the war. In 1948 the Republic entered into a Trade Agreement with Britain, although most of its protective tariffs were retained. Ireland was also a founding member of the Organisation for European Economic Co-operation (OEEC) and the Council of Europe, although it remained relatively isolated from discussions regarding the Common Market. Moreover, Ireland took foreign money for the first time in the form of nearly £150 million in Marshall aid.[33]

The state also adopted a more active role, although again this did not amount to a radical shift in overall stance. Measures during the war included legislation to provide children's allowances and increase local government responsibility for health services. In 1947 a separate Department of Health was established and the state's share of total costs increased to one half of total costs.[34] By the late 1940s public expenditure rose above 25 per cent of GDP for the first time.[35] Some (albeit limited) innovation also occurred in relation to monetary policy. In 1943 the Central Bank was founded, as de Valera put it, to protect 'the integrity of our currency' and 'the welfare of the people as a whole' in terms of credit.[36] In practice, however, monetary policy remained linked to sterling and lending was still concentrated in the City of London. In terms of fiscal policy, some change was evident in a shift towards Keynesianism. In 1948, the finance minister proposed that capital be separated from current items in the budget so that a deficit could be run on the capital side. This innovation remained limited, though, since official policy remained preoccupied with annual fluctuations in the balance of trade and balance of payments.[37] Finally, there were also signs of a shift in approach to industrial relations. Indeed, the minister of industry and commerce, Seán Lemass, advocated that economic management be transformed into genuine corporatism after the war. However, his only proposal to be implemented successfully was the establishment of the Labour Court in 1946, and this soon became a pillar of the free collective bargaining system.[38] Nevertheless, while the broad trend was towards non-interventionism in the 1940s, some counter-tendencies can also be identified.

Stagnation

The 1950s are most often noted as a period of economic crisis in Ireland (see chapter 6). Yet government policy remained characterised by significant continuity for most of the decade. In contrast to other Western European countries and despite changes in government in 1951 and 1954, Ireland retained its broadly protectionist stance.[39] A report in 1957 stated: 'as regards a large sector of existing industries, the Department of Industry and Commerce can see no prospect of their survival even as suppliers of the home market, except with *permanent* protection . . . [and] can see no prospect of a significant expansion of industrial exports from Ireland to the continental part of the free trade area'.[40] The state also retained its 'auxiliary' tendencies, with total social expenditure actually declining from 16 to 14 per cent of GNP in 1951–9.[41] The Central Bank remained small and made no attempts to influence interest rates or the reserves of the commercial banks.

Nevertheless, the tendential nature of the state's broad stance can again be identified. In particular, a number of important steps were also taken to establish the basis of an export-orientated strategy. In 1950 the IDA was established to oversee industry, and in 1952 its role was extended to include the attraction of foreign industry. However, although the IDA had a separate board, it remained subject to the normal administrative controls and the need to acquire formal departmental approval for spending.[42] Despite this, the IDA would later play a major role in the attraction of foreign investment to Ireland (see chapter 3). Further measures included the establishment of the Irish Export Board in 1951 (to help export producers sell to foreign markets) and the introduction of exports tax relief in 1956. The more outward-looking approach was also reflected in Ireland's membership of the World Bank and the IMF in 1957, and Ireland maintained its presence in the Council of Europe (although this was initially used to promote anti-partition policy).[43] Signs of a shift in approach were also evident in other areas such as monetary policy. Indeed, in 1955 and 1956 the government attempted to break the link with sterling, although this was a temporary deviation.[44] The Social Welfare Act of 1952 provided limited benefits but nevertheless established the basis for the current welfare system.[45] Again, while the early to mid-1950s were characterised by much continuity in the state's auxiliary role, some counter-tendencies were nevertheless evident.

From 1958 onwards

Policy turnaround

While the 1950s can be identified as a period of transition, it was at the end of the decade that a decisive shift in approach occurred. In 1958 a White Paper entitled the *Programme for Economic Expansion* was published. Pointing to the emerging Free Trade Area in Europe, this argued that 'protection can no longer be relied upon as an automatic weapon of defence' and that 'we must be prepared to welcome foreign participation'.[46] The *Programme* advocated trade liberalisation, attracting foreign investment, and state investment in capital-intensive, export-oriented production. It was highly interventionist and marked the beginning of Ireland's move towards export-oriented growth.[47] Ireland was one of the first of the late-industrialising nations to adopt such an approach,[48] which in turn helped to lay the foundations for its improved performance in the 1990s (see chapter 3).

In particular, the focus of government policy turned towards Europe. Ireland made its first application for EEC membership in 1961. This collapsed after the French president, Charles de Gaulle, imposed a veto on EEC enlargement in 1963. Nevertheless, Ireland took provisional measures to prepare for EEC membership, including two unilateral reductions in manufacturing tariffs and the signing of the Anglo-Irish Free Trade Area Agreement in 1965 (in which protection against British imports was to be removed progressively in return for much greater access to British markets). In 1969 serious negotiation resumed for EEC membership, with a number of domestic policy measures introduced in order to prepare Irish industry for trade liberalisation (including the creation of committees to help organise industry and the introduction of grants to modernise buildings and plants). Crucially, the government also adopted active measures in order to attract FDI.[49] Export tax relief was quickly extended, giving complete tax exemption on profits generated from export transactions. The Control of Manufactures Act was relaxed in 1958 and then repealed in 1964, meaning that there was no longer any restriction on foreign investment. This represented a major turnaround in policy.

Moreover, the role of the IDA was strengthened and extended from 1958. In particular, the Industrial Development Act of 1969 established the IDA as a separate state agency. This 'marked a major transition in the IDA's development from limited to full autonomy'.[50]

However, the focus of public policy was on national rather than regional development in order to attract foreign investment.[51] Thus, the origins of Ireland's regional inequality (noted in chapter 2) as well as its growth can be traced back many years.

Though not explicitly labelled a 'plan', the *Programme for Economic Expansion* signified Ireland's adjustment to indicative economic planning. It emphasised the need to 'redefine the objectives of economic policy in the light of present-day and probable future conditions'.[52] The targets set were modest, with an annual growth rate of 2 per cent anticipated over five years. While the plan was not followed precisely, GNP grew by 4 per cent in 1958–63, and this was attributed to the plan itself. A Second Programme was thus adopted for the period 1964–7. This was significantly more detailed but failed to meet the targets set, even after they were revised downwards, and was formally abandoned in 1967 (though it was followed by a Third Programme for 1969–72).[53]

The Irish state expanded dramatically during the 1960s. Institutional innovations included the establishment of a number of permanent bodies and forums to advise on economic development, such as the National Industrial and Economic Council (NIEC). Indeed, the number of civil servants rose by a quarter in the space of a decade. This was matched by a significant rise in total public expenditure (from 32 to 42 per cent of GNP in 1960–73). Social expenditure also rose during this period (from 14 to 22 per cent of GNP),[54] with social citizenship considerably expanded as services were improved and income and maintenance payments upgraded and extended.[55] New measures included the child allowance scheme of 1966 and free travel for old-age pensioners in 1967. Spending on education, too, grew enormously, rising from 3.0 to 6.3 per cent of GNP between 1961–2 and 1973–4.[56] This was not least due to the introduction of free post-primary education in 1967 (with accompanying measures including free transport), with a Higher Education Authority (HEA) also established in 1969 to oversee improvements in third-level education. As discussed in chapter 3, Ireland has since reaped the benefits of these reforms, not least in terms of attracting foreign investment.

In the late 1950s and 1960s, the Irish state began to take a more active role in other areas such as monetary policy. For example, in 1958 US dollar securities were used to back Irish currency for the first time, and in 1959 Irish securities were included in the Legal Tender Note Fund. The government also adopted a more interventionist stance in terms of industrial relations. While union leaders and activists remained committed to free collective bargaining, a shift towards neo-corporatism was nevertheless evident during the 1960s.[57] Throughout the decade attempts to encourage consultation were common, and the establishment of bodies such as the NIEC laid the institutional foundations for further state intervention in industrial relations.[58] The origins of the social partnership approach since 1987 therefore date back several decades earlier, again suggesting that the historical context is crucial when understanding more recent developments.

However, it is important not to overemphasise the pace and extent of change in the 1960s. As Ó Gráda notes: 'To describe Ireland's transition as one from protection to free trade is to oversimplify.'[59] For example, the *Programme for Economic Expansion* stated: 'If this country becomes a member of the Free Trade Area, legislation will be promoted to protect Irish industries against dumping or any other form of unfair competition.'[60] In the early 1960s tariff rates remained high and some quotas were even increased. Moreover, the new financial and fiscal incentives to attract foreign investment were designed to complement rather than replace existing indigenous firms. Policy also continued to proceed on a rather *ad hoc* basis, with little attention given to longer-term matters such as the barriers facing indigenous industry and the role of agriculture in the wider economy.[61]

Various authors have also pointed to the limits of state activism after 1958.[62] Indeed, in some respects a shift *away* from state activism is evident. For example, the initiative for meeting growing demand for housing increasingly moved to the private sector. The 1966 Housing Act emphasised the privatisation of the housing market and sought to facilitate tenant purchase of public housing, although a commitment to local authority housing was retained.[63] Nor can the growth in social expenditure be assumed to signify an increase in state control. This can be seen, for example, in relation to education. While state funding increased, the decisions as to how to spend those funds remained in the hands of private institutions such as the church.[64] Thus, while strong tendencies towards state activism were apparent, the state continued to exhibit some auxiliary tendencies, too.

Consolidation

In 1973 Ireland finally gained entry to the EEC, with a transition period of five years agreed to abolish existing tariffs.[65] From the start, governments under both Fianna Fáil and Fine Gael sought to adopt a consistent and constructive role within Europe. While there was some resistance to rules that would burden Irish industry and services, in most areas Irish policy-makers accepted the broad outline of the European Community's (EC's) regulatory strategy. Key aims included the creation of a framework for EC cohesion policy and the preservation of the key principles of the Common Agricultural Policy (CAP).[66] Ireland's integration into Europe gained momentum after 1978 with the decision for Ireland to join the European Monetary System (EMS). This finally brought an end to the monetary union between Ireland and Britain that had existed since 1826.

The 1970s also saw the consolidation of Ireland's outward-looking approach in terms of industrial policy. The emphasis was upon the cultivation of Ireland as an export platform for overseas firms, with relatively little attention and support given to indigenous industry. In particular, the IDA focused upon employment creation and sought to attract industries that were labour-intensive, relied largely on unskilled labour and were far advanced in their product cycle.[67] Policy was based upon large-scale state intervention in the form of grants and tax expenditures but was non-directive. As Sweeney observes: 'The visible hand was more the "open hand" than the "pointing hand".'[68]

In addition, the expansion of the Irish state accelerated in the 1970s (see table 4.1). Between 1973 and 1985 public expenditure rose from 42 to 67 per cent of GNP.[69] This was driven mainly by a rise in

Table 4.1 Expenditure of central government by purpose of expenditure and economic category in Ireland (IR£m, current prices), 1965–6 to 1984

Category	1965–6	1970–1	1975	1980	1984
Defence	14.1	22.4	67.1	176.3	262.6
Other central government services	23.3	37.9	126.3	320.9	607.8
Education	39.8	81.3	222.2	553.7	980.3
Health	15.6	42.7	213.6	697.3	1,102.4
Social security and welfare	57.6	119.1	389.6	925.4	2,133.9
Housing	21.9	37.0	139.1	371.3	626.0
Other community and social services	4.6	8.1	26.7	71.5	142.1
Agriculture, forestry and fishing	60.7	107.4	179.4	333.0	509.1
Mining, manufacturing and construction	15.7	32.0	82.9	261.5	361.0
Transport and communications	25.6	42.4	131.9	345.9	359.3
Other economic services	6.9	15.9	183.8	168.8	302.5
Public debt	38.0	88.6	217.4	1,082.9	2,367.7
Total expenditure	*323.9*	*634.8*	*1,980.1*	*5,305.6*	*9,754.6*

Source: B. Brunt, *The Republic of Ireland* (London: Paul Chapman, 1988), p. 19.

public sector employment, which made up one third of the total workforce by 1980.[70] Social expenditure rose dramatically, from 22 to 34 per cent of GNP,[71] with the proportion of the labour force with full social insurance coverage increasing from 66 to 74 per cent in 1971–81.[72] The education system – and particularly third-level education – was also considerably expanded. This included the building of Regional Technical Colleges and two National Institutes for Higher Education, with the number of places provided at existing universities also greatly extended. In addition, the HEA was given powers to monitor higher education and impose decisions under the HEA Act (1971). Again, Ireland has since reaped the benefits of these policies implemented in the 1970s (see chapter 3).

The decade also saw the adoption of expansionary fiscal policy. A key concern was the need to reduce unemployment, which had reached 9 per cent by 1977.[73] The supplementary budget of 1970 stated that a current account deficit was an option and the budget of 1972 became the first to prepare for this.[74] The government's response to the oil crises of 1972–3 was 'thoroughly Keynesian', with the adoption of the counter-cyclical measure of boosting spending sharply.[75] In 1973–5 the current budget deficit rose from 0.4 to 6.8 per cent and, while the budget deficit was lowered in 1977 to 3.6 per cent, spending again increased after 1978 under Fianna Fáil in order to lift employment.[76] The 'landmark' budget of 1979 sought to increase economic growth by 7 per cent through an Exchequer borrowing requirement of 13 per cent of GDP and, by 1980, the public sector borrowing requirement had risen from 8.6 to 17.3 per cent of GNP since 1972–3.[77] In turn, the total national debt increased from 55 to 81 per cent of GNP in 1973–80.[78]

Finally, significant change occurred in terms of industrial relations. In previous decades Irish industrial relations had continued to follow the British model. However, 1970 saw the adoption of centralised bargaining, initially on a bipartite basis and then with full government participation.[79] This 'expanded bargaining agenda' culminated in the 'National Understanding' of 1979, which covered a variety of issues including state health and education provision.[80] A particularly important institutional development was the replacement of the NISC with the NESC, which was broader in scope and included agricultural interests. This body would later play a central role in the adoption of the social partnership approach from 1987 (see chapter 7).

Again, though, it is possible to overstate the extent of state activism in the 1970s. In particular, authors point to the lack of state policy to reduce Ireland's long-standing social inequalities.[81] Welfare state expansion in Ireland stood 'in stark contrast to the Scandinavian pattern' (characterised by commitments to universalism and equality).[82] While there was the expansion of social coverage through a basic service, there was minimal commitment to reducing inequalities. Indeed, O'Connell and Rottman contend that inequalities were made worse by the extension of social insurance and the universal provision of services.[83] They also point to the essentially 'pay-related' nature of the Irish welfare state, with the supplementing of basic state entitlements with private savings and insurance schemes. Thus, while Irish welfare state expansion reflects the wide range of social rights afforded to Irish citizens, it also reveals 'the degree to which those rights reinforce, rather than mitigate, market inequalities'.[84]

Moreover, a shift *away* from state activism continued to be evident in areas such as housing. The incentives for private ownership were extended in the 1970s, including the withdrawal of rates on domestic dwellings and the introduction of an IR£1,000 grant for first-time house purchasers.[85] It is also worth noting that, despite the consistently Keynesian approach to macro-economic policy, economic planning fell out of favour for much of the 1970s after the Third Plan failed to meet its targets. While it was briefly revived under *National Development* (1977–80), this also failed to meet its targets and marked the end of indicative economic planning in Ireland.[86] Thus, while the Irish state exhibited strong 'activist' tendencies during the 1970s, some 'auxiliary' tendencies also remained apparent.

Transition

Ireland's integration into Europe gathered pace in the 1980s with the negotiation of the Single European Act (SEA). In 1985 Ireland voted with the original six members of the EEC in favour of an inter-governmental conference to draft the SEA. Irish policy-makers emphasised the need for cohesion and solidarity within Europe, using the negotiations with other poorer members to push for greater redistribution policies.[87]

A notable shift in approach is evident in terms of industrial policy. The IDA Strategic Plan for 1982–92 marked a change from the traditional emphasis on attracting the most labour-intensive industries. Rather than focusing upon employment creation alone, the IDA aimed to maximise gains for the economy as a whole, which would in turn produce additional employment. In particular, the IDA aimed to attract the most technologically advanced industries that could achieve high output growth and also invest in Irish services and materials. This included the introduction of a New International Services Programme, which specifically aimed to attract highly successful and employment-intensive service sector companies. Twelve target sectors were outlined, including data processing and software development. However, the emphasis upon fiscal and financial incentives remained, with proposals to reduce grants to foreign firms rejected by the 1984 White Paper. While the rate of corporation tax was increased from zero to 10 per cent in 1981, this was primarily in response to pressure from the European Commission.[88]

Crucially, industrial policy also began to focus upon the need to cultivate indigenous industry from the mid-1980s. The highly controversial Telesis report in 1982 called for a more 'hands on' approach that would 'focus on building competencies within companies'.[89] The government White Paper Industrial Policy (1984) marked a shift in emphasis towards promoting indigenous enterprise (although in practice this did not translate into immediate change).[90] Measures included the creation of a Company Development Scheme and National Linkage Programme in 1985 and a National Development Corporation in 1986. These schemes involved a more directive approach than before in the development of indigenous industry. In particular, the emphasis was upon supporting firms with the most growth potential and that could succeed in the internationally traded sectors. Measures were designed to combat weaknesses in areas such as marketing and technology and encourage subcontracting industries.[91]

The 1980s also saw a shift in macro-economic policy in Ireland. By 1982 total government expenditure had risen to 61.5 per cent of GNP, accompanied by a dramatic rise in the national debt (see table 4.2) – the highest in the EC. The Fine Gael/Labour coalition of 1981 placed particular emphasis upon controlling the public finances. Although the governments of 1981 and 1982 were too brief and unstable for clear policies to emerge, the coalition finally introduced deflationary measures in the budget of 1983. This included a sharp increase in tax rates, which affected the earned income of employees in particular due to the narrow tax base and low rate of corporation tax.[92] Public expenditure was also reduced, with the numbers in the civil service falling from 30,800 to 25,000 between 1981 and 1990.[93] While the spending cuts impacted upon health in particular, they affected a range of other areas, too. For example, spending on local authority housing was reduced by more than half between 1982 and 1987.[94] A rupture

Table 4.2 Government spending and debt in Ireland, 1980–6

Year	Exchequer balance €m	Exchequer balance % GNP	Total government expenditure €m	Total government expenditure % GNP	National (Exchequer) debt €m	National (Exchequer) debt % GNP
1980	−1,545	−13.4	6,245	54.2	10,026	87.0
1981	−2,186	−15.7	8,004	57.6	12,945	93.2
1982	−2,470	−15.5	9,815	61.5	14,817	92.9
1983	−2,253	−13.5	10,847	62.2	18,274	104.8
1984	−2,317	−12.2	11,533	60.9	21,358	112.8
1985	−2,559	−12.1	12,355	58.6	23,493	111.4
1986	−2,724	−12.1	13,052	58.1	27,440	122.2

Source: adapted from Department of Finance, *Budgetary and Economic Statistics: 2002* (Dublin: Department of Finance, 2002), pp. 1–6.

also appeared in the commitment to full employment, with the national plan, *Building on Reality*, foreseeing no immediate fall in unemployment. However, attempts at fiscal retrenchment largely foundered before 1987 due to clashes between the coalition members. The reforms were thus not fully carried out until 1987.[95]

Again, though, a mixed picture emerges in terms of the state's priorities. For example, although education was subject to some cutbacks in spending between 1986 and 1989, it 'continued to receive privileged treatment'.[96] There were also some measures to combat poverty such as the establishment of the Combat Poverty Agency (CPA) through legislation in 1986.

Finally, the 1980s also saw a change in approach to industrial relations. In 1980 a second National Understanding was agreed, which, like its predecessor, included tax concessions and a range of spending commitments.[97] However, this collapsed in 1981, largely due to resistance from the government and employers, marking the end of centralised bargaining until 1987. While the state made *ad hoc* attempts to reduce public sector pay and occasionally called for reductions in private sector pay, its broad stance was that of non-interventionism. It sought both to distance the unions from public policy-making and to uphold the traditions and institutions of free collective bargaining. While various 'rounds' of pay increases occurred during this period, this was quite different from the previous system due to the growing disparities between wage levels and termination dates.[98] Nevertheless, it is important to note that the tripartite bodies established in the 1970s continued to function. As noted earlier, the NESC in particular would later play a central role in the development of social partnership.

If the 1980s can be characterised as a period of transition, it was in 1987 that a radical change in approach occurred. Indeed, Taylor argues that it is 'not in dispute' that 1987 marks the start of Ireland's current 'largesse'.[99] This may be a slight exaggeration, for authors certainly do characterise the present era differently; Ó Gráda, for example, starts it in 1985.[100] Nevertheless, it is clear that 1987 did mark a decisive shift in the government's approach. Irish economic policy from 1987 to the present day will be discussed in the next chapter.

Conclusion

This chapter has provided an overview of Irish economic policy in the period 1921 to 1987. In order to do so, it has first considered how such change might be conceptualised. In particular, it has argued that the complexities and contingencies of policy change are best characterised in terms of the ebb and flow of tendencies and counter-tendencies rather than in terms of mutually exclusive state forms. The chapter has then used this theoretical framework to explore the trajectory of the Irish state. It has suggested that while Irish economic policy exhibited strong 'auxiliary' tendencies prior to 1958 and strong 'activist' tendencies thereafter, this does not mean that the Irish state shifted from one form (the 'auxiliary state') to another (the 'active state'). Rather, strong counter-tendencies were also apparent during both periods. Nor has the Irish state shifted once again to the model of a 'competition state' – which is the subject of the next chapter.

Notes

1 C. Hay, *Political Analysis* (Basingstoke: Palgrave, 2002), pp. 138–9.
2 Ibid., pp., 144–8, 177; see also P. Kerr, 'Saved from extinction: evolutionary theorising, politics and the state', *British Journal of Politics and International Relations*, 4: 2 (2002), p. 335.
3 Hay, *Political Analysis*, pp. 144–8.
4 M. Bunting, 'Pressure of work', *Guardian* (22 April 2002). I am grateful to Matthew Watson for pointing out this newspaper article.
5 See for instance Kerr, 'Evolutionary theorising, politics and the state', p. 335; Hay, *Political Analysis*, pp. 148–50; P. Pierson, 'Increasing returns, path dependence and the study of politics', *American Political Science Review*, 94: 2 (2000), p. 251.

6 Hay, *Political Analysis*, p. 149.
7 Ibid., pp. 178–80.
8 It should be noted that there is considerable debate as to whether incremental change should be characterised as 'evolutionary'. For example, Kerr argues that an evolutionary approach does not assume *a priori* that change is gradual: see P. Kerr, *Postwar British Politics: From Conflict to Consensus* (London: Routledge/PSA, 2001), p. 72. In this sense, it may be better simply to counterpose rapid change with gradual change, rather than revolutionary change with evolutionary change.
9 See for instance G. Hodgson, 'An evolutionary theory of long-term economic growth', *International Studies Quarterly*, 40: 3 (1996), p. 398; Hay, *Political Analysis*, p. 163; P. John and H. Margetts, 'Policy punctuations in the UK: fluctuations and equilibria in central government expenditure since 1951', *Public Administration*, 81: 3 (2003), pp. 412–14; S. Krasner, 'Approaches to the state: alternative conceptions and historical dynamics', *Comparative Politics*, 16: 2 (1984), pp. 240–4.
10 Hodgson, 'An evolutionary theory of long-term economic growth', p. 396.
11 Kerr, *Postwar British Politics*, p. 67.
12 See for instance R. Breen, D. Hannan, D. Rottman and C. T. Whelan, *Understanding Contemporary Ireland: State, Class and Development in the Republic of Ireland* (Dublin: Gill & Macmillan, 1990), pp. 22–49; B. Brunt, *The Republic of Ireland* (London: Paul Chapman, 1988), pp. 1–55; R. Fanning, *Independent Ireland* (Dublin: Helecon, 1983); D. Keogh, *Twentieth-Century Ireland: Nation and State* (Dublin: Gill & Macmillan, 1994); K. A. Kennedy, T. Giblin and D. McHugh, *The Economic Development of Ireland in the Twentieth Century* (London: Routledge, 1988), pp. 33–94; J. Lee, *Ireland, 1912–1985: Politics and Society* (Cambridge and New York: Cambridge University Press, 1989); R. Munck, *The Irish Economy: Results and Prospects* (London: Pluto Press, 1993), pp. 23–42; C. Ó Gráda, *A Rocky Road: The Irish Economy Since the 1920s* (Manchester: Manchester University Press, 1997), pp. 1–40.
13 See for instance J. Bradley, 'The legacy of economic development: the Irish economy 1960–1987', in C. Ó Gráda (ed.), *The Economic Development of Ireland Since 1870* (Aldershot: Edward Elgar, 1994), p. 139; E. Hazelkorn and H. Patterson, 'The new politics of the Irish Republic', *New Left Review*, 207: 5 (1994), p. 54; M. Hickman, *Ireland and the European Community* (London: PNL Press, 1990), p. 5; Munck, *The Irish Economy*, p. 33; Ó Gráda, *A Rocky Road*, p. 29.
14 Breen et al., *Understanding Contemporary Ireland*, pp. 22–3, 38.
15 M. Hornsby-Smith and C. T. Whelan, 'Religious and moral values', in C. T. Whelan (ed.), *Values and Social Change in Ireland* (Dublin: Gill & Macmillan, 1994), p. 13.
16 Cited in Breen et al., *Understanding Contemporary Ireland*, p. 22.
17 Indeed, 99 per cent of civil servants at this time had previously been employed by the British administration.
18 P. O'Connell and D. Rottman, 'The Irish welfare state in comparative perspective', in J. H. Goldthorpe and C. T. Whelan (eds), *The Develop-*

ment of Industrial Society in Ireland (Oxford: Oxford University Press, 1992), p. 231.

19 See for instance Breen et al., *Understanding Contemporary Ireland*, pp. 22–3; Fanning, *Independent Ireland*, pp. 73–4; Ó Gráda, *A Rocky Road*, pp. 55–6.
20 Bradley, 'The legacy of economic development', p. 139.
21 For example, little use was made of the Agricultural Credit Corporation's facilities during this period.
22 Ó Gráda, *A Rocky Road*, p. 5.
23 N. Collins and T. Cradden, *Irish Politics Today* (Manchester: Manchester University Press, 1997), pp. 11–12; Munck, *The Irish Economy*, pp. 28–9.
24 Fanning, *Independent Ireland*, p. 109.
25 Hazelkorn and Patterson, 'The new politics of the Irish Republic', p. 54.
26 Breen et al., *Understanding Contemporary Ireland*, p. 31.
27 Kennedy et al., *The Economic Development of Ireland*, pp. 258–60.
28 Ibid., p. 44.
29 On average, 12,000 new houses were constructed with state aid each year in 1932–42, compared to an average of 2,000 per year under the previous administration. See O'Connell and Rottman, 'The Irish welfare state', p. 232.
30 T. Cradden, 'Social partnership in Ireland: against the trend', in N. Collins and T. Gradden (eds), *Political Issues in Ireland Today* (Manchester: Manchester University Press, 1999), pp. 51–2; W. K. Roche, 'The liberal theory of industrialism and the development of industrial relations in Ireland', in Goldthorpe and Whelan, *The Development of Industrial Society in Ireland*, p. 31.
31 Ó Gráda, *A Rocky Road*, p. 16.
32 Brunt, *The Republic of Ireland*, p. xi.
33 Hickman, *Ireland and the European Community*, p. 4; P. Sweeney, *The Celtic Tiger: Ireland's Continuing Economic Miracle* (Dublin: Oak Tree Press, 1999), p. 38.
34 Brunt, *The Republic of Ireland*, p. 41.
35 Ó Gráda, *A Rocky Road*, p. 72.
36 E. de Valera, 'Speech to Dail Eireann, 21 November 1951', in M. Moynihan (ed.), *Speeches and Statements by Eamon de Valera, 1917–73* (Dublin: Gill & Macmillan, 1980), p. 548.
37 Ó Gráda, *A Rocky Road*, p. 68.
38 Cradden, 'Social partnership in Ireland', p. 52; Roche, 'The liberal theory of industrialism', p. 311.
39 Munck, *The Irish Economy*, p. 32.
40 Cited in D. McAleese, 'European integration and the Irish economy', in Ó Gráda, *The Economic Development of Ireland Since 1870*, p. 79.
41 O'Connell and Rottman, 'The Irish welfare state', p. 233.
42 R. Mac Sharry and P. White, *The Making of the Celtic Tiger: The Inside Story of Ireland's Boom Economy* (Cork: Mercier Press, 2000), pp. 185–6.
43 Hickman, *Ireland and the European Community*, p. 6.
44 Ó Gráda, *A Rocky Road*, p. 56.
45 Brunt, *The Republic of Ireland*, p. 47.

46 Government of Ireland, *Programme for Economic Expansion* (Dublin: Stationery Office, 1958), pp. 7, 36–8.
47 Hazelkorn and Patterson, 'The new politics of the Irish Republic', p. 54; Munck, *The Irish Economy*, p. 33.
48 E. O'Malley, 'Problems of industrialisation in Ireland', in Goldthorpe and Whelan, *The Development of Industrial Society in Ireland*, p. 34.
49 This included the placement of advertisements in *Fortune* magazine from 1964, which showed an Irish boy writing 'Yanks please come over' on a brick wall. See Ó Gráda, *A Rocky Road*, p. 144.
50 Mac Sharry and White, *The Making of the Celtic Tiger*, pp. 191–2.
51 R. O'Donnell, 'Regional policy', in P. Keatinge (ed.), *Ireland and EC Membership Evaluated* (London: Pinter, 1991), p. 61.
52 Government of Ireland, *Programme for Economic Expansion*, pp. 7–8.
53 Ó Gráda, *A Rocky Road*, pp. 73–9.
54 Kennedy et al., *The Economic Development of Ireland*, pp. 87–8.
55 O'Connell and Rottman, 'The Irish welfare state', p. 234.
56 Breen et al., *Understanding Contemporary Ireland*, p. 123.
57 Ó Gráda, *A Rocky Road*, pp. 73–9; Cradden, 'Social partnership in Ireland', p. 53.
58 W. K. Roche, 'Pay determination, the state and the politics of industrial relations', in T. V. Murphy and W. K. Roche, *Irish Industrial Relatiens in Practice* (Dublin: Oak Tree Press, 1994), p. 154.
59 Ó Gráda, *A Rocky Road*, p. 55.
60 Government of Ireland, *Programme for Economic Expansion*, p. 36.
61 Kennedy et al., *The Economic Development of Ireland*, pp. 260–1.
62 See for instance Breen et al., *Understanding Contemporary Ireland*, p. 46; Brunt, *The Republic of Ireland*, p. 46; Kennedy et al., *The Economic Development of Ireland*, pp. 258–64; O'Connell and Rottman, 'The Irish welfare state', p. 224.
63 Brunt, *The Republic of Ireland*, pp. 39–40.
64 Breen et al., *Understanding Contemporary Ireland*, p. 99.
65 Haughton thus identifies 1973 rather than 1958 as the key turning point in the Republic's economic history. However, as Laffan notes, Ireland's motivation to join Europe stemmed from the change in policy approach in 1958. The 1970s are best characterised as a period of consolidation and extension of the previous decades' reforms, with the strategy of gaining entry to the EEC part of a consistent and long-term goal. See J. Haughton, 'The historical background', in J. W. O'Hagen (ed.), *The Economy of Ireland: Policy and Performance of a Small European Country* (Dublin: Gill & Macmillan, 1995), p. 37; B. Laffan, 'Managing Europe', in N. Collins and T. Cradden (eds), *Political Issues in Ireland Today* (Manchester: Manchester University Press, 1994), pp. 43–4.
66 Hickman, *Ireland and the European Community*, p. 15; B. Laffan, *Organisation for a Changing Europe: Irish Central Government and the European Union* (Dublin: Policy Institute, 2001), p. 3.
67 Ó Gráda, *A Rocky Road*, p. 117.
68 Sweeney, *The Celtic Tiger*, p. 231.
69 Kennedy et al., *The Economic Development of Ireland*, p. 87.

70 Breen et al., *Understanding Contemporary Ireland*, p. 45.
71 Kennedy et al., *The Economic Development of Ireland*, p. 88.
72 S. Ó Riain and P. O'Connell, 'The role of the state in growth and welfare', in B. Nolan, P. O'Connell and C. T. Whelan (eds), *Bust to Boom? The Irish Experience of Growth and Inequality* (Dublin: Institute of Public Administration, 2000), p. 328.
73 J. Haughton, 'The dynamics of economic change', in W. J. Crotty and D. E. Schmitt (eds), *Ireland and the Politics of Change* (London: Longman, 1998), p. 43.
74 Ó Gráda, *A Rocky Road*, p. 69.
75 Haughton, 'The historical background', p. 38.
76 Haughton, 'The dynamics of economic change', p. 43.
77 Ó Gráda, *A Rocky Road*, pp. 70–1.
78 Kennedy et al., *The Economic Development of Ireland*, p. 89.
79 Cradden, 'Social partnership in Ireland', p. 54.
80 N. Hardiman, 'The state and economic interests: Ireland in comparative perspective', in Goldthorpe and Whelan, *The Development of Industrial Society in Ireland*, p. 345.
81 See for instance Breen et al., *Understanding Contemporary Ireland*, p. 16; Brunt, *The Republic of Ireland*, p. 46; E. Smyth and D. Hannan, 'Education and inequality', in Nolan et al., *Bust to Boom?*, p. 112.
82 Ó Riain and O'Connell, 'The role of the state in growth and welfare', p. 326.
83 Similarly, Breen et al. contend that increased spending and improvements in health services have 'generally favoured the better-off'. For example, they argue that the real cost of private health care has been reduced by government subsidies and tax reliefs on voluntary health insurance. See Breen et al., *Understanding Contemporary Ireland*, pp. 43–4.
84 O'Connell and Rottman, 'The Irish welfare state', pp. 224–5, 238.
85 Brunt, *The Republic of Ireland*, pp. 39–40.
86 Bradley, 'The legacy of economic development', p. 146; Ó Gráda, *A Rocky Road*, p. 78.
87 Hickman, *Ireland and the European Community*, p. 16; B. Laffan, 'The European Union and Ireland', in Collins and Cradden, *Political Issues in Ireland Today* (1999), p. 47.
88 Brunt, *The Republic of Ireland*, pp. 31–2; Mac Sharry and White, *The Making of the Celtic Tiger*, pp. 206–28.
89 Telesis, *A Review of Industrial Policy* (Dublin: National Economic and Social Council, 1982), p. ii.
90 O'Malley, 'Problems of industrialisation in Ireland', p. 43.
91 Brunt, *The Republic of Ireland*, p. 32; J. J. Sexton and P. O'Connell, *Labour Market Studies: Ireland* (Brussels: European Commission, 1996), pp. 170–2; Sweeney, *The Celtic Tiger*, p. 140.
92 Roche, 'Pay determination, the state and the politics of industrial relations', p. 172; Brunt, *The Republic of Ireland*, p. 28; R. O'Donnell, 'Social partnership: principles, institutions and interpretations', in P. O'Connell, *Astonishing Success: Economic Growth and the Labour Market in Ireland* (Geneva: International Labour Office, 1999), p. 48.

93 Brunt, *The Republic of Ireland*, p. 40.
94 Interestingly, incentives for the private sector were increased during this time. For example, the grant for first-time householders was converted to an IR£2,250 grant to the builders of new houses. The government also continued to encourage home ownership in such terms as mortgage tax relief (costing approximately £55 million in foregone taxes in 1983) and grants for local authority tenants to become owner-occupiers. See Brunt, *The Republic of Ireland*; Y. Galligan, 'Housing policy in Ireland: continuity and change in the 1990s', in Collins and Cradden, *Political Issues in Ireland Today* (1999), p. 152.
95 Brunt, *The Republic of Ireland*, pp. 28–9; A. Murphy, 'The "Celtic tiger" – an analysis of Ireland's economic growth performance', Working Paper, San Domenico (2000), p. 7; Sweeney, *The Celtic Tiger*, p. 92.
96 P. Kirby, *The Celtic Tiger in Distress: Growth and Inequality in Ireland* (Basingstoke: Palgrave, 2002), p. 42.
97 Hardiman, 'The state and economic interests', p. 339.
98 Cradden, 'Social partnership in Ireland', p. 55; Roche, 'Pay determination, the state and the politics of industrial relations', p. 172; Sexton and O'Connell, *Labour Market Studies: Ireland*, p. xiii.
99 G. Taylor, *Negotiated Governance and Public Policy in Ireland* (Manchester: Manchester University Press, 2005), p. 6.
100 Ó Gráda, *A Rocky Road*, p. 32.

5

The trajectory of the Irish state (2): 1987 to 2004

In chapter 4 the shape and pace of Irish economic policy change were placed in historical perspective. This chapter considers the more recent trajectory of the Irish state. As discussed in chapter 1, globalisation is often assumed to have redefined (if not eradicated) the role of national economic management, so that states must increasingly prioritise market forces. For some authors, the Irish Republic has indeed shifted towards a more neo-liberal approach. For others, however, the role of the Irish state has become more rather than less important in an era of globalisation.[1] This chapter traces developments since 1987 (which marked the beginning of social partnership) in order to examine whether Irish economic policy is indeed becoming more 'neo-liberal' or, alternatively, more 'statist'. The dynamics behind that policy change – and in particular whether it can be attributed to globalisation – will be considered in the following chapters.

Characterising the contemporary Irish state

Within the Irish literature, there is considerable debate as to the trajectory of the Irish state since 1987. On the one hand, authors such as Ó Riain and O'Connell assert that Ireland's experience simply cannot be characterised as a 'story of neoliberal globalisation'. Rather, the Irish state continues to play a central role in economic and social development and, as such, can be classified as essentially distributive and developmental.[2] Sweeney, too, argues that Ireland has moved in the 'opposite direction' to neo-liberalism, pointing for example to the revival of social partnership.[3] On the other hand, scholars such as Allen and Kirby are highly sceptical. For Allen, social partnership is a 'myth' that masks a 'decade of social vandalism'. Though Ireland has done so pragmatically, it has 'joined the neo-liberal revolution'.[4] While

Kirby suggests that Allen overstates his case, he too points to the emergence of a distinctive 'Irish' neo-liberalism in recent years. He thus characterises the Irish state in terms of Cerny's 'competition state', in which social policy is subordinated to the needs of the market.[5]

As we shall see, there is something to be said for both perspectives. On the one hand, strong tendencies towards prioritising economic competitiveness are indeed apparent. Yet this does not make Ireland a 'competition state'. Rather, some 'distributive' and 'developmental' tendencies are also apparent and, indeed, change in significance over time. This highly complex (and, at times, contradictory) picture suggests that Ireland is not easily characterised as 'neo-liberal' or as 'distributive/developmental', for economic policy since 1987 has entailed elements of both. Rather than defining the Irish state in terms of what it 'is', then, it is preferable to consider the Irish state in terms of what it 'does'.[6] After all, particular tendencies (such as those towards prioritising competitiveness) are not confined to a particular 'model' but are instead compatible with a range of state forms. Once again, this highlights the need to conceive change in terms of the ebb and flow of particular tendencies and counter-tendencies rather than assuming that it must be defined in terms of mutually exclusive state forms such as the 'distributive/developmental state' or the 'competition state'.

Social partnership

Perhaps the most controversial and contested element of Irish economic policy is the social partnership approach. The negotiation of the first centralised agreement in 1987 represented the start of a new era in Irish politics, with social partnership forming a central pillar of macro-economic policy ever since. It has involved a series of negotiations between government and key economic and social interests in the form of the Programme for National Recovery (PNR) for 1988–90, the Programme for Economic and Social Progress (PESP) for 1991–3, the Programme for Competitiveness and Work (PCW) for 1994–5, Partnership 2000: Employment, Competitiveness and Inclusion (P2000) for 1997–2000, the Programme for Prosperity and Fairness (PPF) for 2000–3 and Sustaining Progress for 2003–5. Broadly similar in form, these agreements have been characterised by a trade-off between moderation in wage demands on the one hand and social benefit improvement and income tax reduction on the other. The agreements have also covered a wide variety of other issues such as Ireland's adherence to the Maastricht criteria.[7]

At first sight, the adoption of social partnership since 1987 might be seen as *prima facie* evidence that Ireland has shifted towards a more 'statist' approach. By definition, macro-political bargaining represents active state involvement in economic affairs. Indeed, as noted in chapter 3, liberal economists have criticised the social partnership approach on precisely the grounds that it represents excessive state intervention. However, various authors have questioned the extent to which macro-political bargaining in Ireland can indeed be characterised as 'statist'.[8] Teague, for instance, contends that social partnership in Ireland simply cannot be described as 'social corporatist'. The Irish approach, he contends, is much more weakly developed than classical neo-corporatist models, particularly at enterprise level. He also notes that the approach arose as a response to economic crisis (see chapter 6) rather than reflecting a genuine desire for redistribution. In turn, this has meant that social partnership has failed to combat wage inequality.[9] Similarly, Allen argues that Ireland has 'quite simply one of the worst records on earnings dispersion in the developed world'. Social partnership, he argues, has exacerbated rather than reduced this inequality: for example, the ratio of earnings of the top to bottom decile for male full-time workers rose from 3.5 to 5 times in 1987–94.[10] In addition, Allen argues that the distribution of tax benefits under macro-political bargaining is 'highly inequitable and disproportionately benefits the higher paid'.[11] For example, a study commissioned by the NESC found that the level of inequality for post-tax income was little different in 1994 from 1987 and actually rose in 1994–8.[12] Allen argues that, rather than offering a 'real alternative to neo-liberalism', then, social partnership is designed to facilitate 'redistribution in favour of the wealthy'.[13] While authors such as Taylor and Kirby take a less extreme approach, they nevertheless contend that neo-corporatism in Ireland is increasingly geared towards market forces rather than social needs.[14] In turn, this is seen as part of a wider process in which the Irish state is being resituated as the model of a 'competition state'.[15]

Yet the picture is rather more complex than this. Certainly the decision to alter radically the state of the public finances was an important element of the social partnership approach. However, as O'Donnell observes, the adoption of neo-corporatism in Ireland is not so different from that in other countries, such as Belgium and the Netherlands, where there have been similar 'emergency packages'. While the structures and procedures of Irish social partnership are weak when compared to classical neo-corporatist models, this is changing over time. New institutional arrangements have included the creation of a National Centre for Partnership and Performance (NCPP) in order to promote enterprise-level partnership.[16]

Moreover, as Hardiman notes, the social partnership has changed considerably in character over time, from managing crisis to managing growth.[17] It has increasingly widened in scope in terms of the issues addressed and the actors involved. Non-pay issues such as long-term unemployment and poverty have received much greater attention over time, with a variety of new initiatives including the National Anti-Poverty Strategy under P2000. Measures to extend involvement beyond the traditional partners have included the extension of NESC membership from 1994 onwards, with a wide range of social and economic interests now involved in the partnership negotiations.[18]

Nor has social partnership unambiguously failed to benefit the less well off. For example, Barrett, Fitz Gerald and Nolan find that wage dispersion did indeed increase between 1987 and 1997. However, they also find that this was concentrated in the period 1987–94 rather than in the period of rapid growth in 1994–7. In terms of hourly earnings, they find that it was only at the top that wage dispersion accelerated in 1994–7. In contrast, the bottom decile and bottom quartile not only kept pace with the median during this period but actually rose slightly faster (see table 5.1).[19] It also cannot be assumed that higher wage dispersion would not have emerged under free collective bargaining. Rather, pronounced wage dispersion was apparent in the period 1981 to 1986.[20] At the very least, the agreements may have helped counter market forces that would otherwise have resulted in higher levels of wage inequality.[21]

It is also worth noting that wages have increased significantly in absolute terms.[22] Between 1987 and 2001 gross average industrial earnings grew by 25 per cent. Moreover, the centralised agreements have entailed significant cuts in income tax (from 35 to 20 per cent in the lower rate and from 58 to 42 per cent in the higher rate between 1987 and 2001).[23] Indeed, an OECD study finds that Ireland has seen the biggest decline in the tax wedge in the OECD area (by 18.3 per cent for a married person with two children in 1996–2003, followed by Hungary at 9.9 per cent and the US at 8.3 per cent).[24] In turn, this has meant that the growth in real take-home pay has considerably exceeded the rise in gross earnings. For example, the real take-home pay for a single person on average manufacturing earnings increased by

Table 5.1 Distribution of gross hourly and weekly earnings in Ireland, 1987–94

As proportion of median	1987	1994	1997
Hourly earnings (all employees)			
Bottom decile	0.47	0.47	0.48
Bottom quartile	0.73	0.68	0.69
Top quartile	1.37	1.50	1.53
Top decile	1.96	2.24	2.33
Top decile/bottom decile	4.16	4.77	4.81
Weekly earnings (full-time employees)			
Bottom decile	0.49	0.48	0.51
Bottom quartile	0.75	0.72	0.71
Top quartile	1.35	1.43	1.43
Top decile	1.82	1.97	2.02
Top decile/bottom decile	3.68	4.06	3.93

Source: Barrett, A., J. Fitz Gerald and B. Nolan, 'Earnings inequality, returns to education and immigration into Ireland', *Labour Economics*, 9: 5 (2002), p. 668.

60 per cent in 1987–2001 (with the corresponding figure for a married person at 54 per cent).[25]

Clearly, then, some social progress *has* been achieved under the social partnership agreements. Yet it is also important not to overstate this. Despite the concern to widen the partnership process, some groups have claimed that they have not been adequately consulted on important issues. For example, anti-poverty groups staged a walkout of one PPF meeting on the grounds that they had not been consulted by the government on a variety of issues (including the rights of travellers and people with disabilities).[26] Moreover, while net take-home pay has certainly increased, Allen rightly notes that house prices have also risen dramatically. Between 1994 and 1998 the ratio of house prices to the average industrial wage nearly doubled, in turn increasing rents for non-house owners.[27] Thus, a rather mixed picture emerges with respect to social partnership – some progress has been made under the agreements, but much more could be done. The use of ideal types such as the 'distributive state' or the 'competition state' tends to obscure rather than illuminate this complexity. For example, in many countries pressures for tax reduction and reform might be associated with a shift towards neo-liberalism. This has not been the case in Ireland, where there has traditionally been a heavy burden of taxation on employees.[28] This highlights the need for sensitivity towards distinctive national contexts; even when common tendencies are apparent the specific dynamics of change may vary greatly between countries.

Public expenditure

Alongside the debate about social partnership, there has been considerable controversy about public expenditure in Ireland. For authors such as Daly and Yeates, the Irish welfare state is 'on an expansionary course' – not least due to the increasing emphasis given to social policy considerations in the partnership agreements.[29] In contrast, Allen argues that social partnership has undermined rather than enhanced social welfare. For example, the tax reductions have meant that Irish public spending as a proportion of GDP is 'now the lowest by far' in the EU.[30] Similarly, Kirby contends that the Irish welfare state declined in the 1990s, noting for example that Ireland now comes last in terms of social protection expenditure in the EU.[31]

This disparity in opinion in itself reveals a rather complex picture with respect to public expenditure. It is indeed the case that public expenditure has failed to keep pace with economic growth. For example, public expenditure as a proportion of GNP fell by 17 per cent in 1987–2003 (see figure 5.1) and social protection expenditure as a proportion of GDP dropped by a quarter in 1992–2001.[32] Yet Ireland does not score as poorly relative to other EU states as critics such as Allen and Kirby contend. If measured as a proportion of GDP, Ireland's

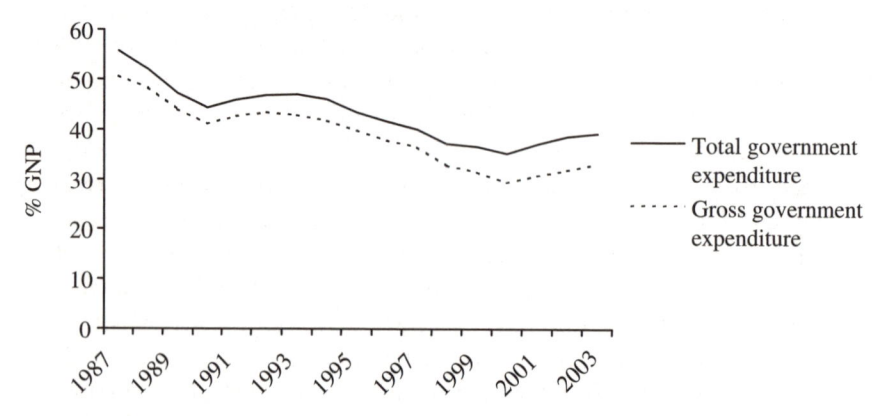

Figure 5.1 Government expenditure in Ireland (% GNP), 1987–2003
Source: Department of Finance, *Budgetary and Economic Statistics: March 2004* (Dublin: Department of Finance, 2004), p. 1.

public expenditure is indeed the lowest in the EU (at 11.8 per cent below the EU average in 2002). However, if measured as a proportion of GNP, Ireland's performance improves considerably (at just 4.7 per cent below the EU average in 2002). Moreover, if public spending is adjusted to exclude interest payments (which are not available for the provision of public services), Ireland is just 3.0 per cent below the EU average.[33] Indeed, when measured in terms of *actual* spending, Ireland scores quite well. For example, total government expenditure per person was slightly higher than the EU average in 2002 (at €11,380 per head of population compared to €11,367 in the EU as a whole).[34] Similarly, while Ireland's social protection expenditure is lower than the EU average (both as a proportion of GNP and in per capita terms),[35] such figures do not take into account the Republic's low old-age dependency.[36] If social protection spending is adjusted to exclude

Table 5.2 Overall government expenditure and social protection expenditure in Ireland (% GDP), 1999 and 2002

	Public expenditure, 2002		Social protection expenditure, 1999	
	Total expenditure (% GDP)	Total non-interest expenditure (% GDP)	Total social protection (% GDP)	Social protection excluding pensions (% GDP)
EU15	47.2	43.7	27.6	14.9
Belgium	48.9	42.7	28.2	16.1
Denmark	53.3	49.8	29.4	18.2
Germany	48.9	45.6	29.6	17.1
Greece	47.4	41.8	25.5	12.6
Spain	39.7	36.8	20.0	10.7
France	52.9	49.8	30.3	16.9
Ireland (GNP)	42.5	40.5	17.2	12.9
(GDP)	35.4	33.8	–	–
Italy	47.5	41.5	25.3	9.1
Luxembourg	43.2	42.9	21.9	12.8
Netherlands	44.8	41.8	28.1	16.4
Austria	51.6	48.2	28.6	15.0
Portugal	46.1	43.0	22.9	12.9
Finland	49.9	47.3	26.7	17.3
Sweden	57.3	54.2	32.9	19.9
UK	41.2	38.9	26.9	14.4

Source: adapted from NESC, *An Investment in Quality, Services, Inclusion and Enterprise* (Dublin: National Economic and Social Council, 2002), pp. 195, 198.

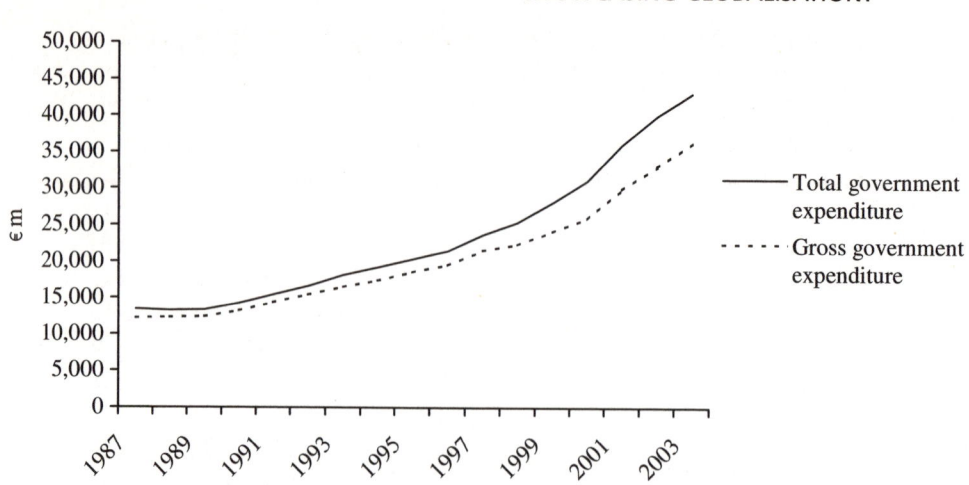

Figure 5.2 Government expenditure in Ireland (€ million), 1987–2003
Source: Department of Finance, *Budgetary and Economic Statistics: 2003* (Dublin: Department of Finance, 2003), p. 1.

pensions, Ireland is only two points below the EU average (see table 5.2). While this performance is still disappointing (particularly given Ireland's rapid economic growth), the statistics are certainly not as damning as the critics suggest.

It is also important to note that while public spending has fallen relative to economic growth, it has nevertheless increased dramatically in absolute terms. Indeed, it rose nearly fourfold in 1987–2003 (see figure 5.2). Similarly, total social welfare expenditure has grown substantially, more than doubling in 1993–2003 and, crucially, rising faster than the rate of inflation (see figure 5.3). In addition, real spending on health increased by a massive 78 per cent in 1987–97 and real spending on education rose by 50 per cent during this period.[37] Far from there being disentitlement in the 1990s, the Irish welfare state has become significantly more inclusive. For example, total insurance coverage has been considerably extended to include such groups as the self-employed, with total coverage rising from 72 to 96 per cent in 1991–7. Similarly, free third-level education for all students was introduced for the first time in 1994.[38]

Nevertheless, as Ó Riain and O'Connell note, Ireland 'has spent more on the welfare state, but it has made less welfare effort'.[39] This is evident not only in the declining share of public spending in national wealth but also in the persistence of marked socio-economic inequalities. For example, while social welfare rates have risen significantly in

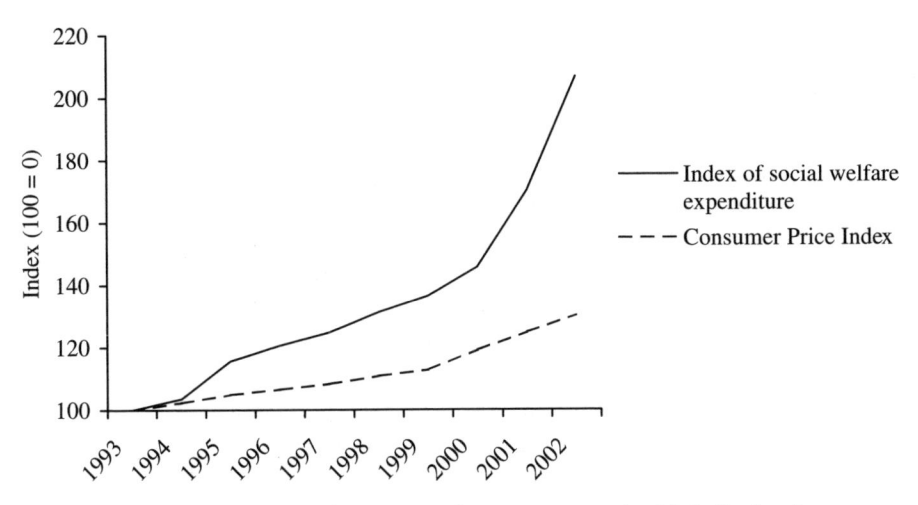

Figure 5.3 Social welfare expenditure compared with inflation in Ireland, 1993–2002

Source: Department of Social and Family Affairs, *Statistical Report on Social and Welfare Services, 2002* (Dublin: Stationery Office, 2003), p. 3.

real terms, they have failed to keep pace with the average take-home pay for employees and average disposable incomes. This has meant that the disparity between average incomes and households dependent on social welfare has risen over time.[40] Despite the provision of free third-level education, significant inequalities persist in terms of educational participation and attainment.[41] Indeed, the *Irish Times* reports that school leavers in some middle-class areas are ten times more likely to go on to higher education than those from poorer areas.[42] Similarly, while there is universal provision of a basic level of free hospital care, commentators point to lengthy waiting lists for those without private health insurance.[43]

In some respects, moreover, there has been a shift away from state intervention. One notable example is that of housing. Spending in the public building programme was reduced dramatically after 1987, from 5 to 2.5 per cent of total public expenditure between 1987 and 1990. This has led to a sharp decline in the share of social housing in new house construction, which has fallen to less than 10 per cent of the total since 1987 (compared to levels of 20–30 per cent in earlier decades).[44] Private housing, by contrast, has been actively encouraged by Irish governments, as is evident for example in the introduction of a 40 per cent discount on the purchase price of local authority houses in 1989, the placing of the new tenant purchase scheme on a permanent basis in 1993, and the abolition of property tax on expensive houses in 1996.[45]

Even in areas where there have not been dramatic spending cuts, commentators argue that priority is nevertheless given to market requirements. Ó Riain and O'Connell argue that the Irish state has retained its essentially 'pay-related' approach to welfare, with a mixture of public and private provision. While there is now the near universal provision of a basic level of social citizenship, this is supplemented by market-generated resources.[46] For example, the proportion of the population with private health insurance increased from one fifth to nearly half in the 1980s and 1990s. A bias towards private patients is also identified in the fact that consultants are paid a fee for service for private care, but a salary to treat public patients.[47]

For Kirby, Ireland is thus 'far from a successful model of a distributive state'. Such a characterisation 'misses the ways in which a distinctive Irish variant of neo-liberalism has emerged with the Celtic Tiger'. Whilst the state 'has not been lacking in extensive social action', it has failed to achieve significant redistribution and address social exclusion. Rather, social development is subordinated to the needs of international competitiveness. For Kirby, Ireland is best characterised in terms of Cerny's 'competition state', in which social policies are designed to serve market forces.[48] Similarly, Taylor argues that even where reform is 'marginally inclusive' it is primarily motivated by the need to achieve flexibility rather than equity and redistribution.[49]

Yet, while strong tendencies towards prioritising competitiveness are apparent, this does not mean that the Irish state is being resituated as a 'competition state'. In fact, there is nothing particularly new about this emphasis upon economic growth over social development. Rather, the Irish welfare state has been essentially 'pay-related' since the 1960s, with little attempt made to counter market inequalities throughout the post-war era (see chapter 4). The general thrust of housing policy, for instance, has remained largely unchanged for decades, with the priority long having been private rather than public ownership.[50]

Indeed, it is in more recent years that some (albeit limited) reforms have been adopted. For example, after commissioning the Bacon Report on house prices in 1997, the government adopted measures to increase the supply of serviced land, reduce excessive investor demand and assist lower-income house purchasers.[51] Other developments include the Affordable Housing Initiative, which aims to increase affordable housing by 10,000 units. Explicit attempts have also been made to address social disadvantage. In terms of educational policy, for instance, there has been a clear shift from a concern with equality of opportunity to an emphasis upon addressing inequality and under-representation. This has included a variety of measures such as the Early Start Programme (to provide early childhood education to children in disadvantaged areas) and Breaking the Cycle (to provide additional funds for schools serving disadvantaged populations).[52] Total spending on access measures rose threefold in 1997–2001.[53] The government has also taken steps towards addressing poverty, most notably with the launch of the National Anti-Poverty Strategy in 1997. While this initially aimed to cut poverty from 9–15 per cent to 5–10 per cent by 2007, this target was nearly reached in 1999 and was therefore revised down to 5 per cent by 2004.[54] A Cabinet Committee on Social Inclusion has also been established and all major policy proposals must now be evaluated for their impact on poverty.

However, the significance of these counter-tendencies should not be exaggerated. For example, whilst the housing initiatives stemming from the Bacon Report have impacted positively on the cost of houses for prospective owner-occupiers, they have failed to address the needs of those unable to buy their own homes in the public and private rental sectors.[55] Similarly, the education schemes do not cover a significant number of pupils from disadvantaged backgrounds. Since many of the programmes have not been systematically evaluated, the effectiveness of the interventions is as yet unclear.[56] The National Anti-Poverty Strategy has also been strongly criticised by the CPA for its focus on 'consistent' rather than 'relative' poverty, with the latter rising considerably in the 1990s (see chapter 2).[57] Nevertheless, it is clear that some attempts to address issues of social justice have been made in recent years. This complex picture suggests that Ireland cannot be described empirically as a 'distributive' or 'competition' state, for there are tendencies in both directions that also change over time.

Industrial strategy

There is controversy not only about whether the Irish state is 'distributive' in terms of its social role but also about whether it is 'developmental' in terms of its approach to the economy. For Ó Riain and O'Connell, the Irish state has been 'deeply implicated in the entire process' of managing economic development – not least in terms of its proactive industrial policy.[58] In contrast, O'Hearn argues that Ireland has pursued a 'neo-liberal growth model' based upon the attraction of foreign investment through low corporate taxation and minimal interference in business.[59]

Once again, a rather complex and varied picture emerges. O'Hearn quite rightly observes that the government has continued to offer generous fiscal incentives to foreign investors, even during its programme of fiscal adjustment after 1987. Indeed, in 1990 the 10 per cent rate of corporation tax was extended until 2010. While the government later agreed to increase this to 12.5 per cent, this was largely in response to pressure from the EU (see chapter 6). The Irish state has also offered substantial grants to foreign investors. While the IDA tightened up its grants provisions to industry after 1987 (making firms legally obliged to repay grants that failed to meet job targets), state aid to private industry and services has risen significantly (from IR£155 million to IR£300 million in 1988–97). For example, the IDA provided a huge grant package of IR£87 million to Intel in 1989, equivalent to 80 per cent of the IDA's capital grant allowance. For O'Hearn, the IDA therefore effectively 'bought economic tigerhood'.[60]

Yet this is only part of the picture, for Irish industrial policy has in fact shifted considerably since the 1980s. Increasingly, the IDA has moved towards a 'rifle-shot' (as opposed to a 'scatter-gun') approach in order to target leading international firms in high technology sectors such as pharmaceuticals (see also chapter 3). In so doing, it has moved away from an emphasis upon fiscal incentives as the principal means to attract FDI. Between 1985 and 1992 the proportion of the industrial budget going to capital investment fell from 61 to 47 per cent, whereas the share for marketing rose (from 11 to 17 per cent), as did that on science and technology (from 11 to 21 per cent).[61] Greater emphasis has also been given to developing indigenous industry. This has included significant institutional restructuring, with the IDA split into separate divisions in 1988 and then in 1993–4 into separate agencies. A new body, Forfás, now oversees IDA Ireland (responsible for foreign industry) and Enterprise Ireland (responsible for indigenous industry). This has meant that a full body of state agency staff is now able to concentrate solely on indigenous enterprise.[62] Policy has continued to emphasise export-driven growth for indigenous firms in order to reduce their dependence on the domestic market. Increasingly, it has focused upon sectors that are high-innovation, quality-driven, productivity-driven and high value-added.[63] In 1991 An Bord Tráchtála (ABT) was established in order to assist industry through direct grants, tailored market intelligence and on-the-ground support from a range of advisory, information and promotional services. Indigenous development is now seen as 'essential to the economy as a whole', forming 'part of a balanced portfolio of economic activities, which prepare the economy against technology, sector or market-specific shocks'.[64] In interviews, senior policy-makers also emphasised the importance of indigenous industry to the wider economy.

For Ó Riain and O'Connell, the Irish state has thus 'played a central role in upgrading industry and deepening Ireland's production and innovation capabilities in the 1990s'.[65] It has gone 'well beyond merely gathering information and upgrading infrastructure', instead playing a 'critical role' in encouraging the development of local technical industry.[66] For example, the IDA has actively developed a network of groups including industry and trade associations, universities and innovation and technology centres. Though semi-autonomous or outside the state, these bodies have most often been created and funded by state initiatives (such as the Applied Research Programme and the Mentorship Programme). Rather than seeking to interfere with specific business or technology decisions, the Irish state has instead sought to shape the overall development of industry.[67] Ó Riain thus classifies Ireland as a 'flexible developmental state', as distinct from the East Asian-style 'bureaucratic developmental states'. Whereas the latter are characterised by the coherence of their state bureaucracy and manage dependency through protectionism, subsidies and domestic banking, the former is 'defined by its ability to nurture post-Fordist networks of production and innovation, to attract international investment, and to link these local and global technology networks together in ways that promote development'.[68]

However, Kirby is highly critical of this characterisation of the Irish state. In particular, he argues that Ó Riain conflates development with the upgrading of certain industrial sectors and does not consider how this might relate to wider national development goals.[69] In turn, he argues, Ó Riain 'neglects the wider, more liberalised macroeconomic context which today limits the extent to which a state can aspire to manipulate the market for development purposes'.[70] Like O'Hearn, Kirby points to Ireland's reliance on inward investment, whereas the East Asian states were able to retain relative autonomy from foreign capital. Rather than contributing to Ireland's development, he argues, foreign firms remain weakly embedded in the Irish economy. For example, although absolute expenditure by foreign enterprise has increased, this does not translate into a deepening of linkages between foreign and indigenous firms (see also chapter 2). Kirby therefore contends that Ireland is better characterised as a 'competition state' in which economic growth is prioritised over economic and social development. The fact that economic rather than social issues dominate is 'no accident' but 'derives from the central feature of Ireland's industrialisation' – the attraction of FDI through low corporate taxation.[71]

Yet there is much to be said for both perspectives. Kirby is right to suggest that the Irish state is far from 'developmental' in some aspects of industrial policy – not least in terms of its continued commitment to low corporate taxation. But in some respects there *has* been a shift towards a more 'developmental' role for the state. In particular, industrial policy has shifted from 'maximis[ing] growth' to 'maximis[ing] *sustainable* growth'.[72] The Department of Enterprise, Trade and Employment now identifies its three key targets as: greater geographical evenness in employment distribution; increased job quality; and the greater embeddedness of foreign firms.[73] This shift in priorities is also reflected in the social partnership agreements. For example, the PPF placed 'particular emphasis on vulnerable sectors' and aimed to 'reposition indigenous manufacturing enterprises generally to achieve scale', in order to upgrade to higher-value activities with higher-quality jobs.[74] Actions include supporting in-company training, expanding trade promotional activities and developing and deepening linkages between Irish and foreign firms. The government has also embarked upon a National Spatial Strategy in order to address the long-term spatial implications of policy. The IDA, Enterprise Ireland and the Department of Enterprise, Trade and Employment have already 'refocused their operations' in order to reduce regional disparities.[75] For example, the Border, Midlands and West region has increased its share of jobs gains – from 18.1 per cent of gross job gains in industry-assisted enterprises in 1999 to 26.0 per cent in 2003 (which is more in line with the region's share of population of 26.5 per cent).[76]

This is not to overstate the significance of these counter-tendencies. For example, the Department of Enterprise, Trade and Employment's *Strategy Statement* for 2001–3 argued that 'many weaknesses persist', including the low productivity and profitability of indigenous enterprise and low expenditure on R&D. The statement also pointed to the need for greater emphasis upon embedding companies and the need to pay closer attention to the nature and location of foreign investment.[77] Nevertheless, the recent changes in industrial policy illustrate the dynamic and multifaceted nature of policy change. This complexity is obscured by the use of labels such as the 'competition' or 'developmental' state to describe the Irish experience. While such ideal types may be useful in heuristic terms, they simply cannot be used as empirical desciptors for Ireland's policy trajectory.

Privatisation

That having been said, in some aspects of economic policy there clearly *has* been a shift away from state interventionism. Not the least of these is privatisation. This did not occur immediately after 1987: indeed, Fianna Fáil initially promised that no industry in the commercial semi-state sector would be sold.[78] Within a decade, however, there had been extensive commercialisation and deregulation of the state-owned companies, including the monopolies. Companies to be restructured radically and privatised include Irish Steel, Irish Sugar, Irish Life, Telecom Éireann, Aer Lingus, ESB and Bord na Mona. Indeed, by the end of 1997 Ireland was one of the least regulated OECD countries in terms of barriers to entry, market openness and labour markets.[79]

Yet, while privatisation in Ireland might at first seem to represent an unambiguous shift towards neo-liberalism, the picture is once again more complicated than this. In fact, the Irish approach to privatisation and regulatory reform has been quite different from the 'ruthless' programme pursued in Britain. For example, Irish privatisations have taken place with trade union support (in part due to the success in job creation) and 'have not, to date, involved any major rip-off of the taxpayer'.[80] As one economic adviser noted: 'it's an issue of a case-by-case basis, looking at whether it is best for the economy as a whole and also for the stakeholders within the particular entity'. For example, he pointed to the case of Eircomm, in which 'there was quite a drive from government to make sure that the workers within the entity were getting a share of it . . . It wasn't a question of "we're selling off to the highest [bidder]".'[81]

Moreover, while privatisation and regulatory reform in Ireland have reflected the explicit desire to enhance economic competitiveness (see chapter 7), this does not make Ireland a 'competition state'. Rather, such tendencies are compatible with a range of state forms and may occur in different ways and for different reasons within particular countries. In fact, as the OECD notes, the dynamics behind market liberalisation in Ireland have been rather unusual. For example, regulatory reform has been seen as a means to counter infrastructural bottlenecks and manage inflationary pressures. In this sense, Ireland is not just the 'familiar story' of a move away from statist policies.[82] Once again, then, while particular *tendencies* are apparent this does not mean that Ireland has been resituated as the model of a 'competition state'.

European membership

Finally, important developments have also taken place since 1987 with respect to Ireland's membership of Europe. As with the other areas of policy discussed, a rather complex picture emerges. On the one hand, in recent years Ireland has embraced the broader shift towards a market-oriented approach in the EU. By signing up to the SEA in 1987, Ireland agreed to the further liberalisation and opening-up of the economy to external markets. Similarly, the signing of the Treaty on European Union (or Maastricht Treaty) in 1993 laid the basis for Ireland's full participation in EMU. In turn, this has reduced considerably the policy tools available to Irish governments to pursue economic and social goals (discussed further in chapter 7).

In some respects, though, the Irish government has attempted to resist supposedly 'neo-liberal' pressures from the EU. In particular, tensions between Ireland and the EU recently emerged in terms of budgetary policy. The budget of 2001 provided the 'biggest tax and social welfare package in the history of the State', including IR£850 million in social welfare, IR£5.3 billion in health services and over IR£1.2 billion in tax benefits.[83] The European Commission considered the 2001 budget to be 'inappropriately expansionary' and inconsistent with its broad economic guidelines.[84] However, the Irish government saw the budget surplus as an 'unprecedented opportunity' to spread Ireland's wealth more evenly.[85] Despite receiving a formal reprimand from the EU in February 2001, the government refused to alter its budgetary policy.[86] Irish policy-makers have also resisted market-oriented pressures from the EU in areas such as agricultural policy – not least by pressing to maximise the size of the CAP budget. With EU reforms to liberalise agriculture and cut agricultural subsidies, it is 'not beyond the realms of reason to suppose that Irish governments would re-nationalise agriculture, at least to some extent'.[87] In addition, the Irish government has pushed for a more interventionist approach in areas such as employment policy. In this sense, while Ireland has embraced market-oriented measures such as EMU, counter-tendencies also exist. This will be discussed in more detail in the following chapter.

Conclusion

This chapter has explored the trajectory of the Irish state since 1987. It has outlined several main areas of policy: privatisation, social partnership, public expenditure, industrial policy and membership of the EU. In so doing, the chapter has argued that while strong market-oriented tendencies are apparent, counter-tendencies are also evident and indeed change in significance over time. Rather than characterising the Irish state *either* as 'neo-liberal' *or* as 'developmental/distributive', economic policy has instead entailed elements of both.

To acknowledge that policy has shifted towards prioritising competitiveness in recent years is one thing; to attribute this to globalisation is clearly another. In order to examine this issue it is necessary to consider in detail the dynamics behind economic policy change in Ireland. This is the subject of the next chapter.

Notes

1. K. Allen, *The Celtic Tiger: The Myth of Social Partnership in Ireland* (Manchester: Manchester University Press, 2000), p. 100; P. Kirby, *The Celtic Tiger in Distress: Growth and Inequality in Ireland* (Basingstoke: Palgrave, 2002), pp. 143–4; S. Ó Riain and P. O'Connell, 'The role of the state in growth and welfare', in B. Nolan, P. O'Connell and C. T. Whelan (eds), *Bust to Boom? The Irish Experience of Growth and Inequality* (Dublin: Institute of Public Administration, 2000), p. 311.
2. Ó Riain and O'Connell, 'The role of the state in growth and welfare', p. 334; see also B. Nolan, P. O'Connell and C. T. Whelan, 'Introduction', in Nolan et al., *Bust to Boom?*, p. 2.
3. P. Sweeney, *The Celtic Tiger: Ireland's Continuing Economic Miracle* (Dublin: Oak Tree Press, 1999), p. 107.
4. Allen, *The Celtic Tiger*, p. 100.
5. Kirby, *The Celtic Tiger in Distress*, pp. 143–4, 160.
6. D. Wincott, 'Welfare regimes: model or mirage?', Working Paper, Department of Political Science and International Studies, University of Birmingham (2002), manuscript.
7. See for instance R. O'Donnell and C. O'Reardon, 'Social partnership in Ireland's economic transformation', in G. Fajertag and P. Pochet (eds), *Social Pacts in Europe* (Brussels: European Trade Union Institute, 2000), pp. 47–64; T. Cradden, 'Social partnership: a "rising tide lifts all boats"?', in N. Collins and T. Cradden (eds), *Political Issues in Ireland Today* (Manchester: Manchester University Press, 2004), pp. 89–98.
8. See for instance Allen, *The Celtic Tiger*, p. 114; P. Teague, 'Pay determination in the Republic of Ireland – towards social corporatism', *British Journal of Industrial Relations*, 33: 2 (1995), p. 263.

9 Teague, 'Pay determination in the Republic of Ireland', pp. 263–9.
10 Allen, *The Celtic Tiger*, p. 76.
11 He also cites a trade union study, which found that a worker on four times the average industrial wage received 36.1 per cent in net tax benefit in 1987–98 compared to 18.8 per cent for a worker on half the average industrial wage. See ibid., pp. 83–4.
12 NESC, *An Investment in Quality: Services, Inclusion and Enterprise* (Dublin: National Economic and Social Council, 2003), pp. 121–2.
13 K. Allen, 'Neither Boston nor Berlin: class polarisation and neo-liberalism in the Irish Republic', in C. Coulter and S. Coleman (eds), *The End of Irish History? Critical Reflections on the Celtic Tiger* (Manchester: Manchester University Press, 2003), p. 71.
14 G. Taylor, 'Negotiated governance and the Irish polity', in G. Taylor (ed.), *Issues in Irish Public Policy* (Dublin: Irish Academic Press, 2002), pp. 28–51; Kirby, *The Celtic Tiger in Distress*, pp. 135–8.
15 Kirby, *The Celtic Tiger in Distress*, pp. 142–4.
16 R. O'Donnell, 'Social partnership: principles, institutions and interpretations', in P. O'Connell, *Astonishing Success: Economic Growth and the Labour Market in Ireland* (Geneva: International Labour Office, 1999), pp. 49–52.
17 N. Hardiman, 'Social partnership, wage bargaining and growth', in Nolan et al., *Bust to Boom?*, p. 289.
18 For example, parties to the *Sustaining Progress* negotiations included the Irish National Organisation of the Unemployed (INOU), the Conference of Religious in Ireland (CORI), the National Women's Council of Ireland (NWCI) and the National Youth Council of Ireland (NYCI).
19 A. Barrett, J. Fitz Gerald and B. Nolan, 'Earnings inequality, returns to education and immigration into Ireland', *Labour Economics*, 9: 5 (2002), pp. 666–7.
20 J. J. Sexton and P. O'Connell, *Labour Market Studies: Ireland* (Brussels: European Commission, 1996), p. xiv.
21 W. K. Roche, 'Pay determination, the state and the politics of industrial relations', in T. V. Murphy and W. K. Roche (eds), *Irish Industrial Relations in Practice* (Dublin: Oak Tree Press, 1994), p. 197.
22 Kirby does acknowledge this.
23 NESC, *An Investment in Quality*, p. 121.
24 OECD, *Taxing Wages* (Paris: OECD, 2004).
25 NESC, *An Investment in Quality*, p. 61.
26 'Partnership under pressure', *Irish Times* (30 April 2002).
27 Allen, *The Celtic Tiger*, p. 94.
28 O'Donnell, 'Social partnership', p. 48.
29 M. Daly and N. Yeates, 'Common origins, different paths: adaptation and change in social security in Britain and Ireland', *Policy & Politics*, 31: 1 (2003), p. 94.
30 Allen, 'Neither Boston nor Berlin', p. 69.
31 Kirby, *The Celtic Tiger in Distress*, pp. 133–5; see also J. S. O'Conner, 'Welfare state development in the context of European integration and

economic convergence: situating Ireland within the European Union context', *Policy & Politics*, 31: 3 (2003), pp. 387–404.
32 European Commission, *European Social Statistics: Social Protection Expenditure and Receipts* (Luxembourg: European Commission, 2004), p. 14.
33 NESC, *An Investment in Quality*, pp. 194–9.
34 European Commission, *Economic Data Pocketbook – Spring 2002 Economic Forecasts*, (Luxembourg: Eurostat, 2002), p. 28.
35 European Commission, *European Social Statistics*, pp. 14, 16.
36 NESC, *An Investment in Quality*, pp. 194–9; O'Conner, 'Welfare state development in Ireland', p. 393.
37 Ó Riain and O'Connell, 'The role of the state in growth and welfare', pp. 328–30.
38 Ibid., p. 328.
39 Ibid., p. 331.
40 B. Nolan, 'Income inequality during Ireland's boom', *Studies*, 92: 366 (2003), p. 137.
41 E. Smyth and D. Hannan, 'Education and inequality', in Nolan et al., *Bust to Boom?*, p. 125.
42 E. Oliver, 'Report finds deep inequalities in college access', *Irish Times* (26 March 2002).
43 See for instance Allen, *The Celtic Tiger*, p. 99; Ó Riain and O'Connell, 'The role of the state in growth and welfare', p. 327.
44 Ó Riain and O'Connell, 'The role of the state in growth and welfare', p. 331; T. Fahey and J. Williams, 'The spatial distribution of disadvantage in Ireland', in Nolan et al., *Bust to Boom?*, p. 237.
45 Y. Galligan, 'Housing policy in Ireland: continuity and change in the 1990s', in N. Collins and T. Cradden (eds), *Political Issues in Ireland Today* (Manchester: Manchester University Press, 1999), pp. 152–9.
46 Ó Riain and O'Connell, 'The role of the state in growth and welfare', p. 333.
47 Kirby, *The Celtic Tiger in Distress*, pp. 61–2. Similarly, Taylor argues that education (and particularly higher education) became increasingly instrumental in the 1990s. He cites the Green Paper (1992), which argued for the rationalisation of provision and more attention to costs, efficiency and quality. Such developments have formed 'part of a wider political project designed to deliver an education system attuned to the demands of the new global economy'. See G. Taylor, *Negotiated Governance and Public Policy in Ireland* (Manchester: Manchester University Press, 2005), p. 83.
48 Kirby, *The Celtic Tiger in Distress*, pp. 139–44, 160.
49 Taylor, *Negotiated Governance and Public Policy in Ireland*, p. 94.
50 Galligan, 'Housing policy in Ireland', p. 149; indeed, Taylor himself acknowledges this point.
51 Ibid., p. 148.
52 S. McCoy and E. Smyth, 'Educational expenditure: implications for equality', in T. Callan, A. Davis and D. McCoy (eds), *Budget Perspectives 2004* (Dublin: Economic and Social Research Institute, 2003), p. 91.

53 Department of Education and Science, 'Press release: over 80 per cent of leaving Cert students now progress to further and higher education' (2002), www.gov.ie/educ/press/press260302c.htm.
54 Kirby, *The Celtic Tiger in Distress*, p. 138.
55 Galligan, 'Housing policy in Ireland', pp. 157–61.
56 Smyth and Hannan, 'Education and inequality', p. 113.
57 M.-A. Wren, 'No fall in numbers living in poverty despite boom years', *Irish Times* (17 April 2002).
58 Ó Riain and O'Connell, 'The role of the state in growth and welfare', p. 310.
59 D. O'Hearn, 'Macroeconomic policy in the Celtic tiger: a critical reassessment', in Coulter and Coleman, *The End of Irish History?*, p. 35.
60 D. O'Hearn, 'Globalisation, "new tigers," and the end of the developmental state? The case of the Celtic tiger', *Politics & Society*, 28: 1 (2000), p. 74.
61 Sexton and O'Connell, *Labour Market Studies: Ireland*, p. 166.
62 E. O'Malley, 'The revival of Irish indigenous industry 1987–97', in T. J. Baker, D. Duffy and F. Shortall (eds), Quarterly Economic Commentary, April 1998 (Dublin: ESRI, 1998), p. 56.
63 Department of Enterprise Trade and Employment, *Productive Sector Operational Programme 2000–2006* (Dublin: Government of Ireland, 2000), p. 33.
64 Ibid., pp. 14–15.
65 Ó Riain and O'Connell, 'The role of the state in growth and welfare', p. 320.
66 S. Ó Riain, 'The flexible developmental state: globalisation, information technology and the "Celtic tiger"', *Politics & Society*, 28: 2 (2000), pp. 165–6.
67 Ibid.; Ó Riain and O'Connell, 'The role of the state in growth and welfare', pp. 320–2.
68 Ó Riain, 'The flexible developmental state', p. 158.
69 Kirby, *The Celtic Tiger in Distress*, pp. 131–2.
70 Ibid., p. 144.
71 Ibid., pp. 140–3.
72 Interviews.
73 Department of Enterprise Trade and Employment, *Productive Sector Operational Programme 2000–2006*, pp. 35–6. When interviewed, a senior civil servant within the department also gave these areas as the 'three enterprise priorities that have been prevailing specifically within the remit of this department'.
74 Government of Ireland, *Programme for Prosperity and Fairness* (Dublin: Stationery Office, 2000), p. 59.
75 Department of Enterprise Trade and Employment, *Strategy Statement 2001–2003* (Dublin: Government of Ireland), p. 18.
76 Forfás, *End of Year Statement 2003* (Dublin: Forfás, 2004), p. 5.
77 Department of Enterprise Trade and Employment, *Strategy Statement 2001–2003*, p. 16.

78 Taylor offers an anecdote in which an anonymous referee rejected his paper on privatisation on the grounds that it would never happen in Ireland.
79 OECD, *OECD Reviews of Regulatory Reform in Ireland* (Paris: OECD, 2001), p. 2.
80 Sweeney, *The Celtic Tiger*, pp. 109–10.
81 Interviews.
82 OECD, *OECD Reviews of Regulatory Reform in Ireland*, pp. 1–3.
83 Department of Finance (ed.), *Budget 2001: An Information Update from the Department of Finance* (Dublin: Department of Finance, 2001), pp. 1–3.
84 European Commission 'Commission Recommendation for the 2001 Broad Guidelines of the Economic Policies of the Member States and the Community' (Brussels: European Commission, 2001), p. 38.
85 B. Ahern, 'Moving towards a truly fair, equal and inclusive Ireland', in Department of Finance, *Budget 2001*, p. 4. This view was also reflected in interviews.
86 Indeed, the minister of finance responded to Commission proposals to strengthen economic policy co-ordination by arguing: 'It is no accident that in all European countries, there is growing support for people who want to step back'. Cited in D. Staunton, 'McCreevy questions pace of EU economic integration', *Irish Times* (8 May 2002).
87 Sweeney, *The Celtic Tiger*, p. 221.

6

The dynamics behind policy change (1): the international economic context

It is often assumed not only that the trajectories of contemporary political economies have radically shifted in recent years but that this change is in itself a response to globalisation. Such a perspective is not least evident in the Irish literature, in which it is widely regarded as self-evident that the small and open Irish economy should be subject to the competitive imperatives of globalisation. This chapter unpacks and interrogates this assumption and questions whether the structural economic factors that are often cited as evidence of 'globalisation' can indeed be characterised in these terms. In so doing, it questions whether Irish policy change has occurred primarily as a response to external economic conditions or whether such factors are in fact limited in explaining the trajectory of the Irish state.

The Irish literature and globalisation

Despite the considerable debate as to the nature and shape of policy change in contemporary Ireland, many accounts have one thing in common: an emphasis upon 'globalisation'.[1] While few commentators explain Ireland's developmental trajectory in terms of globalisation alone, many nevertheless stress its importance in the Irish case. It is perhaps surprising, then, that few authors seek to engage explicitly and systematically with the globalisation literature in examining Ireland's political economy. As Kirby writes: 'due to this lack of clarity about what is meant by globalisation, it is not at all clear what is being claimed for the Irish case'.[2]

Nevertheless, it is possible to identify several key perspectives with respect to globalisation.[3] The hyperglobalist thesis finds its closest expression in the work of authors such as O'Hearn and Murphy. Both emphasise the role of foreign direct investment and low corporate

THE INTERNATIONAL ECONOMIC CONTEXT 141

taxation in Ireland's economic growth. O'Hearn is pessimistic about such developments, arguing that 'the sustainability of this model is highly questionable', for the Irish state has 'no real control' over multinational corporations and is therefore left 'vulnerable to changing flows in international capital'.[4] Murphy, by contrast, views Ireland's participation in the global economy rather more favourably. He argues: 'rather than demonising and fearing these processes . . . they may actually be viewed as highly beneficial to a country such as Ireland'.[5]

The sceptical approach to globalisation finds little expression in the Irish literature. Allen does reject the 'myths of globalisation' that both 'systematically disempower people' and 'paint an idealised picture of capitalism as the neo-liberal economists might like it to appear'.[6] But it is not globalisation itself that Allen rejects as a myth but rather the normative assumption that it is a positive development. Indeed, he argues that the 'Irish economy needs to be viewed against the background of the global system' and that '[g]lobal capitalism is such a dynamic and chaotic system that no planning is possible'.[7] This implies that the Irish state is ultimately subordinate to market forces, which for Allen lead to 'inevitable' class inequality.[8] In this sense, Allen has much in common with hyperglobalists such as Greider and Gray,[9] who are critical of globalisation in normative terms but nevertheless present it as a harsh material reality.

The 'complex' approach to globalisation can be seen in the work of Kirby. Drawing upon the work of complex theorists such as Falk, Gill, Cox and Cerny, he writes: 'globalisation is forcing not so much the retreat of the state as the resituating of the state "into a subordinate relationship with global market forces"'.[10] In so doing, he points to the importance of ideas and institutions in supporting market forces, most notably in the form of neo-liberalism and a subservient state. However, while Kirby does devote some attention to the role of agency and ideas, this is ultimately subordinated to the economic superstructure. Assessments of practicality, he argues, must address 'what is feasible within the limitations of global forces'. Indeed, globalisation is the 'starting point' for any discussion of Irish strategy.[11]

A similar argument is put forward by O'Conner, who emphasises the 'profound implications of globalisation' in shaping Ireland's economic and policy development. Like Kirby, O'Conner identifies a shift towards neo-liberalism in Ireland, pointing for example to the persistence of marked social inequalities despite rapid economic growth (see chapter 5). In turn, she explains this in terms of the need for Ireland to compete on global markets. She writes: 'As a small and progressively more open economy in a globalised trading situation [Ireland] is competing not only for export markets but for foreign direct investment. *This has led to* the achievement and maintenance of competitiveness becoming the primary orientation in public policy' (emphases added).[12] In this sense, policy outcomes are seen to derive directly from the globalisation of the Irish economy.

However, it is the new institutionalist approach to globalisation that has most in common with the mainstream Irish literature. Like the new institutionalists, authors such as Nolan, O'Connell and Whelan, Sweeney, and Ó Riain dismiss claims that globalisation is necessarily associated with a shift towards neo-liberalism.[13] As Nolan, O'Connell and Whelan write: 'the Irish growth experience and its distributional consequences is not a simple story of globalisation, forced withdrawal of the state and the promotion of neo-liberalism'. Rather, the Irish state has been 'deeply implicated in the entire process, managing both economic development and the welfare state'.[14] For example, Ó Riain argues that the state has played a vital role in mediating between the local and global levels by providing the infrastructural and institutional conditions for both local and foreign industry to flourish.[15] Like scholars such as Weiss and Hobson,[16] the mainstream Irish literature sees globalisation as both enabling and constraining. As Ó Riain and O'Connell write, the 'intensification of global processes has actually made the role of the state more important' in Ireland.[17]

To take one final example, Taylor attempts to question more simplistic accounts of globalisation in relation to the Irish case. He writes: 'reform and change cannot be understood in terms of a simple, causal process; that globalisation leads to a particular trajectory of policy'. Taylor devotes considerable attention to the role of discourse and ideology in shaping policy outcomes in Ireland. In turn, these are 'influenced, shaped and constrained by the particular economic, political and ideological terrain'. Again, though, Taylor seems to subordinate this within the economic superstructure, for the 'overall trajectory of a political project is shaped and constrained by the structural conditions of capitalism'. Indeed, his core artument is that 'Irish political institutions have altered radically in response to the pressures of competing in the global economy.'[18] In this sense, Taylor has much in common with Vivien Schmidt, for while he points to globalisation discourse this is ultimately seen to derive from the 'reality' of globalisation itself.

Hence, there has been considerable debate about the impact of globalisation in the Irish case. While some authors have taken the view that globalisation has been good for Ireland, others have sought to highlight its 'darker side', particularly in social terms.[19] However, while a number of authors have sought to question globalisation in normative terms, there has been surprisingly little attempt to challenge it in analytical terms. A variety of authors have explored *how* and *why* Ireland has been globalised, but no one has confronted the view *that* Ireland has been globalised. This is not to contend that the Irish literature adopts a crude hyperglobalist approach. As we have seen, many commentators embrace much more subtle and nuanced interpretations put forward by 'complex' and 'new institutionalist' theorists alike. But even in more critical accounts it seems to be regarded as self-evident that the small and open Irish economy has been 'globalised'. In this sense, it is not globalisation *per se* that is questioned but rather the extent to which its impact is detrimental to Ireland's economic and social development.

However, it is possible to understand Ireland's developmental trajectory without any reference to globalisation in analytical terms. This is partly for empirical reasons. There is simply no evidence to suggest that the mechanisms of policy change in Ireland are actually 'global'. If anything, Ireland's patterns of trade and investment are becoming more rather than less concentrated in geographical terms. More fundamentally, the concept of 'globalisation' can also be questioned on theoretical grounds. Both the globalisation and Irish literatures tend to confuse structure and agency questions, often presenting globalisation itself as the agent of change. Yet, as a 'process without a subject', globalisation cannot actually *do* or explain anything (see chapter 1).

This is not to suggest, however, that policy change is independent of the economic context in which it is constituted. As we shall see, economic factors (such as trade openness) have indeed influenced the trajectory of the Irish state. Crucially, though, such factors *do not represent 'globalisation'*. Nor can they in themselves explain how and why particular policies are adopted. For, as Hay notes, while economic conditions may shape the *context* in which political decisions are made, they do not ultimately determine the *conduct* of political agents. After all, structures do not just constrain agents but can also facilitate them, be exploited by them and be altered by them. Ultimately, it is the conduct of agents that determines the extent to which such opportunities are realised.[20] In turn, this points to the role of interpretation and ideas, for actors clearly do not possess perfect information of the world in which they find themselves but must instead interpret their context. The way in which actors behave is thus informed by the ideas they hold about the context in which they find themselves rather than the context itself.[21]

While these points may seem intuitively obvious, they are all too often neglected. Though rarely stated explicitly, it is often implied that policy change occurs as a direct and inevitable response to underlying economic conditions. This sort of assumption is not least evident in claims that globalisation has driven a shift towards neo-liberalism in Ireland. Yet, as we shall see, the trajectory of the Irish state simply cannot be understood in these terms. The remainder of this chapter will focus on the role of economic factors – and whether or not they represent 'globalisation' – in shaping Irish policy change. The role of other factors – including, crucially, that of *ideas* about globalisation – will be discussed in the following chapter.

The domestic economic context in historical perspective

Before exploring wider international conditions, it is worth considering the domestic economic context, since the two are separable but not separate. In so doing, it is important to place more recent developments in historical perspective. For, just as policies do not remain static over time, so too we should avoid a 'snap-shot' approach with respect to the economic context in which such policies are constituted. After all, the factors that shape policy adaptation and/or transformation are themselves open to change over time.[22] Rather than immediately focusing on more recent developments, then, it is instructive to examine *over time* the relationship between political outcomes and their economic context in Ireland.

As we saw in chapter 4, the path of economic policy prior to 1958 was characterised by considerable continuity. Even the birth of the new Irish state in 1921 did not mark a radical change in approach. This can in part be attributed to the massive infrastructural and other damage caused by civil war, evident for example in the systematic destruction of the railways. The fact that agriculture remained the key priority for the new administration is also unsurprising, given that Ireland was primarily agricultural at this time.[23] Yet, as Breen et al. note, the little room for innovation that did exist was not pursued.[24] Agriculture, for instance, declined significantly in the 1920s. While this can partly be attributed to changing conditions in international markets, the government failed to counter this by supporting prices or providing loans.[25] As will be outlined in chapter 7, this can be attributed in large part to Cumann na nGaedheal's ideological stance and, in particular, their commitment to laissez-faire government. In turn, this meant that they did not intervene in the economy even when it would have been pragmatic to do so.[26]

In fact, there was significant pressure for change by the time Fianna Fáil came to power in 1932. Both agriculture and industry had failed to thrive,[27] and laissez-faire was increasingly hard to sustain in the light of world depression and growing protectionism in other countries. In this context, it does not seem remarkable that a key aim for the new administration was for Ireland to become self-sufficient through the expansion of indigenous industry. Yet, as will be discussed in chapter 7, the rationale behind economic nationalism in Ireland was primarily political rather than economic: indeed, Fianna Fáil were quite prepared to sacrifice economic prosperity for ideological goals.[28] Although industry did grow quite rapidly at first (with industrial production rising by 50 per cent in 1931–8), this expansion lasted only for the time it took the infant firms to capture domestic demand.[29] With production geared towards Ireland's small internal market, there was little scope for further industrial expansion.[30] Agriculture, too, failed to thrive under Fianna Fáil, with the export of live animals hit particularly hard by the introduction of tariffs.

For all these limitations, protectionism remained a fundamental policy aim for several decades. Again, this can in part be explained by the economic context. While industrial output fell by about one fifth during World War II, enforced autarky served to hide the true limits of import substitution.[31] In the immediate post-war years, economic recovery 'produced the illusion that protection was doing no harm'.[32] All sectors of the economy experienced recovery, but the most rapid growth was achieved in industrial production, which rose by an average of 10.7 per cent between 1946 and 1951.[33] Yet the economic context alone cannot explain why Irish governments remained committed to protectionism, whereas other European countries embarked upon a process of post-war restructuring and modernisation. As will be discussed in chapter 7, the government's ideological stance played an important role in this.

Nevertheless, structural conditions cannot be seen as static but instead change over time. By the 1950s, Ireland's domestic economic context had changed markedly. While other European economies experienced rapid growth, Ireland's GNP actually declined in 1950–8. Total employment fell (to lower than its 1926 level in 1961), whereas migration rose dramatically (indeed, four fifths of people born in the 1930s emigrated).[34] To make matters worse, there were also recurrent crises in the balance of payments and increased inflation in the 1950s. The shift in policy approach from 1958 is thus often characterised as an inevitable response to economic failure. Breathnach, for example, writes: 'The resultant crisis forced a reversal of economic policy and a switch to export-oriented industrial growth based on the attraction of foreign investment.'[35] Similarly, Sachs argues: 'The changes forced on Irish policy-makers by economic collapse were fundamental and far-reaching.'[36] Yet, while economic factors undoubtedly played an important role in this policy shift, they did not make such change inevitable. Indeed, the extent of Ireland's economic 'crisis' in the 1950s is often overstated. As Haughton rightly notes, to characterise Ireland's performance in these terms is a 'half-truth'. In fact, real product per capita grew by 2.2 per cent per year between 1950 and 1960, 'possibly the fastest rate recorded up to then'. Industrial output rose by 2.8 per cent per annum and output per farmer increased by a 'respectable' 3.4 per cent per year. Thus: 'Ireland's performance looks disappointing only by the standards of neighbouring countries, not by historical standards.'[37] Nor can the 'crisis' of the Irish economy in the 1950s be attributed to protectionism alone. As O'Malley notes, Ireland's industrial decline had already been evident throughout the nineteenth century under conditions of free trade. Indeed, protectionism may initially have generated greater industrial expansion than continuing free trade would have.[38] This suggests that other factors were at work – including the very *perception* of economic crisis – in explaining the shift towards a more active, export-oriented approach in 1958. These factors will be explored in chapter 7.

As outlined in chapter 4, the change in strategy from 1958 marked the beginning of a period of export-oriented growth. Industrial output in the 1960s and 1970s rose at more than three times the rate of the 1950s.[39] Manufactured exports grew particularly rapidly (by an average of 23 per cent per annum in 1958–73). This can 'largely be attributed to the arrival of the multinationals',[40] with indigenous firms showing no overall gain in export market shares.[41] By the early 1970s Ireland was no longer a simple agrarian economy, but instead had experienced rapid industrialisation and urbanisation.[42] Yet, despite economic growth, significant structural weaknesses remained. A self-sustaining industrial base was simply not achieved after 1958. Despite economic growth, total employment did not increase and total unemployment rose dramatically. This affected not only agriculture but also, crucially, the industrial sector, with manufacturing employment falling by one fifth between 1979 and 1987.[43] As Munck writes: 'De-industrialisation was a worrying trend for an economy which had only in recent years began to industrialise.'[44] While GNP rose by an average of 4.8 per cent per annum in the 1960s and early 1970s, it rose by just 2.2 per cent in the mid- and late 1970s, and virtually halted altogether in the 1980s.[45]

By 1987 the state of the Irish economy had deteriorated significantly. Unemployment levels were at 'record highs' and inflation averaged 20.5 per cent in 1982–7.[46] Emigration in the 1980s was double that of its level in the 1970s (at 208,000 compared to 104,000).[47] In addition, the national debt had increased to 129 per cent (compared to 52 per cent in 1973), the highest in the EU. In 1986 the cost of servicing this debt accounted for 94 per cent of all tax from personal income tax.[48] The shift in approach from 1987 is often directly attributed to the conditions of economic failure. For example, Sexton and O'Connell write: 'One thing is certainly clear: the recent return to centralised bargaining in Ireland was born out of crisis.'[49] Roche, too, identifies the new approach as 'the outcome of profound crisis'.[50] Yet, while the adoption of social partnership in 1987 was certainly influenced by underlying economic conditions, it was by no means inevitable. Rather, as will be discussed in chapter 7, the narrative of crisis was crucial in shaping the new political paradigm.[51]

In turn, as outlined in chapter 5, the new policy paradigm has changed considerably over time. This can, in part, be explained by the experience of rapid economic growth. For example, the National Anti-Poverty Strategy has been adopted precisely on the grounds that Ireland's prosperity has created the resources for the state to combat persistent poverty and social exclusion. Yet Ireland's rapid economic growth cannot explain why the government has made 'less welfare effort' in recent years, with social and welfare expenditure failing to keep pace with GNP.[52] It is for this reason that authors such as Kirby and O'Conner point to the role of globalisation in constraining the policy alternatives available to Irish governments.[53] Having examined Ireland's domestic economic context, it is to the so-called 'globalisation' of the Irish economy that we now turn.

A small, open economy

Clearly, Ireland's domestic economic context cannot be seen as independent of the broader international environment in which it is situated. The role of the external structure is widely seen as particularly important to Ireland's development due to the small and open nature of the Irish economy.[54] As discussed in chapter 3, this is in itself cited as *prima facie* evidence of Ireland's 'globalisation' in recent years.

Once again, however, it is important to place more recent developments in historical perspective. In fact, Ireland's experience simply cannot be characterised as a dramatic shift from a closed national economy to an open global one. Indeed, the Irish economy has never been truly closed. Rather, the importance of external transactions has remained an 'enduring and distinctive' feature throughout the twentieth century.[55] In particular, Ireland's economy has long been closely integrated with that of the UK. While political independence from Britain was achieved in 1921, the UK remained Ireland's biggest market for exports and a key source of industrial goods. The advent of protectionism did not serve to break these close economic ties. While Ireland and Britain engaged in an 'Economic War' of tariffs between 1932 and 1938 (sparked by Ireland's refusal to pay land annuities), this did not result in the redirection of trade. Quite the contrary: it served to highlight the importance of Britain to the Irish economy. For example, in 1924–50 the proportion of Irish exports to the UK fell by just 6 per cent (from 99 to 93 per cent).[56] Hence, as Bradley notes, the change in approach after 1958 did not represent a move towards openness *per se*, for the Irish economy was already relatively open when compared to other small European states (see table 6.1). Instead, it

Table 6.1 Openness of small EU economies, 1960

	Exports of goods and services (% of GDP)	Imports of goods and services (% of GDP)
Luxembourg	85.6	72.4
Netherlands	45.7	44.2
Belgium	39.0	39.2
Denmark	32.7	34.5
Ireland	30.4	35.5
Austria	23.7	24.4
Sweden	22.7	23.3
Finland	22.5	23.2
Portugal	16.0	21.3
Greece	7.1	14.2

Source: Bradley, J. 'The Irish economy in international perspective', in W. Crotty and D. E. Schmitt (eds), *Ireland on the World Stage* (Manchester: Manchester University Press, 2002), p. 48.

THE INTERNATIONAL ECONOMIC CONTEXT

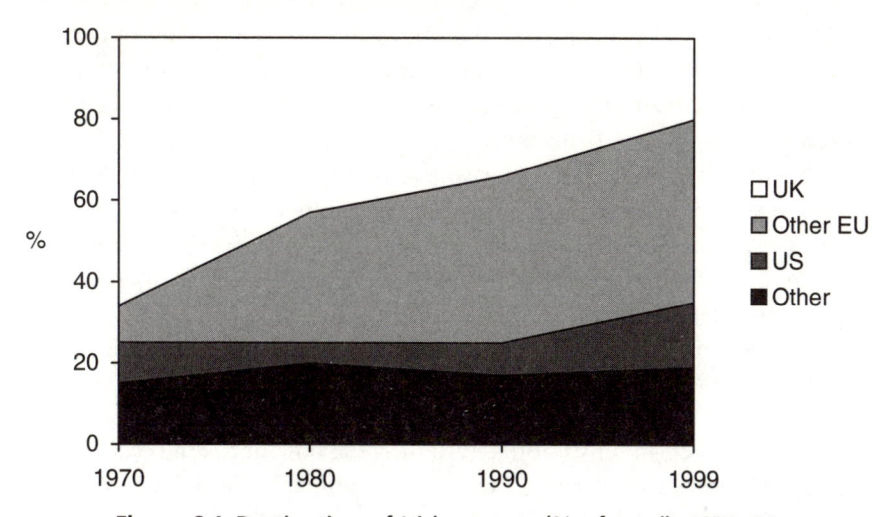

Figure 6.1 Destination of Irish exports (% of total), 1970–99
Source: OECD, *Economic Surveys: Ireland 2000–2001* (Paris: OECD, 2001), p. 30.

marked the beginning of a shift away from the heavy dependence on UK markets (see figure 6.1).[57]

If the Irish economy has not shifted from being 'closed' to 'open', nor has it moved from being a 'national' economy to a 'global' one. For, as Watson writes: 'If physical distance is no longer relevant to economic activity, then economic activity should no longer be discriminating with respect to space ... There should be no identifiable patterns of privileged trading routes – be that trade in commercial goods, trade in investment capital or trade in financial assets.'[58] Such a description simply does not reflect the pattern of Ireland's external trade, which is in fact highly concentrated. As figure 6.1 above reveals, exports to EU-European countries other than the UK have increased steadily in recent decades, from just 9 per cent in 1970 to 45 per cent in 1999. Irish exports to the US have fluctuated, although in 1999 they were above their level in 1980. In contrast, Ireland's trade with the rest of the world was actually slightly *less* in 1999 (at 19 per cent) than in 1980 (at 20 per cent). If anything, this points to a process of integration into the diad of the EU and the US, but it certainly does not point to a broader process of 'globalisation'.

Not only are Ireland's trade patterns highly regionally concentrated but they are also highly country-specific (see also chapter 3). While trade between Britain and Ireland has diminished, the UK remains the Republic's most important European trading partner by far. For example, in early 2005 the UK sourced over a quarter of total imports to Ireland (nearly as much as imports from all other EU countries combined) and also received one-sixth of total Irish exports (again, considerably higher than any other EU country), Behind the UK, Germany is the most significant source of imports by some considerable distance, whereas Belgium is the most important destination for Irish exports. But while Ireland remains primarily EU–European in terms of trade (in that the EU accounts for nearly two thirds of exports and imports), it is notable that the US (rather than the UK) is now Ireland's most important export partner (accounting for one fifth of total Irish exports in early 2005 – see table 6.2 for detailed figures).

Clearly, then, the Irish economy is simply not competing on 'global' markets in terms of trade. Rather, the bulk of trading relations are with other EU–European economies (primarily the UK) and the US. Thus, while Ireland's trade patterns have certainly changed considerably over time, the Irish economy remains distinctly international (and, on the whole, EU–European) rather than 'global' or 'de-temitorialised' in character.

To contend that Ireland is not subject to globalising economic imperatives is *not* to suggest that the Irish economy is unexposed to the external economic environment. Nor is it to claim that policy choices are not influenced by the small and open nature of the economy. Yet it is also vital to avoid the common assumption that policy outcomes emerge as a direct and unmediated response to external economic pressures. The fact that the Irish economy is highly open in terms of trade cannot in itself explain the shift towards prioritising economic competitiveness or, indeed, the decline in welfare effort. Quite the contrary: the correlation between trade openness and public spending in other EU countries is positive rather than negative (see chapter 1), and the welfare generosity of other small open economies such as Denmark and Norway has also risen over time.[59] If Ireland's policy trajectory could be explained in terms of trade openness, then, we might reasonably expect state expenditure to have *risen* as a share of GNP over time. The fact that quite the opposite has occurred suggests that other factors have been at work in shaping policy developments. In particular, the very perception that Ireland is competing on global markets has played a powerful role in driving the shift towards prioritising economic competitiveness (see chapter 7).

Table 6.2 Ireland's trade by geographical origin, January–March 2005

Country	Imports (€m)	Exports (€m)
Great Britain	3653.1	3195.8
Northern Ireland	244.8	322.9
Austria	40.2	87.8
Belgium	251.6	2963.7
Cyprus	1.7	5.7
Czech Republic	47.7	46.3
Denmark	227.1	130.9
Estonia	3.2	2.9
Finland	62.8	70.2
France	570.1	1374.8
Germany	1066.5	1481.6
Greece	10.3	74.3
Italy	279.0	1038.8
Latvja	8.5	1.3
Lithuania	6.5	2.2
Luxombourg	6.9	35.8
Hungary	37.4	32.5
Malta	0.6	2.8
Netherlands	512.2	99.4
Poland	27.0	56.4
Portugal	45.5	80.7
Slovakia	2.4	6.1
Slovenia	2.4	4.0
Spain	204.7	564.3
Sweden	133.7	250.0
EU country not specified	105.6	21.5
Total EU	*7551.3*	*12847.6*
of which EU-15	*7413.9*	*12687.5*
Australia	32.9	151.5
Brazil	53.5	32.7
Canada	68.9	75.1
China	770.7	196.1
Hong Kong	118.2	182.9
India	69.7	25.1
Japan	614.6	579.7
Malaysia	155.7	127.9
Mexico	28.8	107.4
Norway	285.7	147.2
Philippines	28.2	53.4
Russia	23.8	35.3
Singapore	181.5	181.7
South Africa	28.8	55.6
South Korea	283.3	88.7
Switzerland	126.8	828.8
Taiwan	231.3	74.0
Thailand	91.0	44.1
Turkey	132.4	66.2
USA	1701.2	4136.3
Other countries	273.9	506.9
Country unknown	13.1	63.5
Unclassified estimates	246.4	13.6
Total	*13111.6*	*20621.3*

Source: CSO, *External Trade* (Cork: Central Statistical Office, 2005), p. 6.

Foreign direct investment

While a dramatic shift from a closed to open economy is not evident in terms of trade, the same cannot be said for FDI. Starting from a zero base in the late 1950s, the rise in export-oriented FDI in manufacturing to Ireland has been 'quite phenomenal'.[60] By 1982 foreign companies accounted for more than 70 per cent of manufactured exports.[61] Foreign investment in Ireland traditionally tended to involve low-skill assembly and packaging work across a wide range of sectors, with few local linkages and high profit repatriation. For example, new foreign firms (excluding those in the food sector) purchased just 11.2 per cent of materials and components from Irish firms in 1974.[62] However, since the late 1980s FDI inflows to Ireland have increased in technologically sophisticated sectors such as electronics and pharmaceuticals (see chapter 3). In addition, the proportion of US FDI in services industries has risen dramatically. While manufacturing accounted for more than half of total stock in 1994, service industries made up two thirds of the total in 2000. This translates into an increase of sevenfold, a rate of accumulation that is more than double that of manufacturing.[63]

It is important to proceed with a certain degree of caution when examining the changing patterns of Ireland's inward investment. In fact, historical estimates do not provide comprehensive coverage of FDI activity – most notably in terms of inflows to the offshore International Financial Services Centre (IFSC). Since only a small proportion of IFSC flows is invested in the domestic economy, they serve to skew the true nature of Ireland's investment. New figures collected by the CSO do provide a breakdown of inflows by type and geographical origin but are not comparable with the earlier series.[64]

Nevertheless, from the data that *is* available, it is possible to gain some understanding of Ireland's foreign investment patterns. Turning first to the data for the 1990s (more specifically, the period 1987–98 – see table 6.3), it is clear that the US was the single biggest investor in Ireland during this period. Inflows from the US increased from 36 to 78 per cent of total inflows in 1987–98. Ireland received no investment at all from Association of South East Asian Nations (ASEAN) countries, and very little from non-OECD countries, during this period.[65] This points to Ireland's integration into the diad of the US and EU rather than a broader process of globalisation. Moreover, as noted in chapter 3, the origins of Ireland's FDI in the 1990s were highly concentrated along national lines. For example, the UK

Table 6.3 Foreign direct investment inflows to Ireland by geographical origin (IR£m), 1987–98

Country	1987	1988	1989	1990	1991	1992	1993	1994	1995	1996	1997	1998
Australia	–	1	1	1	–	1	–	3	–	1	–	–
Austria	–	–	–	–	–	1	1	–	–	–	–	–
Belgium/Luxembourg	16	1	1	1	2	1	1	1	–	1	1	–
Canada	2	3	2	–	3	–	–	–	–	–	6	–
Denmark	4	1	–	–	–	–	–	–	–	–	–	–
France	7	15	3	2	2	1	–	5	–	2	3	–
Germany	18	18	10	15	25	28	8	7	8	8	5	6
Italy	1	–	1	1	1	1	–	–	–	5	6	–
Japan	20	8	7	9	15	8	8	4	21	10	7	4
Netherlands	5	6	3	7	8	8	6	2	1	3	5	7
Norway	2	–	–	–	–	–	3	3	–	1	–	5
Spain	–	1	–	–	–	–	–	–	–	–	–	–
Sweden	2	5	2	1	5	4	1	2	–	–	3	–
Switzerland	2	1	1	1	14	11	22	–	7	–	–	40
UK	58	21	18	16	13	16	17	26	12	27	25	27
US	77	86	83	65	113	135	192	153	184	300	323	324
Non-OECD	2	2	5	6	31	7	2	1	3	1	1	–
World	217	169	136	125	232	221	261	207	235	360	383	415
EU	112	67	38	43	56	59	33	42	21	47	49	41
NAFTA	79	89	85	65	116	135	193	154	184	301	329	324
ASEAN	–	–	–	–	–	–	–	–	–	–	–	–

Source: OECD, *International Direct Investment Statistics Yearbook 1999* (Paris: OECD, 1999), pp. 176–7.

accounted for nearly half of total EU investment between 1987 and 1988. While the UK's share fluctuated year by year, it did not fall over time (indeed, it was considerably higher in 1998 than in 1987, rising from 52 to 66 per cent). Germany was also a significant investor, accounting for an average of 26 per cent of total EU investment during this period (again fluctuating but remaining as high in 1998 as 1987). As with Ireland's external trade, then, Ireland's FDI in the 1990s was characterised by highly specific geographies rather than being 'global' or 'deterritorialised'.

A similar picture appears with respect to the more recent data. As noted in chapter 3, while there was significant disinvestment by US firms in 2001 this was partly offset by inflows to Ireland from Europe and, more specifically, from the Netherlands. Indeed, as figures 6.2 and

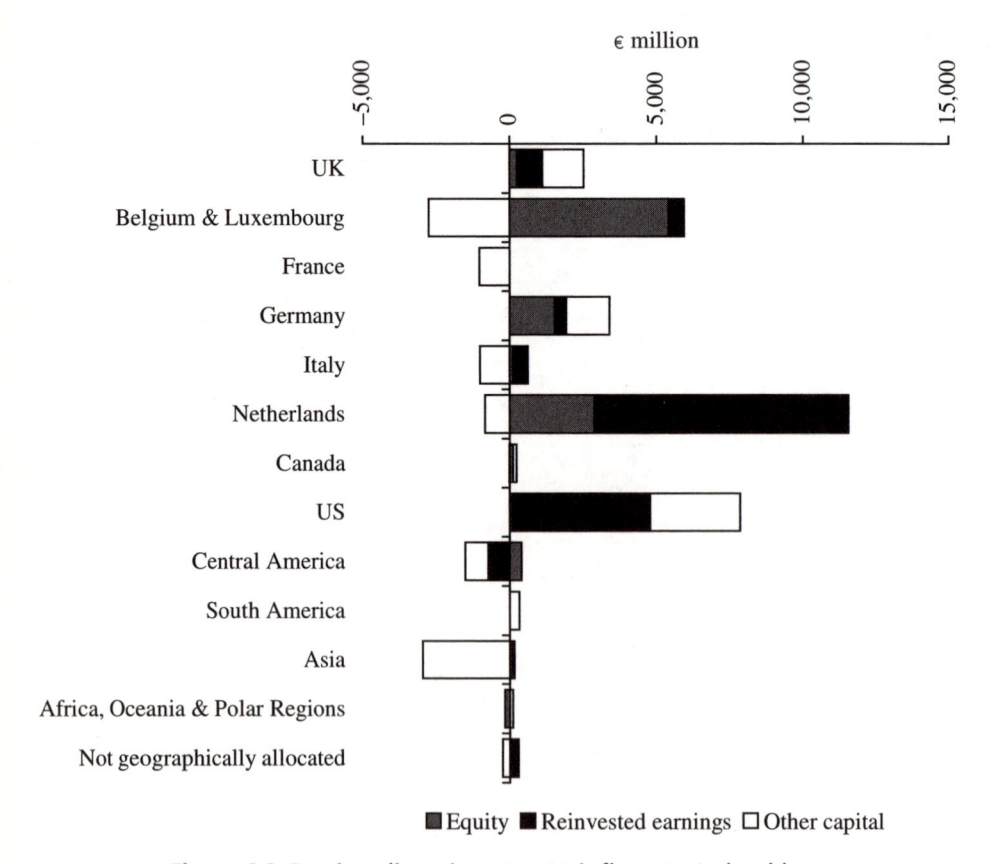

Figure 6.2 Foreign direct investment inflows to Ireland by geographical location, 2002

Source: adapted from CSO, *Foreign Direct Investment 2001 and 2002* (Cork: Central Statistical Office, 2003), p. 4.

THE INTERNATIONAL ECONOMIC CONTEXT 155

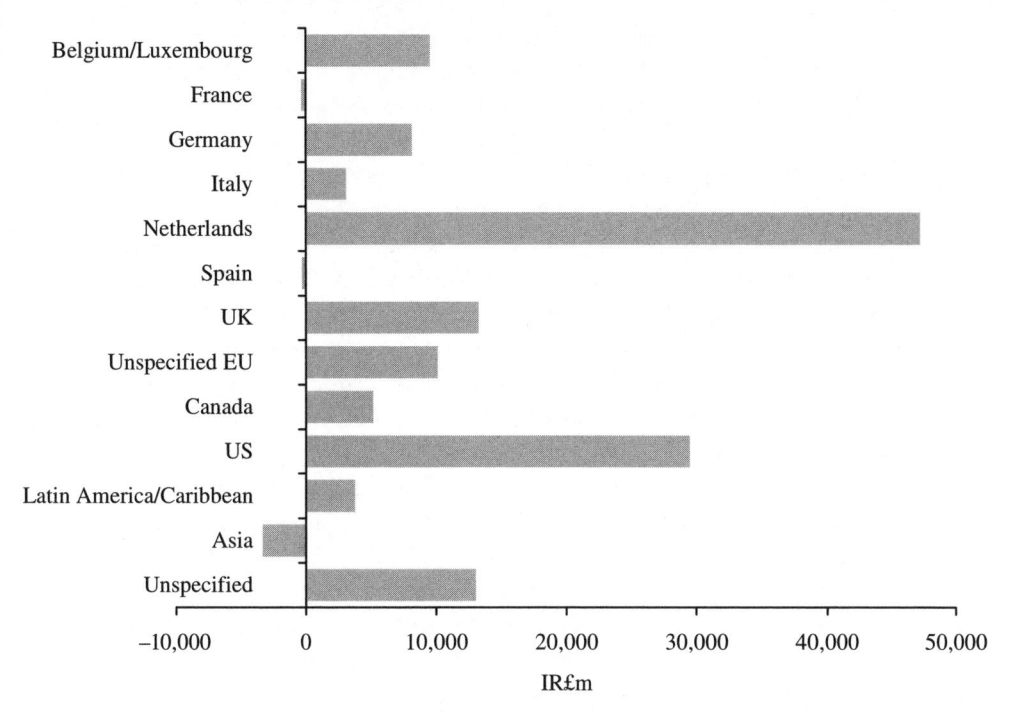

Figure 6.3 Foreign direct investment stocks in the Irish economy by geographical origin, 2002

Source: adapted from UNCTAD, *WID Country Profile: Ireland* (Geneva: United Nations, 2004), p. 11.

6.3 reveal, the Netherlands accounted for by far the largest share of both FDI inflows (largely reinvested earnings) and FDI stocks. Yet we must be careful not to deduce from this that the US no longer plays a major role in the Irish economy. For, as the CSO observes, a great deal of American investment is channeled through foreign intermediary subsidiaries, so that a 'sizeable portion' of Dutch investment in Ireland is likely to have originated from the US.[66] Nevertheless, as discussed in chapter 3, this in itself reflects a process of integration into the diad of the EU and US rather than a broader shift towards globalisation.

It is also worth examining Ireland's patterns of outward investment. As noted in chapter 2, while the share of outward investment as a proportion of total investment is low in Ireland, outward FDI stocks have nevertheless risen significantly in absolute terms (from US$202 million to US$15 billion in 1985–99). The limited evidence available suggests that the US and the UK are the two main recipients of Irish investment, together accounting for 85 per cent of Irish companies' total spend on overseas acquisitions in 1995–7. Indeed, by the late 1990s the stock of Irish FDI in the US had nearly caught up with US FDI stock in Ireland (reaching $18 billion in 1999, just $1.8 billion less than US assets in Ireland).[67] As with Ireland's inward FDI, then, the Republic's outward FDI is not becoming more global in scope but is instead characterised by highly specific geographies.

But the lack of empirical evidence is not the only reason to be sceptical of claims about Ireland's 'globalisation'. They can also be challenged on theoretical grounds. For, as has been noted, there is a common tendency not only to *describe* Ireland's development in terms of globalisation but also to *explain* it in these terms. More specifically, it is often assumed that Ireland's exposure to FDI has served to drive the shift towards prioritising competitiveness at the expense of social justice. As outlined in chapter 5, it is indeed the case that Irish economic policy has become increasingly market-oriented – not least in terms of attracting FDI. Yet Ireland's exposure to FDI cannot in itself explain such factors as the continued commitment to low corporate taxation and the decline in welfare effort. In fact, the evidence suggests that foreign investors are *not* primarily attracted to low-cost locations. Quite the contrary: higher-cost locations have received an ever-increasing share of FDI in recent years (see chapter 1). Once again, this suggests that other factors are at work – not least Irish policy-makers' *perception* of the need to reduce costs due to the 'competitive imperatives of globalisation' (see chapter 7).

Membership of the European Union

The pressures for policy change in Ireland are by no means solely discursive, however. While the 'competitive imperatives of globalisation' have been greatly exaggerated, one external economic pressure that *has* had a crucial impact on Irish economic policy is membership of the EU. This has provided the 'road map' for both economic and social development in Ireland.[68] It has entailed the extensive adaptation of Irish government and politics, involving both opening up to Brussels and shifting domestic policy management.[69]

Clearly, a central element of Ireland's integration into Europe has been participation in the internal market. The Treaty of Rome in 1957 established a customs union for the free movement of goods, services and capital. Irish policy-makers have accepted the broad outline of the

EC's regulatory strategy.[70] Yet it is important not to characterise Ireland's shift towards trade liberalisation as a direct result of European membership. Rather, Ireland's participation in the Common Market was the 'logical outcome' of policies pursued since the 1950s.[71] Nevertheless, the drive towards trade liberalisation accelerated with the SEA in 1987. This marked a shift in emphasis from the quantitative removal of barriers towards qualitative liberalisation, including the introduction of common standards and practices. As Lintner writes, the single market was 'firmly rooted in the move toward a more market-friendly form of governance for the EU'.[72]

Given the significance of the single market, it is 'not surprising' that competition policy is one of the most developed areas of EU policy.[73] This aims to minimise different forms of anti-competitiveness behaviour, including monopolies, cartels and state aids to industry. Prior to the 1990s, Ireland had a limited competition policy and little anti-trust legislation. While the Restrictive Practices Commission could issue orders in the case of anti-competitive practices, only ten such orders were issued before 1991.[74] However, Irish competition policy has developed considerably in the 1990s, with legislation now paralleling what is decided in Brussels.[75] This played a central role in stimulating the commercialisation, deregulation and privatisation of the state-owned utilities in the 1990s.[76]

A further crucial development in recent years has been Ireland's full participation in EMU. Since the late 1980s Irish macro-economic policy has been formulated within the parameters of the criteria set out at Maastricht. With control of Irish monetary policy in the hands of the European Central Bank since 1999, EMU has significantly limited the economic policy tools available to Irish policy-makers. While this is true of all EMU member states, the policy constraints on Ireland are particularly severe. This is because the Irish economy cycles out of phase with that of the EU due to its heavy dependence upon the UK and US. Since currency devaluation is no longer an option, EMU leaves Ireland less able to adjust to asymmetric (that is, country-specific) shocks. In turn, this means that the government must rely upon fiscal policy and labour market flexibility to adjust to shocks.[77] Yet such policies are potentially constrained under the terms of the Stability and Growth Pact, which imposes a 3.0 per cent deficit limit on national budgets. Taken together, these factors represent a 'serious loss of economic independence' for Ireland.[78] Ireland's participation in EMU can thus be seen as a vital factor in the government's desire to restrain public expenditure increases. In interviews, the Stability and

Growth Pact in particular was seen to represent a 'huge constraint' on Irish budgetary policy.[79]

Yet, while Ireland's EU membership can help explain the more market-oriented approach in recent years, it by no means represents a single systemic process of neo-liberalism.[80] As Teague writes, the EU has a 'much stronger social dimension than any other regional trading bloc in terms of the laws it passes, the forms of social action it engenders amongst policy communities and labour market actors and the discussions it generates on topics such as the future of employment regulation'.[81] For example, the Treaty of Rome included articles governing equal pay, the free movement of workers and the upward harmonisation of social security systems. Under the SEA, articles on health and safety, the working environment and new, clearly defined areas of social policy competence were introduced. One crucial development was the Social Charter in 1989, which set out twelve principles to guide social policy development. The Social Action Programme in 1990 contained specific measures to see these aims realised. Hourihan also points to the 'less discernible but equally important' impact of European Court of Justice decisions, most notably in areas such as equality and pensions.[82]

Certainly it is important not to overstate the significance of such developments – indeed, as Grahl notes, there has been 'little EU activity in the field of social protection outside the general legal requirement'.[83] Nevertheless, the fact that the EU's general market-oriented tendency is offset by a number of social initiatives may in itself help to explain why a similar pattern has emerged in Ireland. One area in which the EU has played a 'more subtle but more profound role' in Irish economic policy is that of social partnership.[84] This has been an important element in EU social policy, evident for example in the Cologne process, which aims to coordinate economic policy and improve interaction between wage development and monetary, budgetary and fiscal policy through macro-economic dialogue. As the NESC notes, this has meant that national social partners have been brought into 'structured, regular macroeconomic policy dialogue' with the EU.[85]

While Ireland's EU membership has played a powerful role in shaping the overall policy agenda, it is important not to conceive political outcomes as a direct and unmediated response to European integration. Indeed, in some respects Ireland has sought to resist pressure from the EU – not least in terms of the corporate tax rate. While the Republic did agree to increase its tax rate to 10 per cent in 1981 and then to 12.5 per cent in 2003 in response to pressure from the European Commission, it continues to have the lowest rate in the EU. As the NESC (rather defiantly) argued in 1999: 'tax harmonisation is beyond the current remit of the European Union. Indeed in the past, the EU has always acknowledged that taxation is a matter for *national* governments except where approximation is needed to complete the internal market, as is the case of excise duties and value-added tax' (original emphasis).[86] A similar picture emerged with respect to the Irish government's refusal to back down over its 2001 budgetary policy (see chapter 5).

It is also important not to conceptualise European integration as a simple 'top-down' process imposed on Irish policy-makers from above. In actual fact, participation has enabled Ireland to play some role in influencing decisions made at the European level. For example, one European Commission representative pointed to the role of specific individuals such as Peter Sutherland, Ray Mac Sharry and David Byrne in shaping the European Union's policy agenda in such areas as competition policy and social policy.[87] As Hickman notes, the Irish have seen the strengthening of the EU's institutional structure as a key way to prevent larger states from exercising excessive influence.[88] For example, Laffan points to the management of the 1996 presidency in which 'the Irish system deployed a number of flexible and very effective tools of co-operation'.[89] These included intensive ministerial and cabinet involvement, interdepartmental committees and specialised training. Laffan also points to the proactive approach adopted by Irish policy-makers towards Agenda 2000, including the management of the negotiations by an inter-departmental group and the maintenance of 'excellent links' between Dublin and Brussels.[90] In 2001, Ireland demonstrated its potential to hinder rather than facilitate European integration. While it did not reflect the government's position, the Irish people's rejection of the Nice Treaty on EU enlargement illustrates the impact that individual nations can have on the wider European agenda.

This is not to overstate the influence that Ireland has. Clearly the Republic does not possess the weight of larger states such as Germany and France due to its small size. In the words of one senior civil servant: 'if push comes to shove, people walk all over us . . . Where we've scored is by moving between the big boys and avoiding push coming to shove.'[91] While Ireland has helped shape the agenda in certain areas, in many others the Republic is a 'taker rather than shaper of EU policy'.[92] Yet in some respects this can be attributed to the approach of the Irish government itself. As Laffan notes, the Irish system remains 'too informal and ad hoc' given the complex and changing nature of

EU integration.[93] There is no 'Bible' on EU affairs for the overall system or even for separate departments and (in contrast to the case in Britain) no set of guidelines for horizontal matters. This means that significant developments are missed – for example, Laffan found in interviews that the Irish system was seen to have responded inadequately to shifts in policies on state aids.[94]

The highly complex and differentiated nature of European integration suggests that it is best conceived in tendential terms rather than as a simple linear process. Clearly, the dynamics of European integration cannot be characterised as static but instead change over time. For example, the balance of power between large and small states is likely to be radically altered by the inclusion of many more small states due to EU enlargement.[95] As a tendency (to which there are counter-tendencies), European integration can be seen to shape but not determine the context of policy-making and implementation in Ireland.

Finally, it is worth reiterating the argument (stated in chapter 3) that Ireland's EU membership cannot in itself be cited as evidence of 'globalisation'. While Ireland's participation in both the Single Market and EMU has encouraged it to open its borders to external trade and investment flows, this has not led to a broader process of globalisation. Indeed, as Leddin and Walsh note, the Euro-zone is far from genuinely open but instead represents a large but closed economy.[96] Nor can the dynamics of Ireland's EU membership be seen as primarily economic. For example, as Honohan and Walsh note, the decision to join EMU was taken on political rather than economic grounds – indeed, policy-makers 'expected the new regime to result in appreciation for the Irish pound against sterling (which had been notably weak since the mid-1960s), and subsidies were granted from Europe to ease the burden of adjusting to a tougher regime'.[97] In interviews, senior Irish policy-makers also emphasised the importance of political rather than economic factors in shaping the decision to join EMU. Once again, appeals to the 'competitive imperatives of globalisation' cannot capture these complex dynamics.

Conclusion

This chapter has unpacked and interrogated the widely held assumption that Irish economic policy has developed as a response to globalisation. Crucially, it has *not* argued that economic factors do not serve to shape policy change. Indeed, the entire chapter has been devoted to examining the economic context in which Irish policy has been constituted, exploring in particular the role of domestic economic factors, external trade, foreign investment and European integration. In so doing, the chapter has made two central claims. First, it has argued that economic conditions cannot in themselves explain the character of policy change (as is so often implied, if not stated explicitly). Such factors create the *context* for policy change, but they do not determine the *conduct* of political decision-makers. This suggests that other factors have been at work in shaping Irish economic policy change. Second, the chapter has argued that these economic conditions cannot be conflated with 'globalisation', for there is simply no evidence to suggest that they are becoming increasingly global in scope.

This disparity between claims made about globalisation and the evidence for such claims invites the question as to why globalisation is so widely invoked politically.[98] As various authors have suggested, globalisation's real power may lie not so much in its 'material reality' as in its discursive construction. In acting as if globalisation were real, policy-makers may produce the very outcomes they attribute to globalisation itself (see chapter 1). The discursive construction of globalisation is the subject of the following chapter.

Notes

1 See for instance P. Kirby, 'Contested pedigrees of the Celtic tiger', in P. Kirby, L. Gibbons and M. Cronin (eds), *Reinventing Ireland: Culture, Society and the Global Economy* (London: Pluto Press, 2002), pp. 30–1; B. Nolan, P. O'Connell and C. T. Whelan, 'Introduction', in B. Nolan, P. O'Connell and C. T. Whelan (eds), *Bust to Boom? The Irish Experience of Growth and Inequality* (Dublin: Institute of Public Administration, 2000), p. 2; J. Fitz Gerald, 'Ireland – a multicultural economy', in W. Crotty and D. E. Schmitt (eds), *Ireland on the World Stage* (Manchester: Manchester University Press, 2002), p. 80; D. E. Schmitt, 'Ireland on the world stage: conclusions and challenges', in Crotty and Schmitt, *Ireland on the World Stage*, p. 189; J. S. O'Conner, 'Welfare state development in the context of European integration and economic convergence: situating Ireland within the European Union context', *Policy & Politics*, 31: 3 (2003), pp. 390–400; R. O'Donnell, 'The future of social partnership in Ireland', Discussion Paper prepared for the National Competitiveness Council (2001), p. 3.
2 P. Kirby, *The Celtic Tiger in Distress: Growth and Inequality in Ireland* (Basingstoke: Palgrave, 2002), p. 6.

3 Kirby offers a categorisation of the Irish literature with respect to the literature on globalisation. As his conceptual framework he uses Held et al.'s classification of the globalisation literature as the 'hyperglobalist', 'sceptical' and 'transformationist' theses. While Kirby's discussion has a great deal to offer, some of his classifications are rather misleading. For example, he argues that the mainstream Irish literature can be characterised as 'hyperglobalist', when in fact it has much in common with the new institutionalist position. Perhaps the core claim of the hyperglobalists is that nation-states are no longer important actors in the global economy – a view that is clearly not shared by authors such as Nolan, Whelan and O'Connell. See Kirby *The Celtic Tiger in Distress,* pp. 195–9; D. Held, A. McGrew, D. Goldblatt and J. Perraton, *Global Transformations: Politics, Economics and Culture* (Stanford, CA: Stanford University Press, 1999), pp. 2–5.

4 D. O'Hearn, 'Globalisation, "new tigers," and the end of the developmental state? The case of the Celtic tiger', *Politics & Society*, 28: 1 (2000), p. 87.

5 A. Murphy, 'The "Celtic tiger" – an analysis of Ireland's economic growth performance', European University Institute Working Paper, San Domenico (2000), p. 24.

6 K. Allen, *The Celtic Tiger: The Myth of Social Partnership in Ireland* (Manchester: Manchester University Press, 2000), pp. 186–7.

7 Ibid., pp. 23–4.

8 Ibid., p. 37.

9 W. Greider, *One World, Ready or Not: The Manic Logic of Global Capitalism* (New York: Simon & Schuster, 1997); J. Gray, *False Dawn: The Delusions of Global Capitalism* (New York: New Press, 1998).

10 Kirby, *The Celtic Tiger in Distress*, p. 6.

11 Ibid., p. 189.

12 O'Conner, 'Welfare state development', p. 400.

13 Nolan et al., 'Introduction', p. 1; S. Ó Riain, 'A tale of two globalisations: the Irish software industry and the global economy', Working Paper, University of California (1998); P. Sweeney, *The Celtic Tiger: Ireland's Continuing Economic Miracle* (Dublin: Oak Tree Press, 1999), pp. 82, 135, 187.

14 Nolan et al., 'Introduction', pp. 1–2.

15 S. Ó Riain, 'An offshore silicon valley? The emerging Irish software industry', *Competition and Change*, 2 (1997), p. 208.

16 L. Weiss, 'Introduction: bringing domestic institutions back in', in L. Weiss (ed.), *States in the Global Economy: Bringing Domestic Institutions Back In* (Cambridge: Cambridge University Press, 2003), pp. 7–14; J. M. Hobson, 'Disappearing taxes or the "race to the middle"? Fiscal policy in the OECD', in Weiss, *States in the Global Economy*, p. 38.

17 S. Ó Riain and P. O'Connell, 'The role of the state in growth and welfare', in Nolan et al., *Bust to Boom?* p. 311.

18 G. Taylor, *Negotiated Governance and Public Policy in Ireland* (Manchester: Manchester University Press, 2005), pp. 5, 9, 96–7; see also G. Taylor,

'Negotiated governance and the Irish polity', in G. Taylor (ed.), *Issues in Irish Public Policy* (Dublin: Irish Academic Press, 2002), p. 36.
19 Kirby, 'Contested pedigrees of the Celtic tiger', p. 30.
20 C. Hay, 'Structure and agency', in D. Marsh and G. Stoker (eds), *Theory and Methods in Political Science* (London: Macmillan, 1995), p. 205; C. Hay, *Political Analysis* (Basingstoke: Palgrave, 2002), p. 198.
21 C. Hay and B. Rosamond, 'Globalisation, European integration and the discursive construction of economic imperatives', *Journal of European Public Policy*, 9: 2 (2002), p. 148.
22 P. Kerr, *Postwar British Politics: From Conflict to Consensus* (London: Routledge/PSA, 2001), pp. 68–9.
23 Indeed, the Republic emerged with virtually no manufacturing sector, and over half the productive workforce was employed in agriculture. While Irish industry had already declined in the nineteenth century, the situation was made far worse by partition, for the bulk of Irish exports came from the Belfast region. See R. Fanning, *Independent Ireland* (Dublin: Helecon, 1983), pp. 72–3.
24 R. Breen, D. Hannan, D. Rottman and C. T. Whelan, *Understanding Contemporary Ireland: State, Class and Development in the Republic of Ireland* (Dublin: Gill & Macmillan, 1990), p. 2.
25 For example, by 1924–5 the volume of gross agricultural output had fallen to 13 per cent below its pre-World War I level. Between 1920 and 1931 agricultural prices fell from an index of 220 to 110. See K. A. Kennedy, T. Giblin and D. McHugh, *The Economic Development of Ireland in the Twentieth Century* (London: Routledge, 1988), p. 37; R. Munck, *The Irish Rconomy: Results and Prospects* (London: Pluto Press, 1993), pp. 26–7.
26 Breen et al., *Understanding Contemporary Ireland*, p. 2; T. Cradden, 'Social partnership in Ireland: against the trend', in N. Collins (ed.), *Political Issues in Ireland Today* (Manchester: Manchester University Press, 1999), p. 51.
27 Despite some recovery, agriculture was still 4 per cent lower than its pre-World War I level in 1930. Similarly, while the total volume of industrial output increased by 8.5 per cent in 1926–9, it declined to less than 2 per cent in 1929–31. See Kennedy et al., *The Economic Development of Ireland*, pp. 38–9.
28 This can be seen, for example, in the Irish government's rejection of British proposals relating to storage and trans-shipment during World War II. This led to serious wartime shortages in Ireland, as the British response was to allow only very limited supplies of coal, and no fats, sugar or wheat, to be shipped to Ireland. See J. T. Carroll, *Ireland in the War Years* (New York: David and Charles, 1975), pp. 83–5.
29 Munck, *The Irish Economy*, p. 30.
30 Manufacturing exports (excluding food, drink and tobacco) made up just 6 per cent of total output in 1951 – see E. O'Malley, 'The problem of late industrialisation and the experience of the Republic of Ireland', *Cambridge Journal of Economics*, 9 (1985), p. 144.
31 C. Ó Gráda, *A Rocky Road: The Irish Economy Since the 1920s* (Manchester: Manchester University Press, 1997), p. 110.

32 Ibid., p. 49.
33 Kennedy et al., *The Economic Development of Ireland*, p. 58.
34 B. Brunt, *The Republic of Ireland* (London: Paul Chapman, 1988), pp. 14–5; J. Haughton, 'The dynamics of economic change', in W. J. Crotty and D. E. Schmitt (eds), *Ireland and the Politics of Change* (London: Longman, 1998), p. 42.
35 P. Breathnach, 'Uneven development and Irish peripheralisation', in P. Shirlow (ed.), *Development Ireland: Contemporary Issues* (London: Pluto Press, 1995), p. 17.
36 J. Sachs, 'Ireland's growth strategy: lessons for economic development', in A. Gray (ed.), *International Perspectives on the Irish Economy* (Dublin: Indecon Economic Consultants, 1997), p. 58.
37 Haughton also attributes high emigration to rising wages in other countries, particularly Britain, rather than to Ireland's failure. J. Haughton, 'The historical background', in J. W. O'Hagen (ed.), *The Economy of Ireland: Policy and Performance of a Small European Country* (Dublin: Gill & Macmillan, 1995), p. 34.
38 O'Malley, 'The problem of late industrialisation', p. 144.
39 Ibid.
40 Ó Gráda, *A Rocky Road*, p. 114.
41 O'Malley, 'The problem of late industrialisation', pp. 144–8.
42 Munck, *The Irish Economy*, pp. 33–4.
43 E. O'Malley, 'Industrialisation in Ireland', in P. Clancy, E. O'Malley, L. O'Connell and C. Van Egeraat (eds), *Ireland and Poland: Comparative Perspectives* (Dublin: Department of Sociology, University College Dublin, 1992), p. 107.
44 Munck, *The Irish Economy*, p. 39.
45 Ibid., p. 38.
46 Taylor, 'Negotiated governance and the Irish polity', p. 10.
47 Sweeney, *The Celtic Tiger*, p. 37.
48 Haughton, 'The dynamics of economic change', p. 43.
49 J. J. Sexton and P. O'Connell, *Labour Market Studies: Ireland* (Brussels: European Commission, 1996), p. 89.
50 W. K. Roche, 'Pay determination, the state and the politics of industrial relations', in T. V. Murphy and W. K. Roche (eds), *Irish Industrial Relations in Practice* (Dublin: Oak Tree Press, 1994), p. 195; see also N. Hardiman, 'The political economy of growth', in Crotty and Schmitt, *Ireland on the World Stage*, pp. 169–70; E. Hazelkorn and H. Patterson, 'The new politics of the Irish Republic', *New Left Review*, 207: 5 (1994), p. 56; B. Laffan, 'The European Union and Ireland', in Collins, *Political Issues in Ireland Today*, p. 94; Munck, *The Irish Economy*, p. 39; P. O'Connell, *Astonishing Success: Economic Growth and the Labour Market in Ireland* (Geneva: International Labour Office, 1999), p. 69; R. O'Donnell, 'Social partnership: principles, institutions and interpretations', in O'Connell, *Astonishing Success*, p. 55.
51 See also G. Taylor, 'Hailing with an invisible hand: a "cosy" political dispute amid the rise of neoliberal politics in modern Ireland', *Government and Opposition*, 37: 4 (2002), pp. 501–23.

52 Ó Riain and O'Connell, 'The role of the state in growth and welfare', p. 331.
53 Kirby, *The Celtic Tiger in Distress*, pp. 142–4; O' Connor, 'Welfare state development', p. 400.
54 See for instance Kennedy et al., *The Economic Development of Ireland*, pp. 35, 258; Munck, *The Irish Economy*, p. 24.
55 Brunt, *The Republic of Ireland*, p. 4.
56 Kennedy et al., *The Economic Development of Ireland*, p. 49.
57 J. Bradley, 'The Irish economy in comparative perspective', in Nolan et al., *Bust to Boom?* p. 6.
58 M. Watson, *Foundations of International Political Economy* (Basingstoke: Palgrave, 2005), manuscript.
59 P. J. Katzenstein, *Small States in World Markets: Industrial Policy in Europe* (Ithaca, NY: Cornell University Press, 1985), p. 192; D. Rodrik, *Has Globalisation Gone Too Far?* (Washington, DC: Institute of International Economics, 1997), p. 53; C. Hay, 'What's globalisation got to do with it?' (2003), www.bham.ac.uk/POLSIS/department/staff/publications/Hay_inaugural.htm/
60 J. Bradley, 'The history of economic development in Ireland, North and South', in A. F. Heath, R. Breen and C. T. Whelan (eds), *Ireland North and South: Perspectives from Social Science* (Oxford: Oxford University Press, 1999), p. 47.
61 E. O'Malley, 'The revival of Irish indigenous industry 1987–1997', in T. J. Baker, D. Duffy and F. Shortall (eds), *Quarterly Economic Commentary, April 1998* (Dublin: Economic and Social Research Institute, 1998), p. 104.
62 O'Malley, 'The problem of late industrialisation', p. 150.
63 Forfás, *International Trade and Investment Report 2001* (Dublin: Forfás, 2002), p. 33.
64 Forfás, *International Trade and Investment Report 2003* (Dublin: Forfás, 2004), p. 33.
65 OECD, *International Direct Investment Statistics Yearbook 1999* (Paris: OECD, 1999), pp. 176–7.
66 CSO, *Foreign Direct Investment 2001 and 2002* (Cork: Central Statistical Office, 2003), pp. 1–8.
67 Forfás, *Statement on Outward Direct Investment* (Dublin: Forfás, 2001), pp. 11–3; Forfás, *International Trade and Investment Report, 2000* (Dublin: Forfás, 2001), pp. 38–40.
68 Laffan, 'The European Union and Ireland', p. 92.
69 B. Laffan, 'Managing Europe', in N. Collins and T. Cradden (eds), *Political Issues in Ireland Today* (Manchester: Manchester University Press, 1994), pp. 53–4.
70 B. Laffan, *Organisation for a Changing Europe: Irish Central Government and the European Union* (Dublin: Policy Institute, 2001), p. 3; see also chapter 5.
71 R. O'Donnell, 'The internal market', in P. Keatinge (ed.), *Ireland and EC Membership Evaluated* (London: Pinter, 1991), p. 7; see also chapter 5.

72 V. Lintner, 'The development of the EU and the European economy', in G. Thompson (ed.), *Governing the European Economy* (London: Sage, 2001), p. 61. Similarly, for Wincott, the single market 'illustrates and strengthens the idea of a society organised around the market'. See D. Wincott, 'Globalisation and European integration', in C. Hay and D. Marsh (eds), *Demystifying Globalisation* (London: Macmillan, 2000), p. 184.
73 R. O'Donnell, 'Competition policy', in Keatinge, *Ireland and EC Membership Evaluated*, p. 90.
74 Ibid., p. 93.
75 OECD, *Economic Surveys: Ireland 2000–2001* (Paris: OECD, 2001), p. 84.
76 See for instance Sweeney, *The Celtic Tiger*, p. 109.
77 A. Leddin and B. Walsh, *The Macro-Economy of Ireland* (Dublin: Gill & Macmillan, 1998), p. 561.
78 Ibid., p. 563.
79 Interviews.
80 See for instance Wincott, 'Globalisation and European integration', pp. 171–2.
81 P. Teague, 'EU social policy: institutional design matters', Institute of European Studies, Queen's University of Belfast, Queen's Papers on Europeanization (2000), p. 1.
82 F. Hourihan, 'The European Union and industrial relations', in Murphy and Roche, *Irish Industrial Relations in Practice*, p. 416.
83 J. Grahl, '"Social Europe" and the governance of labour relations', in Thompson, *Governing the European Economy*, p. 158.
84 Laffan, 'The European Union and Ireland', p. 94.
85 NESC, *Opportunities, Challenges and Capacities for Choice* (Dublin: National Economic and Social Council, 1999), pp. 127–8.
86 Ibid., p. 120.
87 Interviews.
88 M. Hickman, *Ireland and the European Community* (London: PNL Press, 1990), p. 15.
89 Laffan, *Organisation for a Changing Europe*, p. 91
90 Ibid., pp. 91–2.
91 Interviews.
92 Laffan, *Organisation for a Changing Europe*, p. 101.
93 Ibid., p. 100.
94 Ibid., pp. 92–5, 100.
95 Ibid., p. 10.
96 Leddin and Walsh, *The Macro-Economy of Ireland*, p. 536.
97 P. Honohan and B. Walsh, 'Catching up with the leaders: the Irish hare', Brookings Panel on Economic Activity, Washington, DC (4–5 April 2002), p. 9.
98 C. Hay and N. J. Smith, 'Horses for courses? The political discourse of globalisation and European integration in the UK and Ireland', *West European Politics*, 28: 1, p. 125.

7

The dynamics behind policy change (2): the political discourse of globalisation

So far, the book has focused upon globalisation in material terms – rejecting rather than affirming its analytical utility in relation to the Irish case. Yet it is also important to consider the role of globalisation in ideational terms. If policy-makers believe in globalisation, it may serve to shape policy outcomes irrespective of its 'real' existence. This chapter considers the role of political discourses in shaping policy change in the Irish Republic. In so doing, it first places more recent developments in historical perspective, and then focuses on contemporary discourses of competitiveness and globalisation. The chapter seeks to unpack both how and why such discourses have come to be deployed in Ireland and, in turn, considers how they are changing over time.

The role of discourse

In recent years there has been growing interest in the role of discourses of globalisation and European integration in shaping political outcomes. This reflects a broader 'ideational turn' within the social sciences. As various authors have suggested, there are strong *a priori* reasons for suggesting that discourses may play a powerful role in shaping social and political outcomes.[1] For, as has been noted in previous chapters, if we accept that actors are not blessed with flawless knowledge of their environment then we must acknowledge the role that ideas play. Ultimately, it is these ideas – rather than the context itself – that serve to shape the way in which actors formulate and act upon decisions.[2] In this sense, globalisation's real power may lie in its discursive construction rather than its material 'reality'. This suggests that the political discourse of globalisation should be treated as an important object of enquiry in its own right. In fact, the very concept of a 'globalisation discourse' needs to be unpacked. As Hay and Rosamond note, there is no single unifying discourse of globalisation; rather, the concept is used in different ways in different contexts. Moreover, in some cases it is European integration rather than globalisation that is appealed to as an external economic imperative.[3] This highlights the need for the detailed empirical analysis of contemporary appeals to globalisation and European integration within specific national contexts. The aim of this chapter is to do precisely this with respect to the Irish case.

Discursive continuity and change

Before turning to more recent developments, though, it is useful to consider the historical background. After all, discourses do not remain static but instead may change markedly over time. As with policy change, then, it is desirable to adopt a diachronic approach in order to examine discursive developments in Ireland. In turn, such an approach can help to illuminate how political discourses have served to shape the trajectory of Irish economic policy over the decades.

How then have political discourses developed in Ireland? As outlined in chapter 4, the first decade of the Irish state was marked by considerable continuity in policy-making. The fact that even the most limited innovation was not pursued can be understood in terms of the government's ideological stance. Cumann na nGaedheal 'set much store by continuity';[4] indeed, they professed to be the most conservative revolutionaries in history. The new government was also strongly committed to economic liberalism, the paradigm favoured by most Irish economists and civil servants at this time. This can be seen, for instance, in the government's refusal to intervene when faced with high levels of unemployment in the late 1920s, relying instead on emigration to alleviate this problem. As the minister for industry and commerce, Patrick McGilligan, stated at this time: 'it is no function of government to provide work for anybody'.[5]

Ideas can also help explain the adoption of economic nationalism under Fianna Fáil. The party leader, Eamon de Valera, had been one of the key figures in the civil war and had a 'particular vision of Ireland'.[6] He outlined Fianna Fáil's purpose in 1926 as 'the reuniting of the Irish people' through such measures as the 'making of Ireland as an economic unit, as self-contained and self-sufficient as possible'.[7] Above all, the priority was to reduce Ireland's dependence on Britain, even if this meant a lower standard of living. In this sense, economic nationalism was simply a means to an end rather than an end in itself.[8] This nationalist rather than economic emphasis was highlighted by the 'Economic War' with Britain, which was very costly for the Irish government. As de Valera told his party: 'What is involved is whether the Irish nation is going to be free or not.'[9] The persistence of the dominant nationalist paradigm can, in turn, help explain the striking lack of policy change in Ireland after World War II. Whereas other countries embarked upon a process of restructuring, Irish policy-makers and opinion-formers continued to take protectionism 'for granted'.[10] Even in the face of new issues such as the Cold War, traditional nationalist concerns remained paramount.[11]

Nevertheless, ideas cannot be seen as static but instead may change over time. As outlined in chapter 4, the 1950s marked a period of transition in Irish policy-making. Certainly the changing domestic and international context contributed to this change – whereas other countries flourished, Ireland appeared to stagnate. Yet, as outlined in chapter 6, to characterise Ireland's performance in terms of failure is a 'half-truth'. What was distinctive about the 1950s was the growing *perception* of crisis and the need for change.[12] In the 1950s, Ireland's failure to thrive was seen no longer as situational (that is, due to depression or war) but deep-rooted. This can be seen, for example, in the response to the budget deficits of 1950 and 1951. In fact, Ó Gráda attributes the deficits to a severe decline in the terms of trade due to the sterling devaluation of 1948 and the worsening of the Korean War in 1950. However, the Irish government interpreted the adverse balance as 'a structural problem requiring drastic surgery' and therefore adopted a series of panic fiscal measures.[13] In 1956 the finance minister saw economic failure as so significant that he argued that 'our economic independence' was at stake.[14] In this sense, Ireland's stagnation was seen as a crisis of the system itself, requiring more than a change in government. Indeed, multi-party coalitions (led by Fine Gael) had been no more successful in tackling the public finances than had Fianna Fáil.

While the traditional discourse had largely broken down by the mid-1950s, the process of paradigm shift had yet to be completed. The considerable continuity in approach, despite the widespread recognition of the need for change, can be attributed to the lack of alternative ideas. Neither the Central Bank nor the Department of Finance proposed a shift away from protectionism, and the IDA even sanctioned some tariff increases.[15] Nevertheless, 'some new thinking was going on behind the scenes'.[16] Paradoxically, this can in part be attributed to very success of political nationalism. Many now took this for granted, particularly after Ireland's break with the Commonwealth in 1948. This helped pave the way for new issues to take centre stage. In particular, the language of nationalism was replaced by the language of economics as the dominant theme in political debates.[17] It was in this context that a new paradigm could come to the fore. In particular, the role of T. K. Whitaker, who became secretary of the Department of Finance in 1953, is widely cited as crucial.[18] Whitaker was commissioned by the government to prepare his report, *Economic Development*, which called for a re-examination of policy 'without regard to past views or commitments' and argued that 'sooner or later, protection will have to go'.[19]

While the publication of *Economic Development* in 1958 provided the ideational basis for policy shift it cannot in itself account for the dramatic change in approach. After all, ideas cannot actually 'do' anything in themselves but must be appropriated by political agents capable of acting upon them.[20] Crucially, the wider government debate that led to *Economic Development* corresponded to a debate within Fianna Fáil itself.[21] The role of Séan Lemass – who succeeded de Valera as leader of Fianna Fáil in 1959 – can be seen as significant in facilitating this change. Though originally committed to protectionism, Lemass was essentially a pragmatist[22] and had become increasingly influenced by Keynesian ideas. During the 1950s he attempted to move the party away from its extreme nationalist roots towards an explicit recognition of the need for foreign capital and Keynesian public policy. In particular, he gave a widely publicised speech in 1955 calling for change. This new political project was embedded in the government's *Programme for Economic Expansion* in 1958, which provided the framework for the more outward-looking and activist strategy pursued from then on.

This is not to contend, however, that no ideational continuity was retained at all. Rather than being rejected altogether, the nationalist emphasis was instead rearticulated. For example, Lemass argued that economic growth would reduce the disparity of interests between nationalists and unionists in the North.[23] As Breen et al. observe: 'Henceforth, Irish nationalism proceeded from an assumption that the primary objective was to reap the benefits from full economic participation in the world economy.'[24] This can help explain the failure to address social inequalities explicitly. Reforms in education, for example, were articulated as being valuable to the nation as a whole rather than to a specific class.[25] Paradoxically, nationalist concerns were also important in Ireland's decision to surrender some autonomy by joining the EEC. As Laffan writes: 'Put simply, [Europe] provided the Republic with an arena to assert its independence from Britain, the historic goal of Irish nationalism.'[26]

It was not until the 1980s that this policy paradigm began to break down. Despite rising public borrowing in the 1970s, successive governments remained committed to the Keynesian ideal of full employment. In the 1980s, however, growing alarm about the rate of public borrowing began to shake the existing paradigm. Yet, while Fianna Fáil's *The Way Forward* of 1982 and the Fine Gael coalition's *Building on Reality* of 1984 both emphasised budgetary targets, little progress was made in reducing the current budget deficit. Once again, this can to be attributed to the lack of an alternative vision, with little consensus about an appropriate future strategy. As in the 1950s, though, some new thinking had been going on behind the scenes. In particular, the role of the NESC (which had been established in the 1970s) is widely recognised as crucial.[27] In its 1986 report, *A Strategy for Development*, the NESC identified Ireland's national debt as the central policy issue to be addressed. At the same time, it emphasised the need 'to foster a greater degree of consensus in Irish society if these measures are to be implemented without giving rise to conflict'.[28] In so doing, the report provided the ideational framework for a new approach based upon macro-political bargaining. Again, though, such ideas must be adopted by political agents capable of acting upon them. In interviews, senior policy-makers and opinion formers identified the role of Charles Haughey (leader of the new Fianna Fáil government in 1987) and Ray Mac Sharry (the minister for finance and tánaiste) as pivotal in pushing through the new approach. In the words of one senior civil servant, Haughey was 'sufficiently adept as a politician, he had a sufficiently clear view, that he led the public system and the consensus'.[29] Mac Sharry recalls his own sense of determination on coming to office: 'I knew the day of fiscal reckoning had arrived. It was time to call a stop – and mean it.'[30]

Crucially, it was through the narrative of crisis that a new consensus could be forged.[31] As Haughey told the Dáil in 1986: 'The present crisis is different in its nature from anything that we have ever witnessed before in this country. It is comprehensive and total. It is felt everywhere. It permeates every sector of our national life.'[32] One senior civil servant recalls: 'there was a sense of imperative about the policy goals so there wasn't really much room for political debate'.[33] Indeed, the leader of the opposition, Alan Dukes, outlined Fine Gael's tacit support for the government's approach, stating: 'If it is going in the right direction, I do not believe that it should be deviated from its course.'[34] Mac Sharry also recounts how Haughey wrote to all ministers in May 1987 giving them ten days' notice to submit a paper on proposed expenditure cuts. This letter was leaked to the press but: 'Far from being an embarrassment, the leaked document was seen, publicly, as a measure of the government's determination to bring public expenditure under control.'[35] This new political project was enshrined in the *Programme of National Recovery* of 1988.[36]

Discourses of competitiveness and globalisation

It is in this context that ideas about competitiveness have come to the fore in Ireland. In *A Strategy for Development* the NESC identified the fundamental problem with Ireland's economy to be the low level of national output. Only by achieving economic growth, it argued, could Ireland address its high unemployment levels. Crucially, the NESC emphasised the need to enhance Ireland's international competitiveness in order to achieve economic growth. As the report stated: 'It is the internationally traded sectors, embracing enterprises which compete on overseas markets and those which compete with imports on the home market, which comprise the locomotive of growth.'[37] This emphasis upon competitiveness was explicitly embraced in the social partnership agreements – not least in the (aptly titled) *Programme for Competitiveness and Work*, which aimed, critically, to deepen the competitiveness of the Irish economy.[38] Indeed, *Partnership 2000* even led to the creation of a National Competitiveness Council (NCC) in 1997. In interviews, this was seen to provide an important stimulus for the shift towards privatisation and deregulation in Ireland. In the words of one economic adviser: 'that is the key issue going forward I think for the economy, the whole issue of competitiveness'.

Yet, while the concept of 'competitiveness' has come to play a central role in Irish political discourse, this has not translated into a commitment to stark neo-liberalism. Indeed, in interviews senior civil servants and opinion formers were very keen to distinguish the dominant ideology in Ireland from that of Thatcherism in the UK. In part, this is due to the way in which competitiveness is defined. Rather than being characterised in terms of low cost, competitiveness is seen much more broadly in terms of 'design, quality, marketing, customer service and that special factor at which Irish companies excel – relationships'.[39]

Nor is competitiveness justified purely in terms of market needs. Rather than being an end in itself, it is instead articulated as a means to an end. As one senior civil servant outlined: 'it's not a one-track mentality that we are purely competitive but we recognise that we need to be competitive to achieve a higher host of social standards'.[40] With rapid economic growth combined with inequality, the issue of social justice has become more rather than less prominent over time. Indeed, one senior civil servant described it as the 'new issue'. As the taoiseach, Bertie Ahern, told his party in 2000: 'In the late 1980s, we conquered the national debt. In the 1990s, we conquered unemployment. In the first decade of the 21st century, we will conquer poor infrastructure and poverty through filling the major gaps in our public services.'[41]

Yet, despite claims that 'economic dynamism and social justice go hand in hand',[42] the two are not treated equally. For it is not social justice but economic competitiveness that is seen as a 'guiding principle of economic and social policy'.[43] Indeed, as *Partnership 2000* states: 'the competitiveness of the Irish economy is a pre-condition for the pursuit of all other economic and social goals'.[44] Thus, social aims can be pursued – but, in the words of one senior policy-maker, 'without killing the goose that laid the [golden] egg'.[45] In this sense, it is economic competitiveness rather than social justice that is seen as the more urgent priority, for the latter is seen as contingent upon – and, by implication, subordinate to – the former.[46]

Crucially, it is globalisation that has increasingly provided the rationale for this emphasis upon competitiveness.[47] The very fact that economic efficiency has come to be seen as the principal objective of economic and social policy has in turn increasingly been justified in terms of the harsh economic pressures unleashed by globalisation.[48] As the *Programme for Competitiveness and Work* argued: 'The emphasis on competitiveness derives from the fact that the degree of competition is increasingly globally and on the domestic market'.[49] *Partnership 2000* outlined this view in more detail:

> The economic environment is now characterised by an unrelenting drive for competitiveness brought about by the increasing globalisation of economic activity and international competition in world markets. Technological advances, which have fuelled much of the growth in globalisation and competition, are continuing apace and show no signs of abating. As a result, the world economy is increasingly dynamic, open and internationally competitive.[50]

Similarly, the *Programme for Prosperity and Fairness* pointed to 'the new and intensified competitive forces unleashed by such factors as globalisation, the Single European Market, EU enlargement and the pace of technological change'.[51]

This is not to suggest, however, that globalisation is presented in negative terms. Quite the contrary: Irish policy-makers tend to articulate globalisation as highly positive to domestic audiences. In particular, it has been closely linked with the 'Celtic tiger' discourse (see also chapter 2). As minister of state Liz O'Donnell argued in 2001, for instance: 'Here in Ireland our national economic progress in recent years has been achieved through our ability to harness globalisation to promote our national development and trade.'[52] Despite Ireland's subsequent economic slowdown, globalisation continues to be presented in glowing terms. As the tánaiste, Mary Harney, argued to the social partners in 2002: 'While some countries have floundered under the pressures of globalisation Ireland has flourished.'[53] In its 2002 election manifesto Fianna Fáil referred to Ireland as 'one of the most successfully globalised countries in the world' and highlighted the fact that Ireland came first in the A. T. Kearney Globalisation Index.[54]

Yet this is a double-edged sword. By this logic, Ireland's ability to thrive depends upon the extent to which it responds to global economic forces. Ireland may have flourished under conditions of globalisation but is ultimately constrained by it. In this sense, globalisation is presented as a non-negotiable external economic constraint. As the Department of Enterprise, Trade and Employment states: 'As trade barriers fall and the process of economic globalisation continues inexorably, the key to future trade success lies in the ability of companies to compete with the best on international markets.'[55] Similarly, the Department of Public Enterprise declares: 'there is no getting away from the fact that for some sectors, globalisation is becoming both a threat and an opportunity . . . No sector is immune from such competition . . . The best antidote to the challenge posed by external competitors in the domestic market is to be as competitive as possible.'[56] Globalisation is thus presented in highly deterministic terms. In turn, this reflects a tendency to reify the concept: it is *globalisation* that is the agent of change. This is reflected in such claims as that globalisation '*requires* the Irish economy to perform to the highest standards'[57] and is '*driving* moves towards regulatory reform' (emphases added).[58] Indeed, the NCC states simply: 'Globalisation will determine policy choices.'[59]

This is not to imply that the role of the Irish state is no longer seen as relevant. For instance, while the NESC stated in *Strategy into the 21st Century* that globalisation has 'profound effects' and has 'brought to the fore the importance of achieving national competitiveness', it also emphasised the crucial role of the state (not least through social partnership) in mediating globalisation. It therefore argued that the successful state acts not only as a 'facilitator' but also 'in a proactive manner and regularly as a joint partner'.[60] Thus, while globalisation is presented as driving a shift towards economic competitiveness in Ireland, this is not in turn articulated in terms of stark neo-liberalism.

It should be noted, though, that while Irish policy-makers frequently appeal to globalisation as an external economic imperative within the domestic context, it is articulated in rather different terms to international audiences. In particular, Irish politicians have been rather more equivocal about globalisation on the international stage. At an international conference on health in 1997, minister of state Liz O'Donnell stated:

> Over recent years, some Governments in developed countries have suffered from what has been tersely but accurately called 'aid fatigue'. They point to demands at home as a reason for giving less to developing countries; they remark hopefully on forces of globalisation and private capital investment as a panacea that will lift all boats in all countries, rich or poor. It needs to be said, in blunt terms, that this attractive vision is at best an exaggeration, at worst untrue. Africa is a stark example of this fallacy of what might be termed Darwinian economics. Private aid flows to many developing countries have, it is true, increased notably in recent years but these have almost totally bypassed impoverished countries of Sub-Saharan Africa. Globalisation has made these countries not more prosperous but more marginalised.[61]

Critical though this clearly is of the content of 'actually existing globalisation', as it were, this has not translated into resisting globalisation *per se*. For, rather than rejecting globalisation, the strategy would seem to be one of steering globalisation in a more defensible direction. As Liz O'Donnell argued at the launch of the UN Human Development Report in 1998: 'Just as we gain from globalisation, so also do we have a responsibility for ensuring that it is based on foundations of fairness and equity. And it cannot be based on firm foundations if half the world is excluded from these benefits.'[62] Indeed, globalisation is often presented as the *only* solution to such problems. As Bertie Ahern told the United Nations in 2003:

> Fair and open international trade is essential for global peace and prosperity . . . I understand the frustration of those who consider themselves unfairly treated in global markets. But if we turn our back on the multi-

lateral trading system, and allow trade and investment to be diverted and distorted by bilateral and regional arrangements, we will damage, perhaps irreparably, the best tool available to us to make serious inroads into poverty and to raise standards of living on a global basis.[63]

Here globalisation is presented as an economic reality that can nevertheless be shaped. Similarly, in an address to the IMF and the World Bank, Charlie McCreevy emphasised the need for 'managing globalisation in more positive ways' and argued: 'There is a very great deal to be done to create a more prosperous, secure and equitable world ... The Bank and the Fund are successes, not failures, despite some popular scepticism. However, we need to do more to get across to the public what we are doing.'[64] Thus, while globalisation is not represented as unambiguously positive (as in the domestic context), it is nevertheless articulated as something that can (and indeed must) be shaped to benefit all. In contrast to the domestic context, then, globalisation is presented as contingent upon the strategies of political actors.[65]

Indeed, in some contexts it is European integration rather than globalisation that is presented as an external pressure on economic policy-making. As with globalisation, this is consistently articulated in highly positive terms. As Bertie Ahern has told his party, for instance: 'After independence itself, the European Union more than any other factor gave Ireland its place among the nations.'[66] Similarly, he declared to the Dáil Éireann: 'If we had not joined Europe, much of what today we take for granted would have been an unimaginable dream.'[67] Like globalisation, moreover, European integration is articulated to domestic audiences as an external economic imperative. More specifically, it is the Stability and Growth Pact that is frequently appealed to as a non-negotiable external constraint. In their programme for government, for example, Fianna Fáil and the Progressive Democrats stated: 'The EU Stability and Growth Pact provides the overriding framework for our budgetary policy. Under the pact Ireland has given a sovereign commitment to keeping the finances of general government close to balance or in surplus.'[68] Yet, on the international stage, European integration is presented not as an external imperative but as a political project that must be made defensible. In turn, this is linked to calls to steer globalisation in a more defensible direction. Addressing the European Foundation Forum in 2002, for instance, Ahern argued:

> The European Union is *the* model for the regulation of economic globalisation that extends beyond trade ... From an Irish perspective, it is clear that Europe offers a new model of globalisation: one that goes far beyond free trade, constrains the naked use of economic and diplomatic power

... The great challenge is how the European model of society can be combined with the European model of economic and political globalisation ... The social dimension is an absolute requirement for a Europe that engages the trust of, and works to the benefit of, the people.[69]

As with globalisation, then, discourses of European integration simply do not translate into the espousal of stark neo-liberalism in Ireland. Rather, Irish politicians continue to emphasise the need for social justice, particularly to international audiences. But while neither globalisation nor European integration is seen to destroy the distributive and developmental capacities of the Irish state, the two are nevertheless presented either as constraining social and economic outcomes (to domestic audiences) or as the medium through which such outcomes can be realised (to international audiences).

The mediation of discourse

As the above discussion reveals, Ireland's political economy is frequently situated with respect to globalisation, but there is no one consistently articulated discourse of globalisation. Rather, the concept is deployed in different ways in different contexts, and on occasion it is European integration that is presented as an external pressure. If appeals to globalisation simply reflected an external 'reality', we would not expect such discursive variation to occur. This suggests that such discourses are in large part independent of the 'reality' they purport to represent. As discussed in chapter 6, there is in fact little evidence to show that the Irish economy is indeed subject to the competitive pressures of 'globalisation'. What this suggests is that globalisation as a source of external compulsion is in significant part a (discursive) construction.[70]

Yet while globalisation discourse(s) do not simply reflect the material 'fact' of globalisation, this does not mean that they float freely. For, while there are strong *a priori* reasons to suggest that discourse always matters, this can tell us little about why particular discourses are successful whereas others are not.[71] In other words, actors always interpret their environment, but why is it that they do so in one way but not in another? This highlights the need to consider not only *how* globalisation discourse(s) are used (as discussed above), but also *why* they have come to the fore. In turn, this points to the need for analysis of the relationship between discourse(s) and the broader economic, political and cultural environment in which they are constituted.

While a number of authors have sought to address this issue,[72] a particularly useful framework is provided by Vivien Schmidt. Schmidt identifies two dimensions of discourse: the ideational and the interactive. In its ideational dimension, discourse performs two functions: a cognitive (by delineating what is logical and necessary) and a normative (by delineating what is desirable and appropriate). In its interactive dimension, discourse also performs two functions: a coordinative (by enabling elites to construct a new policy programme) and a communicative (by persuading the general public of a programme's appropriateness and legitimacy). For discourses to be successful they need to perform all four functions: they must not only provide convincing solutions to problems (the cognitive function) but also appeal to national values (the normative function), provide the basis for elite coordination (the coordinative function) and be translated into a common language capable of convincing the general public of a programme's merits (the communicative function).[73] Here we shall consider each of these discursive elements in turn.

The cognitive function

Despite the obvious difficulties in establishing what political actors actually *believe* (as opposed to what they *say* they believe),[74] it is nevertheless possible to glean some insights into the 'cognitive' element of globalisation discourse in Ireland. In interviews, senior decision-makers and opinion-formers were keen to emphasise the role of globalisation in Ireland's economic transformation. Indeed, globalisation was consistently seen to have had a 'huge' impact on the Irish economy. In turn, this was perceived to have important policy-making implications – not least in terms of the need to prioritise competitiveness. As one senior civil servant noted, in the early stages of social partnership 'the focus was very on the domestic'. In more recent years, though, he points to the 'issue of globalisation', with 'much greater realisation that we are competing with countries in Europe, in Asia'. Other senior civil servants agreed that policy has 'absolutely' been driven by the need to compete on global markets, with one describing policy as having been 'driven very much ... towards grasping the potential that globalisation represents'.[75]

While policy-makers were adamant that globalisation has had an enormous impact on the Irish economy, they were less clear as to how the concept might be defined. In the words of one senior civil servant: 'If you asked me to define globalisation I'd have to scratch my head

... But to the extent that I have any sense as to what globalisation is about it is co-operating much more in a world market, we're world competitors, and as a consequence the international companies/ organisations play a larger role.' Other interviewees pointed to Ireland's openness, attracting FDI, the speed of communications, 'the integration of the European market and international trade agreements and things like that'. At the same time, interviewees also seemed to define globalisation in terms of what it is *not*. Globalisation is 'not Ireland' (and, indeed, 'not Britain'). Rather, it seems to represent the 'rest of the world' – and particularly the US. For example, when asked about the impact of globalisation on Ireland, one senior civil servant said: 'There was a saying here in the past that if Britain sneezes Ireland catches a cold. Now it's a bit like the rest of the world, if America sneezes we feel it here.' Another senior civil servant referred to 'the US, globally you know'.[76] In this sense, the concept of globalisation appears to act as something of a cognitive filter through which Irish policy-makers make sense of the complex world in which they live.

It is worth noting that ideas about globalisation may have cognitive resonance with Irish policy-makers because these ideas feed into existing discourses. Interviewees were keen to note that Ireland has long been dependent upon the outside world due to the small and open nature of the economy. Policy-makers have thus been 'very conscious' of developments in other countries, 'even before they invented the term "globalisation"'. The cognitive power of ideas about globalisation and competitiveness are further reinforced by the fact that Irish policy-makers are exposed to them so frequently.[77] Such ideas have become increasingly influential on the European (and, indeed, the international) stage.[78] In interviews, intellectual links with bodies such as the OECD, the World Bank and (in particular) the EU were felt to have played an important role in shaping the Irish policy agenda. As one interviewee noted: 'big ideas, small ideas have been imported and brought back home and applied'.[79] Such intellectual links may also reinforce the dual commitment to economic strength and social justice in Ireland. A European Commission representative outlined the Commission's own philosophy regarding competitiveness and social justice: 'The two of them are linked together ... You can't actually do all you want to do on to do on social cohesion unless you have the wherewithal to do it, and that comes from your competitiveness.' The fact that Irish policy-makers have tended to pursue a positive and constructive role towards Europe may, in turn, mean that they have been particularly open to such ideas.[80]

The normative function

As Schmidt notes, if discourses are to be successful they cannot rely on their cognitive function alone. Rather, they must also contain a normative element and, in particular, must resonate with underlying values. This indeed appears to be the case with respect to globalisation and European integration in Ireland. In particular, they seem to feed into pre-existing discourses of nationalism and national identity. As noted earlier, the principal goal of Irish nationalism since the 1960s has been to 'reap the benefits from full economic participation in the world economy'.[81] In the words of one senior decision-maker: 'We want to achieve things for Ireland so it's very much a national [focus], that's what we're interested in, that's where we get satisfaction, from being successful for Ireland.'[82]

Rather than undermining national sovereignty, then, both European integration and globalisation were seen by interviewees to provide significant opportunities for Ireland. In political terms, the Republic's membership of Europe was cited as particularly crucial. In the words of one senior civil servant, this enabled Ireland to 'escape from the shadow of Britain' and become an equal on the international stage. Another argued: 'Our membership of the European Union has given us a sense of confidence in ourselves but it has also given us a certain standing with other external bodies.' While European integration was also seen as important in economic terms, it was globalisation that was seen as particularly important in this respect. In turn, this was attributed to Irish policy-makers' positive attitude towards globalisation. In the words of one senior civil servant, globalisation has had 'a *huge* impact here, and it has a huge and favourable impact because we have embraced it and opened up to it'. Another described globalisation as a 'hugely powerful force here that we have turned to our advantage'. Still another declared: 'if it is globalising financial markets, globalising investment, yes please we'll have it thank you'.[83]

Existing national values in Ireland can also help explain the dual commitment to economic strength and social justice. As the European Commission representative argued, the 'sense of levelling economic prowess with a level of social responsibility sits very well on the Irish mentality'. In particular, he pointed to the role of Christian values in shaping this:

> I suppose that you could – without being too sanctimonious – [point to] the sort of Christian morality that underpins decision making . . . we're talking about an ethos that has been ingrained in Irish society over

hundreds of years and did come from the Catholic background . . . I think there's a feeling that economic development of itself is not a sufficient goal, that unless all this economic prowess can pay off in terms of improvement of the quality of life of ordinary people then it doesn't stand up on its own . . . So prosperity . . . stands up very well here and some people have prospered enormously. But there's also a feeling that according as we prosper we owe it to our fellow man to ensure that people are not left in the gutter, that people are helped along through a form of social solidarity.

Similarly, a very senior civil servant pointed to 'a set of implicit shared values which would be based on some sort of common good public interest model'. In turn, he highlighted the role of Catholic values in shaping this emphasis upon social solidarity.[84]

The coordinative function

Alongside these cognitive and normative elements, Schmidt suggests that discourses must also perform a coordinative function by providing a common language, vision and framework through which elites can debate and deliberate over policy programmes.[85] In the Irish case, a number of interviewees pointed to the high level of consensus in the overall policy approach. In the words of one senior civil servant: 'There are occasional head-bangers who want to go with their line and they tend to stick out of the system rather than stick into the system . . . you don't get civil servant A fighting with civil servant B over some issue or policy or ideology, it just doesn't happen.' This consensus was widely perceived to be driven by the need to achieve economic prosperity – and, more specifically, to avoid economic crisis. As one senior policy-maker argued:

There is just a very good national focus here which we didn't come to quickly but which the lessons of the 1980s told us that we had to be internationally competitive, we had to be cost competitive but we had to be competitive in education, in productivity performance, in creating all the conditions that would attract foreign investment and having attracted, hold it and have it added to and deepened and increased in value . . . There is here a much broader and more soundly based national consensus than you will find in any location and what drives it is the crisis points of the '50s and the '80s. That is embedded in the public psyche.

Crucially, this sense of crisis has also enabled the government to garner support from societal groups – most notably the social partners – for the new policy agenda from 1987. For, as Schmidt writes:

no amount of discourse will succeed in promoting a new policy paradigm where it does not address the interests of societal groups, in particular powerful groups. This could simply mean giving voice to such interests. But more likely it also means attempting to overcome entrenched interests, by altering perceptions of interest not only cognitively, by arguing that change is necessary and in the best (material) interests of all, but also normatively, by arguing that change is in the public interest (or common good) and therefore the appropriate thing to do.[86]

So it has been the case with social partnership in Ireland. As noted in chapter 4, both business and unions had traditionally been committed to free collective bargaining. While they had participated in the national understandings of the 1970s, the lack of a shared perspective on issues such as inflation made the agreements increasingly harder to sustain. However, by 1987 there was a growing sense of crisis on both sides. As one representative from the Irish Business and Employers Confederation (IBEC)[87] recalled:

> I suppose the original driver would have been the problems, the awful conditions, in the early to mid-1980s... you had the conundrum that although during that period export growth was relatively strong, jobs were not being delivered, emigration was still high and fundamentally confidence in the economy was weak. So it was an acknowledgement that... a coherent business voice was important.[88]

From the unions' perspective, rising unemployment had undermined their position in the labour market and growing wage dispersion threatened to undermine the cohesion and solidarity of the movement. Many leading unionists therefore saw a return to the national stage as the only way to prevent a further decline in power.[89]

Increasingly, the need to secure the social partners' consent for macro-economic policy has been articulated in terms of the competitive imperatives of globalisation rather than crisis. For example, as Bertie Ahern told the trade unions in 2003:

> While the Irish economy is doing a lot better than most of our partners, the fact is that our achievements are vulnerable. We are a highly globalised economy. That means there is much in our economic performance which is heavily influenced by decisions made elsewhere... We cannot ignore the pressure points that now exist in the economy. Our fiscal position has tightened and so has our range of choices. Now we must temper our expectations and moderate our behaviour to conform with economic reality.[90]

At the same time, this has also been presented in terms of the need to achieve social justice. This dual commitment to economic and social issues has, in turn, offered the means to reconcile the (traditionally competing) aims of business and unions. Indeed, the Irish Congress of Trade Unions (ICTU) explicitly identifies both social justice and economic prosperity as key priorities.[91] Similarly, IBEC has declared: 'The days when social and economic objectives were perceived as competing with rather than complementing each other should be consigned to the past.'[92] Yet it is important not to overstate the extent of this (rather uneasy) alliance in Ireland. Increasingly, the unions have argued that too much emphasis is placed upon competitiveness rather than social justice.[93] Business, by contrast, have urged that it is the former rather than the latter that has 'slipped off the national agenda'.[94] In interviews it was widely felt that the social partnership approach is becoming increasingly tenuous because of this growing disparity in aims. In the words of one senior civil servant, competitiveness and social justice 'were very closely entangled when you had significant unemployment, you could see that there was a direct connection. Now that's less obvious so it is more redistribution rather than attacking social disadvantage through growth. So I do think there is a sense of growing detachment between the two sides of that coin.'[95] As in the 1970s, this lack of a shared perspective between business and unions may make the current policy paradigm harder to sustain.

The communicative function

Yet, even if discourses are able to persuade policy-makers and powerful interests of a policy programme's merits, they must also be capable of convincing the general public. It is here that the 'communicative' function of discourse comes into play.[96] Indeed, as Hay and Rosamond note, whether or not policy-makers deem particular discourses to be true, they may perceive them as highly useful. The 'logic of no alternative' associated with both globalisation and European integration is of use precisely because it provides decision-makers with the perfect alibi for policies (such as welfare retrenchment) that would otherwise prove highly unpopular with electorates.[97] One senior civil servant alluded to this when he remarked: 'I think maybe we're inclined to invoke Europe . . . when actually the lines of policy are what we would do anyway.'[98]

In turn, for such discourses to be successful they must have resonance with voters' perceptions and values. For Hay and Rosamond, globalisation is thus unlikely to be articulated as a non-negotiable external constraint in countries in which it has negative connotations. In France, for instance, globalisation – which is closely associated with Americanisation – is presented as a political project that must be resisted. Instead, it is European integration rather than globalisation that is invoked as an external imperative within the French context. In the UK, by contrast, it is European integration rather than globalisation that is more negatively conceived and, as such, it is the latter rather than the former that is appealed to as a non-negotiable constraint.[99]

In the Irish case, a rather complex picture emerges. As outlined earlier, *both* globalisation *and* European integration are appealed to as external economic imperatives within the domestic Irish context. However, this reinforces rather than undermines Hay and Rosamond's argument, for in Ireland *both* globalisation *and* European integration are conceived in highly positive terms. This is not just by Irish policymakers (see above) but, crucially, by the Irish voters themselves. The Irish electorate has traditionally been highly pro-European, with 83 per cent (of a turnout of over 70 per cent) in favour of joining Europe in the referendum of 1972.[100] This positive attitude has been reflected in a number of Eurobarometer surveys: for example, 82 per cent of Irish

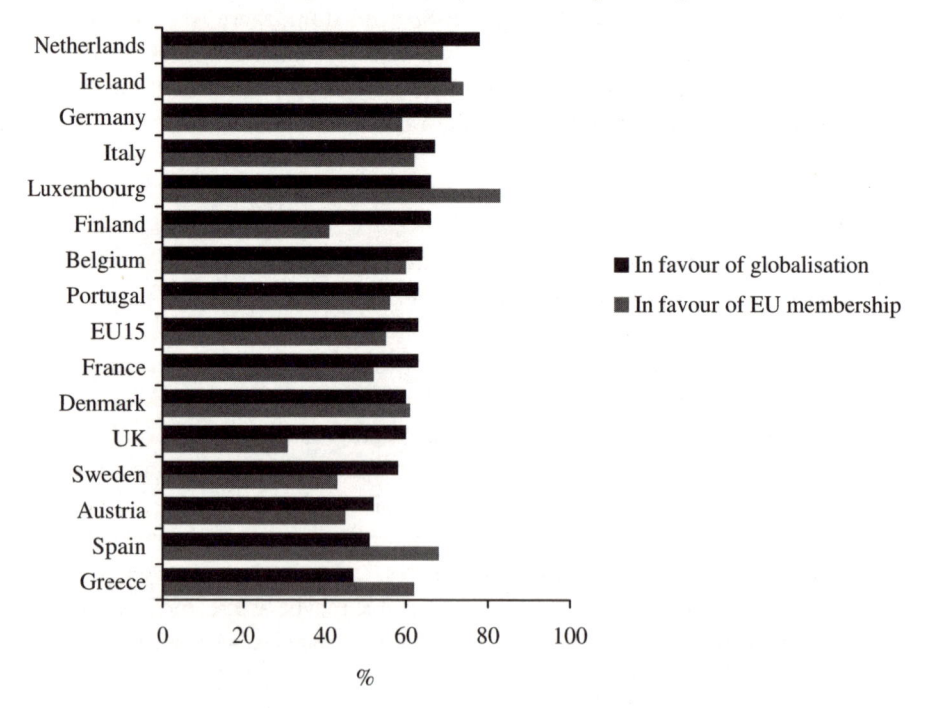

Figure 7.1 Public opinion in the EU of globalisation and European membership

Source: Eurobarometer, *Globalisation* (Brussels: European Commission, 2003), p. 17; Eurobarometer, *Public Opinion in the European Union, October/November 2002* (Brussels: European Commission, 2002), p. 32.

respondents in 2002 felt that Ireland had benefited from membership of the EU (the highest in the EU), with 74 per cent supporting Ireland's membership (the second highest in the EU) and 50 per cent expressing attachment to the Union (the fourth highest in the EU).[101] While rather less research has been undertaken with respect to globalisation, one 2003 survey found that 71 per cent of Irish people were in favour of globalisation's development (the second highest in the EU), 66 per cent were optimistic about the impact for themselves and their families should globalisation intensify (the highest in the EU), and 48 per cent believed that the Irish economy was 'suited to the development of the global economy' (with a further 28 per cent identifying the Irish economy as 'too closed') (see also figure 7.1).[102]

This is not to imply, however, that globalisation and European integration remain uncontested in Ireland. For instance, anti-globalisation protestors have staged a series of protests on issues such as civil liberties and privatisation. In interviews, senior policy-makers expressed concern that such anti-globalisation sentiment was increasingly shared by wider elements of the Irish community. This was, in part, seen to relate to the 'paper tiger' discourse (discussed in chapter 2), with one senior civil servant commenting: 'the biggest cliché in the last few years is this area or this group [saying], "we never saw the Celtic tiger"'. Similarly, while the Irish public generally remains positive towards European integration, Eurobarometer surveys also reveal that their attitudes are becoming more volatile.[103] The Irish electorate's rejection of the Nice Treaty on enlargement in 2001 is a particularly striking example of how their euro-enthusiasm cannot be taken for granted. While this did not appear to represent a rejection of further integration *per se*,[104] it was nevertheless perceived as highly embarrassing by the Irish government. Indeed, the 2001 referendum result may reflect a growing sense of cynicism towards the Irish establishment itself – not least due to the series of corruption scandals in the 1990s. As one senior civil servant remarked, the Nice Treaty was supported by the entire establishment – including the unions – and 'for some reason it got up people's noses'.[105]

In turn, this may mean that appeals to the imperatives of globalisation and European integration are becoming increasingly problematic in Ireland. European integration in particular is no longer simply articulated as 'that which is used to defend' but increasingly as 'that which must be defended'. As Fianna Fáil and the Progressive Democrats urged in their *Programme for Government*, for instance: 'Any perception, either within the Union or outside, that Ireland was other than a fully committed member would be deeply damaging both to our ability to promote our interests in the Union and to our economic development. We have no doubt that there is no alternative to being a fully engaged member of the EU.'[106] In turn, there seems to be a reversion to the narrative of crisis in order to justify unpopular policies – not the least of these being spending restraint. As Charlie McCreevy argued in his 2003 budget speech, for example: 'There are those who want us to forget the lessons of the past. They want me to announce major spending increases, irrespective of the economic situation. However, my view is that the responsible policy is to take a moderate route and to take the necessary decisions now so that we ensure growth in the medium term.'[107]

It is also worth noting that the electoral context can help explain why there has been no shift towards stark neo-liberalism in Ireland. The Irish party system has never been based upon a clear-cut divide between left and right; the traditional social cleavage is that of nationalism rather than class. Irish voters have tended to favour a moderate rather than extreme approach to social and economic policy: indeed, during the 1980s and 1990s centre-right parties won an average of four fifths of the vote, compared to two fifths in all other West European countries combined.[108] In interviews, it was thus felt to be 'highly unlikely that an extremist policy platform would ever come to power here'.[109] Rather, both the main parties, Fianna Fáil and Fine Gael, have tended to lean towards the centre of the political spectrum. But it is Fianna Fáil that can genuinely be described as a 'catch-all' party. While Fine Gael tends to attract more support from large farmers and the professional classes, the level of support for Fianna Fáil across the board is quite striking (see figure 7.2). In turn, this has been reflected in Fianna Fáil's ideology. From the start, it has presented itself as *the* party of the Irish people, not only in territorial terms but also in social terms.[110] While the former element has declined, the latter has remained an important part of the party's discourse – not least in terms of the dual commitment to economic strength and social justice. As the taoiseach, Bertie Ahern, declared in 2000: 'We are not a party whose appeal is sectional. We remain committed to working for all parts of the population in all regions of the country to create a better Ireland for all . . . A truly socially inclusive Ireland is the only Ireland acceptable to Fianna Fáil.'[111]

Yet Ireland's electoral context also appears to be changing over time. While Fianna Fáil has traditionally dominated the Irish party system,[112] since the 1980s its electoral hegemony has increasingly come

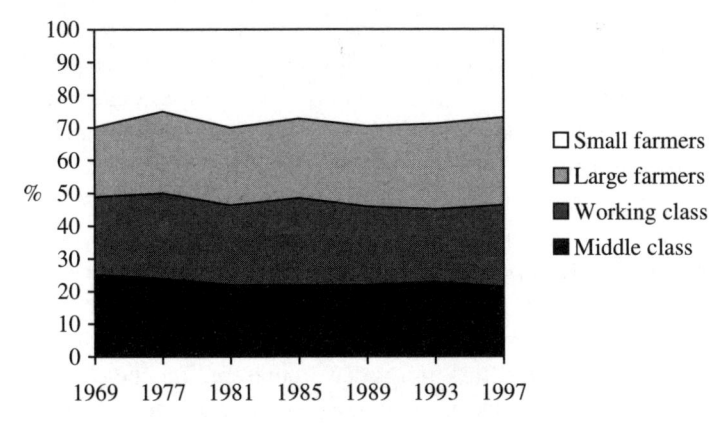

Figure 7.2 Opinion poll support for Fianna Fáil by social group, 1969–97

Source: Coakley, J. and M. Gallagher (eds.), *Politics in the Republic of Ireland* (London: Routledge, 1999), p. 373.

under threat. For the first time, in 1989, Fianna Fáil felt it necessary to form a coalition (with the Progressive Democrats) in order to stay in government. Since then, the party has continued to form coalitions (with the Labour Party in 1992-4 and the Progressive Democrats since 1997). Signs of fragmentation in the party system since the 1980s are also evident in the rise of new parties (not the least of these being the Progressive Democrats).[113] In interviews, moreover, it was felt that class issues are beginning to grow in importance in Ireland, in part due to Ireland's rapid growth with inequality. In the words of one senior civil servant: 'the traditional left–right debate which has been fairly muted in Ireland is probably beginning to emerge'. While it is certainly important not to overstate these developments,[114] it once again suggests that the current policy paradigm may become more difficult to sustain.

Conclusion

This chapter has examined the development of political discourses in Ireland. In so doing, it has first placed the ideas that inform current Irish policy-making in historical perspective, pointing in particular to the narrative of crisis in both the 1950s and 1980s in helping to alter the trajectory of the Irish state. The chapter has then focused in on the development of the current policy paradigm, which has increasingly entailed an emphasis upon achieving economic competitiveness. It is within this context that ideas about globalisation have come to the fore, for globalisation is seen (at least within the domestic context) as a non-negotiable external constraint that drives the need for competitiveness in Ireland. But this is by no means the only way in which globalisation is articulated. In the international context it is presented as a political project that must be defended and also made defensible. In some cases, moreover, it is European integration rather than globalisation that is presented as an external economic imperative. This discursive variation in turn suggests that such discourses are (at least in part) independent of the external 'reality' they purport to represent. Yet the chapter has not sought to claim that such discourses have arisen from thin air. Rather, it has examined in detail why discourses of globalisation and competitiveness have taken hold in Ireland, looking in particular at the 'cognitive', 'normative', 'coordinative' and 'communicative' functions identified by Schmidt. In so doing, the chapter has suggested that the current policy paradigm may be become increasingly difficult to sustain, for the consensus over the main tenets of economic and social policy appears to be fragmenting over time.

Notes

1 See for instance M. Blyth, ' "Any more bright ideas?" The ideational turn of comparative political economy', *Comparative Politics*, (1997), pp. 229–51; C. Hay and D. Marsh, 'Introduction: demystifying globalisation', in C. Hay and D. Marsh (eds), *Demystifying Globalisation* (London: Macmillan, 2000), pp. 1–17; R. Heffernan, ' "The possible as the art of politics": understanding consensus politics', *Political Studies*, 50: 4 (2002), pp. 742–60; B. Rosamond, 'Imagining the European economy: "competitiveness" and the social construction of "Europe" as an economic space', *New Political Economy*, 7: 2 (2002), pp. 157–77; V. A. Schmidt and C. Radaelli, 'Policy change and discourse in Europe: conceptual and methodological issues', *West European Politics*, 27: 2 (2004), pp. 183–210; G. Skogstad, 'Ideas, paradigms and institutions: agricultural exceptionalism in the European Union and the United States', *Governance: An International Journal of Policy and Administration*, 11: 4 (1998), pp. 463–90; J. I. Walsh, 'When do ideas matter? Explaining the successes and failures of Thatcherite ideas', *Comparative Political Studies*, 33: 4 (2000), pp. 483–516.
2 C. Hay and B. Rosamond, 'Globalisation, European integration and the discursive construction of economic imperatives', *Journal of European Public Policy*, 9: 2 (2002), p. 148.

3 Ibid., p. 163; B. Rosamond, 'Discourses of globalisation and the social construction of European identities', *Journal of European Public Policy*, 6: 4 (1999), p. 667.
4 C. Ó Gráda, *A Rocky Road: The Irish Economy Since the 1920s* (Manchester: Manchester University Press, 1997), p. 55.
5 Cited in J. Lee, *Ireland, 1912–85: Politics and Society* (Cambridge and New York: Cambridge University Press, 1989), p. 127.
6 N. Collins and T. Cradden, *Irish Politics Today* (Manchester: Manchester University Press, 1997), p. 11.
7 E. de Valera, 'Press statement, 17 April 1926', in M. Moynihan (ed.), *Speeches and Statements by Eamon de Valera, 1917–73* (Dublin: Gill & Macmillan, 1980), p. 131.
8 P. Neary, 'The failure of economic nationalism', in C. Ó Gráda (ed.), *The Economic Development of Ireland Since 1870* (Aldershot: Edward Elgar, 1994), p. 43; R. Breen, D. Hannan, D. Rottman and C. T. Whelan, *Understanding Contemporary Ireland: State, Class and Development in the Republic of Ireland* (Dublin: Gill & Macmillan, 1990), p. 28; K. A. Kennedy, T. Giblin and D. McHugh, *The Economic Development of Ireland in the Twentieth Century* (London: Routledge, 1988), p. 40.
9 Cited in R. Fanning, *Independent Ireland* (Dublin: Helecon, 1983), p. 113.
10 Ó Gráda, *A Rocky Road*, p. 49.
11 P. Keatinge and B. Laffan, 'Ireland: a small open polity', in J. Coakley and M. Gallagher (eds), *Politics in the Republic of Ireland* (London: Routledge, 1999), p. 322.
12 For detailed discussion of the discursive construction of crisis see C. Hay, 'Narrating crisis: the discursive construction of the "winter of discontent"', *Sociology*, 30: 2 (1996), pp. 253–77.
13 Ó Gráda, *A Rocky Road*, pp. 25–7.
14 Cited in ibid., p. 57.
15 Ibid., pp. 49–50.
16 P. Sweeney, *The Celtic Tiger: Ireland's Continuing Economic Miracle* (Dublin: Oak Tree Press, 1999), p. 38.
17 Breen et al., *Understanding Contemporary Ireland*, p. 4; Neary, 'The failure of economic nationalism', p. 44.
18 Fanning argues that Whitaker's influence was highlighted by one finance minister's claim, when quoting from budget speeches from four different ministers in the 1950s, that 'the same man must have written them all'. See Fanning, *Independent Ireland*, pp. 193–4.
19 T. K. Whitaker, *Economic Development* (Dublin: Stationery Office, 1958), pp. 2–5.
20 C. Hay, 'Crisis and the structural transformation of the state: interrogating the process of change', *British Journal of Politics and International Relations*, 1: 3 (1999), p. 323.
21 Fanning, *Independent Ireland*, p. 194.
22 For example, in 1932 Lemass told one new recruit in 1932 that his specific policies were not sacrosanct and 'the last thing I want is a yes man'. Cited in Lee, *Ireland, 1912–85*, p. 189.

23 M. Hickman, *Ireland and the European Community* (London: PNL Press, 1990), p. 6.
24 Breen et al., *Understanding Contemporary Ireland*, p. 38.
25 Ibid., p. 128.
26 B. Laffan, 'The European Union and Ireland', in N. Collins (ed.), *Political Issues in Ireland Today* (Manchester: Manchester University Press, 1999), p. 89. Similarly, one senior civil servant argued that by joining Europe 'we escaped from the shadow of Britain'.
27 See for instance R. Mac Sharry and P. White, *The Making of the Celtic Tiger: The Inside Story of Ireland's Boom Economy* (Cork: Mercier Press, 2000), p. 44; W. K. Roche, 'Pay determination, the state and the politics of industrial relations', in T. V. Murphy and W. K. Roche (eds), *Irish Industrial Relations in Practice* (Dublin: Oak Tree Press, 1994), p. 172. Interviewees also emphasised the importance of the NESC in this process. As one senior servant recalled: 'in a sense it acted as a catalyst in this period.'
28 NESC, *A Strategy for Development 1986-90: Growth, Employment and Fiscal Balance* (Dublin: National Economic and Social Council, 1986), p. 321.
29 Interviews.
30 Mac Sharry and White, *The Making of the Celtic Tiger*, p. 44.
31 G. Taylor, 'Hailing with an invisible hand: a "cosy" political dispute amid the rise of neoliberal politics in modern Ireland', *Government and Opposition*, 37: 4 (2002), p. 511.
32 C. Haughey, 'Confidence motion, Dail Eireann, 22 October 1986', in M. Mansergh (ed.), *The Speeches and Statements of Charles J. Haughey* (Dublin: Mercier Press, 1986), p. 1162.
33 Interviews.
34 Cited in Mac Sharry and White, *The Making of the Celtic Tiger*, p. 77.
35 Ibid., pp. 68–70.
36 For Taylor, the PNR marked the beginning of the end of crisis in Ireland. In contrast, Hay defines crisis *itself* as a 'moment of decisive intervention'. He writes: 'the struggle to impose a new trajectory on the structures of the state is won and lost *not* in the wake of the crisis moment but in the very process in which the crisis is constituted'. In this sense, crisis represents 'dusk and dawn'. However, Hay therefore seems to imply that a crisis narrative necessitates rather than facilitates decisive intervention. Crisis may better be conceived as presenting a window of opportunity for decisive intervention, the outcome of which is nevertheless contingent. See Taylor, 'Hailing with an invisible hand', p. 511; Hay, 'Narrating crisis', pp. 255, 275.
37 NESC, *A Strategy for Development*, p. 147.
38 Government of Ireland, *Programme for Competitiveness and Work* (Dublin: Stationery Office, 1994), p. 5.
39 NCC, *Annual Competitiveness Report 2000* (Dublin: Forfás, 2000), p. i.
40 Interviews.
41 B. Ahern, 'Speech by the taoiseach', meeting of the Fianna Fáil Parliamentary Party (27 September 2000).

42 Forfás, *Annual Report 2002* (Dublin: Forfás, 2003), p. 5.
43 Bertie Ahern, 'Foreword by an taoiseach', in NCC, *Annual Competitiveness Report 2003* (Dublin: Forfás, 2003), p. iii.
44 Government of Ireland, *Partnership 2000 for Inclusion, Employment and Competitiveness* (Dublin: Stationery Office, 1997), p. 37.
45 Interviews.
46 For further discussion of these issues see C. Hay and N. J. Smith, 'Horses for courses? The political discourse of globalisation and European integration in the UK and Ireland', *West European Politics*, 28: 1, pp. 124–58.
47 It is difficult to establish when the term 'globalisation' was first used in Irish policy discourse. The Culliton report devoted a small section to the 'globalisation of industry' and pointed to 'a new form of global enterprise' in which 'decision-making and management structures, as well as other key corporate functions, are no longer integrated in one country'. J. Culliton, *A Time for Change: Industrial Policy for the 1990s – Report of the Industrial Policy Review Group* (Dublin: Stationery Office, 1992), p. 29.
48 Hay and Smith, 'Horses for courses?', pp. 136–7.
49 Government of Ireland, *Programme for Competitiveness and Work*, p. 57.
50 Government of Ireland, *Partnership 2000*, p. 67.
51 Government of Ireland, *Programme for Prosperity and Fairness* (Dublin: Stationery Office, 2000), p. 47.
52 L. O'Donnell, 'Address by minister of state with special responsibility for overseas development assistance and human rights', annual Christmas lecture on international relations, Dublin City University (18 December 2001).
53 M. Harney, 'Remarks by an tánaiste', plenary meeting of the Programme for Prosperity and Fairness (25 July 2002).
54 Fianna Fáil, *A Lot Done: More to Do – Fianna Fáil Manifesto 2002–7* (Dublin: Fianna Fáil, 2002), pp. 29–30.
55 Department of Enterprise, Trade and Employment, *Statement of National Trade Policy* (Dublin: Department of Enterprise, Trade and Employment, 1998), p. 21.
56 Department of Public Enterprise, 'Statement of strategy' (2001), http://222.gov.ie/tec/publications/statements/dpe7.htm.
57 Government of Ireland, *Partnership 2000*, p. 67.
58 Department of Enterprise, Trade and Employment, *Statement of National Trade Policy*, p. 21.
59 NCC, 'The competitiveness challenge: council summary statement – overview' (1998), www.forfas.ie/ncc/reports/nccsum/overview.htm.
60 NESC, *Strategy into the 21st Century: Main Report* (Dublin: National Economic and Social Council, 1996), pp. 56–8.
61 L. O'Donnell, 'Address by minister of state at the Department of Foreign Affairs with special responsibility for development cooperation and human rights', international conference on sector wide approaches to health, Dublin (12 November 1997).
62 L. O'Donnell, 'Remarks by minister of state at the Department of Foreign Affairs with special responsibility for human rights and development

cooperation', launch of the UN Development Programme Human Development Report (9 September 1998). Similarly, Ireland's *Annual Report* to the IMF and World Bank in 2002 stated: 'The reform of the international financial architecture must be pursued in order to reduce the risks posed by financial globalisation and to ensure that its benefits are shared by all, including the poorest. See Government of Ireland, *Annual Report: Ireland's Participation in the World Bank and the International Monetary Fund* (Dublin: Government of Ireland, 2002).

63 B. Ahern, 'Statement by the taoiseach to the general debate', 58th General Assembly of the United Nations, New York (25 September 2003).

64 C. McCreevy, 'Statement by the governor of the IMF and World Bank for Ireland', joint annual discussion of the Boards of Governors of the IMF and World Bank (29 September 2002).

65 For further discussion of these issues see Hay and Smith, 'Horses for courses?', pp. 138–40.

66 B. Ahern, 'Speech at the opening of the 64th Fianna Fáil Ard Fheiss' (3 March 2000).

67 B. Ahern, 'Speech by the taoiseach on the 26th amendment of the constitution', Dáil Éireann, Dublin (10 September 2002).

68 Fianna Fáil and Progressive Democrats, *An Agreed Programme for Government Between Fianna Fáil and the Progressive Democrats* (Dublin: Fianna Fáil and Progressive Democrats, 2002), p. 7.

69 B. Ahern, 'Speech by the taoiseach: Europe makes a difference – challenges for the European social model', European Foundation Forum, Dublin Castle (29 August 2002).

70 Hay and Smith, 'Horses for courses?', pp. 150–2.

71 Radaelli and Schmidt contend: 'Discourse, just as any other factor, sometimes matters, sometimes does not in the explanation of policy change.' See C. M. Radaelli and V. A. Schmidt, 'Mapping the scope for discourse, Europeanisation and learning in policy change', *West European Politics*, 27: 2 (2004), p. 184. Yet, if we are to assume that actors always interpret their environment, then we must also assume that discourse *always* matters – including during periods of relative continuity (when dominant discourses may serve to constrain perceptions of what is politically possible, even when radical change may be appropriate). For example, as discussed earlier, the fact that Ireland retained its commitment to protectionism after World War II can largely be attributed to the continued dominance of nationalist discourse.

72 See for instance E. Bleich, 'Integrating ideas into policy-making analysis: frames and race policies in Britain and France', *Comparative Political Studies*, 35: 9 (2002), pp. 1054–76; M. Blyth, 'The transformation of the Swedish model: economic ideas, distributional conflict and institutional change', *World Politics*, 54 (2001), pp. 1–26; J. L. Campbell, 'Ideas, politics and public policy', *Annual Review of Sociology*, 28 (2002), pp. 21–38; P. A. Hall, 'Policy paradigms, social learning and the state: the case of economic policymaking in Britain', *Comparative Politics*, 25: 3 (1993), pp. 257–96; Heffernan, 'Understanding consensus politics',

pp. 742–60; J. K. Jacobsen, 'Much ado about ideas: the cognitive factor in economic policy', *World Politics*, 47: 2 (1995), pp. 283–310; Skogstad, 'Ideas, paradigms and institutions', pp. 463–90; Walsh, 'When do ideas matter?', pp. 483–516.
73 V. A. Schmidt, *The Futures of European Capitalism* (Oxford: Oxford University Press, 2002), pp. 277–89.
74 Clearly, the analysis of official documentation, press releases and speeches is particularly limited in this regard. While they can tell us a great deal about the 'interactive' dimension of discourse, they cannot really be seen as reliable sources when exploring the 'ideational' dimension. Semi-structured interviews – though still limited – seem more appropriate to the analysis of this latter dimension. In particular, they provide political actors with the opportunity to speak more informally and in their own words about their attitudes and beliefs with respect to specific issues. Further information on the semi-structured interviews undertaken for this research is provided in the introduction. For detailed discussion of the merits and limitations of semi-structured interviews to social science research, see A. Bryman, *Social Research Methods* (Oxford: Oxford University Press, 2001), pp. 312–33.
75 Interviews.
76 Interviews.
77 Traditionally, Irish civil servants and economists were heavily influenced by British policy paradigms, due to the strong historical links and the common language. However, the Republic has become more intellectually open in recent years, in large part due to its membership of Europe. In the words of one senior economist: 'you've had a feedback effect I think in terms of European policy, European ways of looking at things, onto the domestic policy front'.
78 See for instance A. Verdun, *European Responses to Globalisation and Financial Market Integration: Perceptions of Economic and Monetary Union in Britain, France and Germany* (Basingstoke: Palgrave, 2002); C. Randzio-Plath, 'What future for the economic policy of the Union: speech to the Brussels Economic Forum, 2 May 2002' (Brussels: European Commission, 2002).
79 For instance, one senior ESRI economist pointed to the EU's impact on shaping the wider debate on social issues. Prior to the late 1980s, he argues, the poverty issue 'didn't have a real existence, it had just become an ideological thing'. However, in the late 1980s individuals within the ESRI decided to analyse the social impact of state policies on Irish households. By chance, they found out about and subsequently joined a wider European Commission project on poverty. This, he argues, had a huge impact on the wider debate in Ireland since 'it actually quantified the nature of it and put it within a comparative European perspective'.
80 This is not to contend, however, that there has been a simple 'top-down' transfer of ideas. Rather, interviewees were keen to emphasise Ireland's own contribution in the transfer of ideas at European level. For example, the ESRI has been the co-ordinator of a 'major' EU project on school-

to-work transitions and has also done 'quite a bit of work' with the Ecofin directorate, the Social Affairs directorate and Eurostat. In this sense 'there's an interplay there that's going on all the time'. With Ireland's rapid economic growth, there has also been growing interest in the Irish model. In the words of one senior civil servant: 'We're beginning to talk to Europeans about using our model, even though if you go back to '87 we were importing a European model. What goes around comes around.' Interviewees also pointed to considerable interest in the Irish case from further afield, including the ASEAN countries.

81 Breen et al., *Understanding Contemporary Ireland*, p. 38.
82 Another argued: 'the fact of there being a strong national identity does mean something like the idea that the country has got to make its way in the world, that puts severe limits on what you can do in terms of wage growth, public services and so on'.
83 Interviews.
84 Interviews.
85 Schmidt, *The Futures of European Capitalism*, p. 210.
86 V. A. Schmidt, 'Democracy and discourse in an integrating Europe and a globalising world', *European Law Journal*, 6: 3 (2000), p. 287. Similarly, Blyth writes: 'under conditions of great uncertainty, such as times of severe economic dislocation, the politics of ideas becomes increasingly important. For under such conditions it is not obvious where agents' best interests may actually lie and therefore what type of institutions would best serve those interests.' Blyth, 'The transformation of the Swedish model', pp. 3–4.
87 The Confederation of Irish Employers and the Confederation of Irish Industry came together to form IBEC in 1993.
88 Interviews.
89 For a more detailed discussion see Roche, 'Pay determination, the state and the politics of industrial relations', pp. 170–8.
90 B. Ahern, 'Speech by the taoiseach', Biennial Conference of Congress (4 July 2003).
91 ICTU, 'Priorities' (2004), www.ictu.ie/html/programme/priority.html.
92 IBEC, *Social Policy in a Competitive Economy* (Dublin: Irish Business and Employers' Confederation, 2002), p. 3.
93 Indeed, at one trade union conference, the ICTU's general secretary, David Begg, said: 'John Bruton, when taoiseach [and Fine Gael leader], once famously replied to a question from a journalist about the peace process – "*F*** the Peace Process*". Being on the receiving end of so much rhetoric about competitiveness I must confess at times to similar feelings.' See D. Begg, 'Address to CIPD conference', CIPD conference, Galway (24 May 2002).
94 T. O'Sullivan, 'Employers focus on competitiveness', *Irish Times* (1 April 2002).
95 Interviews.
96 Schmidt, 'Democracy and discourse', pp. 288–9.
97 Hay and Rosamond, 'Globalisation and European integration', p. 158; see also C. Hay and M. Watson, 'The politics and discourse of globalisa-

tion: "sceptical" notes on the 1999 Reith lectures', *Political Quarterly*, 70: 4 (1999), p. 423.
98 Interviews.
99 Hay and Rosamond, 'Globalisation and European integration', pp. 159–64.
100 Keatinge and Laffan, 'Ireland: a small open polity', p. 323.
101 Eurobarometer, *Public Opinion in the European Union, October/November 2002* (Brussels: European Commission, 2002), pp. 27–34.
102 Eurobarometer, *Globalisation* (Brussels: European Commission, 2003), pp. 8–21.
103 See for instance Eurobarometer, *Irish Public Opinion and European Integration: Autumn 2002* (Brussels: European Commission, 2002).
104 A survey conducted by the European Commission representation in Ireland found that abstention (with a turnout of just 34 per cent) was the key feature of the electorate's behaviour. The turnout was much lower than at previous referendums – indeed, more than half who voted 'yes' to the Amsterdam Treaty in 1997 abstained in the Nice referendum. The most frequent explanation given for abstention was the lack of information, with just 8 per cent believing that they had 'a good understanding' of the treaty. For those who did vote, there was also a marked tendency to follow the maxim 'if you don't know, vote no'. See R. Sinnott, *Attitudes and Behaviour of the Irish Electorate in the Referendum on the Treaty of Nice: Executive Summary* (Dublin: Institute for the Study of Social Change, 2003), pp. i–vii. It should of course also be noted that the Irish electorate subsequently approved the Nice Treaty, in a referendum the following year.
105 Similarly, Fintan O'Toole argued in the *Irish Times* that the 'chance to bloody all their noses with a single swipe was far too good to miss'. F. O'Toole, 'Uneasy electorate gives the establishment a bloody nose', *Irish Times* (9 June 2001).
106 Fianna Fáil and Progressive Democrats, *An Agreed Programme for Government*, p. 4.
107 C. McCreevy, 'Budget 2003: financial statement of the minister for finance' (4 December 2002), www.budget.gov.ie/2003/speech03.asp.
108 P. Mair, 'The changing party system', in Coakley and Gallagher, *Politics in the Republic of Ireland*, p. 129.
109 Interviews.
110 See for instance N. Hardiman and C. T. Whelan, 'Values and political partisanship', in C. T. Whelan (ed.), *Values and Social Change in Ireland* (Dublin: Gill & Macmillan, 1994), p. 184.
111 Ahern, 'Speech at the opening of the 64th Fianna Fáil Ard Fheiss'. As one senior economist argued, Fianna Fáil 'still remains very much a populist party and, at least in terms of its ideology, it will still put a strong emphasis upon the developmental role of the state and the provision of public services and regional development and things like that . . . at least in terms of its ideology it's very strong on those'.
112 Indeed, the pattern of competition in Ireland has tended to reflect that of a two-party system, with Fianna Fáil on the one hand and the remain-

ing parties on the other. See Mair, 'The changing party system', pp. 136–7.
113 Sweeney, *The Celtic Tiger*, p. 120; Mair, 'The changing party system', pp. 145–9.
114 Indeed, Fianna Fáil's share of the vote increased from 39.3 to 41.5 per cent in the general election of 2002.

Conclusion

Rethinking 'globalisation'

While the concept of 'globalisation' is relatively new, the controversy that surrounds it is centuries old. At its heart, the globalisation debate is about the power of capitalism, and whether or not that power ultimately serves to determine the decisions and actions of national governments. But what *is* distinctive about the current era is the common perception that this debate has largely been won. Something called 'globalisation' is widely believed to have unleashed forces which are so strong that governments are left with little option but to pander to the needs of global capital. While there is still controversy about the ways in which governments should do this (for example, should they reduce costs, or enhance human capital?), it is globalisation that is ultimately seen to shape the terrain of social and political possibility.

But can the dynamics of change in contemporary political economies really be understood in these terms? This volume has argued that the concept of 'globalisation' can in fact reveal very little in the analysis of economic and political change. For, if the term is to have any meaning at all, it must refer to processes or tendencies that can be genuinely described as 'global'. There is little evidence to suggest that such tendencies exist. More than this, the focus on globalisation serves to obscure the actual processes of change producing social and political outcomes. For the concept invites reification, suggesting something that is *doing* rather than being *done*, in turn implying that social outcomes are predetermined by exogenous forces rather than contingent upon the conduct of human agents.

Herein lies the real power of globalisation: that is, in the very perception that it is driving change across the world. If political decision-makers believe that the alternatives available are restricted by exogenous global forces, then globalisation *has* in a sense 'won'. For it is the choices and actions of human actors that ultimately shape the social world in which we live, and these choices and actions are increasingly influenced by the perception that globalisation sets limits on what is possible. The discourse of globalisation, if not the reality of globalisation, thus has a powerful impact on social and political outcomes.

All of this highlights the need to examine critically not only *what* globalisation obscures (that is, the actual mechanisms of change producing political outcomes) but also *how* and *why* it does so (that is, the ways in which and reasons why globalisation discourse is used). This has been the task of the current volume. In so doing, it has emphasised the need to consider specific national contexts in order to understand the dynamics of change in contemporary political economies. While international economic pressures certainly provide part of the context in which national governments act, such pressures are in turn mediated by existing national institutional and cultural environments, and by the responses and strategies of political decision-makers themselves.

The Irish case

The volume has thus explored the utility of globalisation in the study of political economy through analysis of a specific country case study, that of the Irish Republic. As indicated, Ireland is perhaps the test case in the study of globalisation. Not only is the Republic hailed as the most globalised country in the world, but its newfound status as the 'Celtic tiger' is seen to demonstrate how nations can prosper under conditions of globalisation. By implication, if other countries are to follow Ireland's success, they too must submit to these exogenous global forces.

This book has sought to challenge such claims. It has argued that there is simply no evidence to suggest that the Irish economy is becoming 'globalised'. For, this would suggest that Ireland's patterns of trade and investment are becoming genuinely global in scope. This is clearly not the case. Instead, Ireland's trade and investment patterns are not only highly concentrated in geographical terms but are also highly nationally specific. In this sense, the Republic can certainly be characterised as an international economy (in that its trade and investment relations are concentrated within a limited number of specific countries) but it cannot be described as a 'global' one. Nor is this a particularly new development. Rather, the Irish economy has long been exposed and open, even during its protectionist phase. What has changed is not that Ireland has shifted from being a closed national economy to an open and 'global' one but that it is no longer dependent upon the UK. While some claim that Ireland is now dependent upon the US instead, it is the Netherlands (and not the US) that is now the single most important investor in the Irish economy. If anything, then, the Irish economy is becoming increasingly EU-European, but this is not translating into a wider process of 'globalisation'. And if the Irish Republic – supposedly the most globalised country in the world – is not in fact being globalised, then this suggests that other nations may not be, either.

Hence, to borrow Hirst and Thompson's argument, Ireland remains 'an open international economy that is still fundamentally characterised by exchange between relatively distinct national economies and in which many outcomes, such as the competitive performance of firms and sectors, are substantially determined by processes occurring at the national level'.[1] For, while Ireland's economic development has certainly been shaped by exogenous factors such as the rise in foreign direct investment, the Irish state has played – and continues to play – a central role in the economy. This is not least in the provision of a highly skilled and technologically adept workforce and in the highly proactive and targeted industrial strategy pursued since the late 1980s. Such factors have played a vital role in Ireland's ability to attract leading international firms in technologically sophisticated sectors such as pharmaceuticals and software, in turn contributing towards the Republic's rapid economic growth in the 1990s. Far from representing a model of free-market capitalism, then, the Irish case highlights how state activism can enhance rather than hinder economic growth. This suggests that other countries, too, could benefit from such a strategy.

Yet one must also be careful of presenting Ireland as a blueprint. The dynamics behind Ireland's growth have not only been highly complex but in some cases (such as the late baby boom) highly unusual. As the OECD states, there has been 'no "silver bullet" – no single, overriding policy that could be adopted elsewhere in order to emulate the Irish experience'.[2] What the Irish case may do is suggest that nations do *not* have to follow a common path, for what matters is not that nations follow the herd but that they adopt policies and strategies that are appropriate to their own contexts. What is dangerous about the globalisation orthodoxy is the sense that there is no alternative but to pursue free-market capitalism, whether or not such strategies are appropriate to specific states. It is for precisely this reason that the World Bank and the IMF have been criticised for their 'one size fits all' approach to developing countries.

There is need for further scepticism about Ireland's model economy status: that economic growth has been accompanied by rising social inequality. It is certainly not the case that Ireland is a 'glaring failure' in social terms, for some important gains have been made – not least in the dramatic reduction of consistent poverty and long-term unemployment. But it is clear that the resources generated by economic growth have not been garnered to tackle Ireland's long-standing inequalities. In contrast to other European countries, where social expenditure as a proportion of economic growth has risen over time, Ireland's welfare effort has actually fallen. Yet it would also be wrong to suggest that Ireland has shifted from one state form (an 'active' or 'distributive' state) to another (a 'competition state'). For, while strong tendencies towards prioritising market forces certainly exist, a number of important counter-tendencies are also apparent, not least in terms of measures explicitly designed to combat social disadvantage. Nor has the competitiveness-oriented approach been confined to the period of rapid economic growth. Rather, Irish policy has been geared towards market needs since the 1960s: indeed, it was not until the 1990s that policies to target social disadvantage were actively pursued. Nevertheless, the fact that such policies have failed to counter the growing disparity between rich and poor in Ireland suggests that it can hardly be regarded a showpiece of social inclusion.

This prompts the question of why more has not been done to tackle Ireland's long-standing inequalities. For many critics, the answer to this is simple: it is because of globalisation. The competitive imperatives of globalisation are believed to have resituated the Irish state so that market forces rather than social needs must increasingly be prioritised. While other commentators are less critical of Ireland's social performance, they too point to the role of globalisation in shaping the overall trajectory of the Irish state. This volume has sought to challenge such claims. It has not only pointed to the lack of empirical evidence for Ireland's 'globalisation' (see above), but has also questioned the common assumption that policy change occurs as a direct and unmediated response to the economic context. While economic conditions such as Ireland's trade openness and high levels of foreign investment have certainly influenced the trajectory of economic policy over time, they cannot in themselves explain the shape and pace of policy change. For instance, Ireland's trade openness cannot explain the decline in welfare effort, for in other European countries there is a clear positive correlation between trade openness and public expenditure.

This relates to a more fundamental theoretical point made by the book: that we should avoid presenting a false dualism between the economic and the political; or, indeed, structure and agency. While (economic) contexts may present opportunities for (policy) change, it is the conduct of agents that determines the extent to which such opportunities are realised. For example, there was nothing inevitable about Ireland's shift towards trade liberalisation, which was instead the result of specific strategies adopted by Irish policy-makers since the late 1950s. Similarly, policy measures associated with European integration (including the Stability and Growth Pact) have not developed inexorably but are 'contingent, contested and, above all, authored politically'.[3] This has crucial implications, not only for Ireland but also for other countries. For, if such developments are contingent upon the actions of human agents rather than predestined by exogenous forces of globalisation, then there may be considerably more room for social and political alternatives than is so often assumed.

Indeed, the main obstacle to such alternatives may be the very *perception* that globalisation shapes the terrain of what is politically possible. The volume has argued that ideas about globalisation have indeed played a crucial role in shaping the responses and strategies of political decision-makers in Ireland. In particular, globalisation has increasingly been seen to drive the need to prioritise market forces in Ireland. While this has not translated into the adoption of stark neo-liberalism, the competitive imperatives of globalisation are nevertheless seen to set limits on what is possible in social terms. In this sense, to paraphrase Hall, economic ideas have yielded considerable political power in Ireland.[4] Again, this has important implications both for Ireland and for elsewhere. For, if we can begin to puncture the *idea* of globalisation, then the scope for social and political alternatives once more opens up.

Notes

1. P. Hirst and G. Thompson, *Globalisation in Question: The International Economy and the Possibilities of Governance* (Cambridge: Polity, 1999), p. 7.
2. OECD, *Economic Surveys: Ireland 1999* (Paris: OECD, 1999), p. 10.
3. C. Hay, 'Contemporary capitalism, globalisation, regionalisation and the persistence of national variation', *Review of International Studies*, 26: 4 (2000), p. 525.
4. P. A. Hall, *The Political Power of Economic Ideas: Keynesianism Across Nations* (Princeton, NJ: Princeton University Press, 1989).

Select bibliography

Allen, K., *The Celtic Tiger: The Myth of Social Partnership in Ireland* (Manchester: Manchester University Press, 2000).
Amin, A. and N. Thrift (eds), *Globalisation, Institutions and Regional Development in Europe* (Oxford: Oxford University Press, 1994).
Auer, P., *Employment Revival in Europe: Labour Market Success in Austria, Denmark, Ireland and the Netherlands* (Geneva: International Labour Office, 2000).
Barrett, A., J. Fitz Gerald and B. Nolan, 'Earnings inequality, returns to education and immigration into Ireland', *Labour Economics*, 9: 5 (2002), pp. 665–80.
Barry, F. (ed.), *Understanding Ireland's Economic Growth* (Basingstoke: Macmillan, 1999).
Barry, F., 'Convergence is not automatic: lessons from Ireland for Central and Eastern Europe', *World Economy*, 23: 10 (2000), pp. 1379–94.
Blyth, M., *Great Transformations: Economic Ideas and Institutional Change in the Twentieth Century* (Cambridge: Cambridge University Press, 2002).
Breathnach, P., 'Exploring the "Celtic tiger" phenomenon: causes and consequences of Ireland's economic miracle', *European Urban and Regional Studies*, 5: 4 (1998), pp. 305–16.
Breen, R., D. Hannan, D. Rottman and C. T. Whelan, *Understanding Contemporary Ireland: State, Class and Development in the Republic of Ireland* (Dublin: Gill & Macmillan, 1990).
Brunt, B., *The Republic of Ireland* (London: Paul Chapman, 1988).
Cerny, P. G., 'Paradoxes of the competition state: the dynamics of political globalisation', *Government and Opposition*, 32: 2 (1997), pp. 251–74.
Clinch, P., F. Convery and B. Walsh, *After the Celtic Tiger: Challenges Ahead* (Dublin: O'Brien Press, 2002).
Coakley, J. and M. Gallagher (eds), *Politics in the Republic of Ireland* (London: Routledge, 1999).
Collins, N. and T. Cradden (eds), *Political Issues in Ireland Today* (Manchester: Manchester University Press, 1st edn 1994, 2nd edn 1999, 3rd edn 2004).
Collins, N. and T. Cradden, *Irish Politics Today* (Manchester: Manchester University Press, 1997).

SELECT BIBLIOGRAPHY

Coulter, C. and S. Coleman (eds), *The End of Irish History? Critical Reflections on the Celtic Tiger* (Manchester: Manchester University Press, 2003).

Cox, R., *Approaches to World Order* (Cambridge: Cambridge University Press, 1996).

Crotty, W. and D. E. Schmitt (eds), *Ireland and the Politics of Change* (London: Longman, 1998).

Crotty, W. and D. E. Schmitt, *Ireland on the World Stage* (Manchester: Manchester University Press, 2002).

CSO, *Foreign Direct Investment 2001 and 2002* (Cork: Central Statistical Office, 2003).

CSO, *Measuring Ireland's Progress* (Cork: Central Statistical Office, 2003).

CSO, *Ireland, North and South: A Statistical Profile* (Cork: Central Statistical Office, 2004).

Culliton, J., *A Time for Change: Industrial Policy for the 1990s – Report of the Industrial Policy Review Group* (Dublin: Stationery Office, 1992).

Daly, M. and N. Yeates, 'Common origins, different paths: adaptation and change in social security in Britain and Ireland', *Policy & Politics*, 31: 1 (2003), pp. 85–97.

Department of Finance, *Budgetary and Economic Statistics: March 2004* (Dublin: Department of Finance, 2004).

Dicken, P., *Global Shift: Reshaping the Global Economic Map in the 21st Century* (London: Sage, 2003).

Duffy, D., J. Fitz Gerald, I. Kearney and F. Shortall (eds), *The Medium-Term Review: 1997–2003* (Dublin: Economic and Social Research Institute, 1997).

Eurobarometer, *Public Opinion in the European Union, October/November 2002* (Brussels: European Commission, 2002).

Eurobarometer, *Globalisation* (Brussels: European Commission, 2003).

European Commission, *European Social Statistics: Social Protection Expenditure and Receipts* (Luxembourg: European Commission, 2004).

Fianna Fáil, *A Lot Done: More to Do – Fianna Fáil Manifesto 2002–7* (Dublin: Fianna Fáil, 2002).

Fianna Fáil and Progressive Democrats, *An Agreed Programme for Government Between Fianna Fáil and the Progressive Democrats* (Dublin: Fianna Fáil and Progressive Democrats, 2002).

Forfás, *International Trade and Investment Report 2003* (Dublin: Forfás, 2004).

Garrett, G., *Partisan Politics in the Global Economy* (Cambridge: Cambridge University Press, 1998).

Gordon, D. M., 'The global economy: new edifice or crumbling foundations?' *New Left Review*, 168 (1988), pp. 24–64.

Government of Ireland, *Programme for Economic Expansion* (Dublin: Stationery Office, 1958).

Government of Ireland, *Programme for Economic and Social Progress* (Dublin: Stationery Office, 1991).

Government of Ireland, *Programme for Competitiveness and Work* (Dublin: Stationery Office, 1994).

Government of Ireland, *Partnership 2000 for Inclusion, Employment and Competitiveness* (Dublin: Stationery Office, 1997).
Government of Ireland, *Programme for Prosperity and Fairness* (Dublin: Stationery Office, 2000).
Government of Ireland, *Sustaining Progress: Social Partnership Agreement 2003–5* (Dublin: Stationery Office, 2002).
Gray, J., *After Social Democracy* (London: Demos, 1996).
Gray, J., *False Dawn: The Delusions of Global Capitalism* (New York: New Press, 1998).
Greider, W., *One World, Ready or Not: The Manic Logic of Global Capitalism* (New York: Simon & Schuster, 1997).
Guéhenno, J., *The End of the Nation-State* (Minneapolis: University of Minnesota Press, 1995).
Hall, P. A., 'Policy paradigms, social learning and the state: the case of economic policymaking in Britain', *Comparative Politics*, 25: 3 (1993), pp. 275–96.
Hall, P. A. and D. Soskice (eds), *Varieties of Capitalism: The Institutional Foundations of Comparative Advantage* (Oxford: Oxford University Press, 2001).
Hay, C., *Political Analysis* (Basingstoke: Palgrave, 2002).
Hay, C., 'Common trajectories, variable paces, divergent outcomes? Models of European capitalism under conditions of complex economic interdependence', *Review of International Political Economy*, 11: 2 (2004), pp. 231–62.
Hay, C. and D. Marsh (eds), *Demystifying Globalisation* (London: Macmillan, 2000).
Hay, C. and B. Rosamond, 'Globalisation, European integration and the discursive construction of economic imperatives', *Journal of European Public Policy*, 9: 2 (2002), pp. 147–67.
Hay, C. and N. J. Smith, 'Horses for courses? The political discourse of globalisation and European integration in the UK and Ireland', *West European Politics*, 28: 1, pp. 124–58.
Hay, C. and M. Watson, 'The politics and discourse of globalisation: "sceptical" notes on the 1999 Reith lectures', *Political Quarterly*, 70: 4 (1999), pp. 418–25.
Heath, A. F., R. Breen and C. T. Whelan (eds), *Ireland North and South: Perspectives from Social Science* (Oxford: Oxford University Press, 1999).
Held, D. and A. McGrew, *Globalisation/Anti-globalisation* (Cambridge: Polity, 2002).
Held, D., A. McGrew, D. Goldblatt and J. Perraton, *Global Transformations: Politics, Economics and Culture* (Stanford, CA: Stanford University Press, 1999).
Hickman, M., *Ireland and the European Community* (London: PNL Press, 1990).
Hirst, P. and G. Thompson, *Globalisation in Question: The Interational Economy and the Possibilities of Governance* (Cambridge: Polity, 1999).
Honohan, P. and B. Walsh, 'Catching up with the leaders: the Irish hare', Brookings Panel on Economic Activity, Washington, DC (4–5 April 2002).

SELECT BIBLIOGRAPHY

Katzenstein, P. J., *Small States in World Markets: Industrial Policy in Europe* (Ithaca, NY: Cornell University Press, 1985).

Kennedy, K. A., T. Giblin and D. McHugh, *The Economic Development of Ireland in the Twentieth Century* (London: Routledge, 1988).

Keogh, D., *Twentieth-Century Ireland: Nation and State* (Dublin: Gill & Macmillan, 1994).

Kerr, P., *Postwar British Politics: From Conflict to Consensus* (London: Routledge/PSA, 2001).

Kirby, P., *The Celtic Tiger in Distress: Growth and Inequality in Ireland* (Basingstoke: Palgrave, 2002).

Kirby, P., L. Gábbons and M. Cronin (eds), *Reinventing Ireland: Culture, Society and the Global Economy* (London: Pluto Press, 2002).

Krugman, P. R., *Pop Internationalism* (Cambridge, MA: MIT Press, 1996).

Laffan, B., *Organisation for a Changing Europe: Irish Central Government and the European Union* (Dublin: Policy Institute, 2001).

Lechner, F. and J. Boli (eds), *The Globalisation Reader* (Oxford: Blackwell, 2000).

Leddin, A. and B. Walsh, *The Macro-Economy of Ireland* (Dublin: Gill & Macmillan, 1998).

Lee, J., *Ireland, 1912–85: Politics and Society* (Cambridge and New York: Cambridge University Press, 1989).

Mac Sharry, R. and P. White, *The Making of the Celtic Tiger: The Inside Story of Ireland's Boom Economy* (Cork: Mercier Press, 2000).

Mansergh, M. (ed.), *The Speeches and Statements of Charles J. Haughey* (Dublin: Mercier Press, 1986).

Moynihan, M. (ed.), *Speeches and Statements by Eamon de Valera, 1917–73* (Dublin: Gill & Macmillan, 1980).

Murphy, A., 'The "Celtic tiger" – an analysis of Ireland's economic growth performance', European University Institute Working Paper, San Domenico (2000).

Murphy, T. V. and W. K. Roche (eds), *Irish Industrial Relations in Practice* (Dublin: Oak Tree Press, 1994).

Navarro, V., J. Schmitt and J. Astudillo, 'Is globalisation undermining the welfare state?', *Cambridge Journal of Economics*, 28 (2004), pp. 133–52.

NCC, *Annual Competitiveness Report 2003* (Dublin: Forfás, 2003).

NESC, *An Investment in Quality: Services, Inclusion and Enterprise* (Dublin: National Economic and Social Council, 2003).

Nolan, B., P. O'Connell and C. T. Whelan (eds), *Bust to Boom? The Irish Experience of Growth and Inequality* (Dublin: Institute of Public Administration, 2000).

Ó Gráda, C. (ed.), *The Economic Development of Ireland Since 1870* (Aldershot: Edward Elgar, 1994).

Ó Gráda, C., *A Rocky Road: The Irish Economy Since the 1920s* (Manchester: Manchester University Press, 1997).

Ó Gráda, C., 'Is the Celtic tiger a paper tiger?', in McCoy, D., D. Duffy, J. Hore and C. Maccoille (eds), *Quarterly Economic Commentary, Spring 2002* (Dublin: Economic and Social Research Institute, 2002), pp. 1–11.

Ó Riain, S., 'A tale of two globalisations: the Irish software industry and the global economy', Working Paper, University of California (1998).

Ó Riain, S., 'The flexible developmental state: globalisation, information technology and the "Celtic tiger"', *Politics & Society*, 28: 2 (2000), pp. 157–93.

O'Brien, R., *Global Financial Integration: The End of Geography* (New York: Council on Foreign Relations Press, 1992).

O'Connell, P., *Astonishing Success: Economic Growth and the Labour Market in Ireland* (Geneva: International Labour Office, 1999).

O'Conner, J. S., 'Welfare state development in the context of European integration and economic convergence: situating Ireland within the European Union context', *Policy & Politics*, 31: 3 (2003), pp. 387–404.

O'Donnell, R., *Ireland and Europe: Challenges for a New Century* (Denver: International Academic, 2000).

OECD, *Economic Surveys: Ireland 1999* (Paris: OECD, 1999).

OECD, *Economic Surveys: Ireland 2000–1* (Paris: OECD, 2001).

OECD, *Economic Surveys: Ireland 2003* (Paris: OECD, 2003).

O'Hearn, D., *Inside the Celtic Tiger: The Irish Economy and the Asian Model* (London: Pluto Press, 1998).

O'Hearn, D., 'Globalisation, "new tigers," and the end of the developmental state? The case of the Celtic tiger', *Politics & Society*, 28: 1 (2000), pp. 67–92.

O'Hearn, D., *The Atlantic Economy: Britain, the US and Ireland* (Manchester: Manchester University Press, 2001).

Ohmae, K., *The Borderless Word: Power and Strategy in the Interlinked Economy* (London: Collins, 1990).

Ohmae, K., *The End of the Nation State: The Rise of Regional Economies* (London: HarperCollins, 1996).

O'Malley, E., *An Analysis of Secondary Employment Associated with Manufacturing Industry* (Dublin: Economic and Social Research Institute, 1995).

Rhodes, M. and Y. Mény (eds), *The Future of European Welfare: A New Social Contract?* (Basingstoke: Macmillan, 1998).

Rodrik, D., *Has Globalisation Gone Too Far?* (Washington, DC: Institute of International Economics, 1997).

Rosenberg, J., *The Follies of Globalisation Theory: Polemical Essays* (London: Verso, 2000).

Ruane, F. and H. Görg, 'Ireland's economic growth', *Economic Review*, 18: 1 (2000), pp. 12–15.

Schmidt, V. A., *The Futures of European Capitalism* (Oxford: Oxford University Press, 2002).

Scholte, J. A., *Globalisation: A Critical Introduction* (London: Macmillan, 2000).

Sexton, J. J. and P. O'Connell, *Labour Market Studies: Ireland* (Brussels: European Commission, 1996).

Sibeon, R., 'Anti-reductionist sociology', *Sociology*, 33: 2 (1999), pp. 317–34.

Sinnott, R., *Attitudes and Behaviour of the Irish Electorate in the Referendum on the Treaty of Nice: Executive Summary* (Dublin: Institute for the Study of Social Change, 2003).

SELECT BIBLIOGRAPHY

Strange, S., *The Retreat of the State: The Diffusion of Power in the World Economy* (New York: Cambridge University Press, 1996).

Sweeney, P., *The Celtic Tiger: Ireland's Continuing Economic Miracle* (Dublin: Oak Tree Press, 1999).

Taylor, G., *Negotiated Governance and Public Policy in Ireland* (Manchester: Manchester University Press, 2005).

Teague, P., 'Pay determination in the Republic of Ireland – towards social corporatism', *British Journal of Industrial Relations*, 33: 2 (1995), pp. 253–73.

Telesis, *A Review of Industrial Policy* (Dublin: National Economic and Social Council, 1982).

UNCTAD, *Handbook of Statistics 2003* (Geneva: United Nations, 2003).

UNCTAD, *WID Country Profile: Ireland* (Geneva: United Nations, 2004).

United Nations, *Human Development Report 2003: Millennium Development Goals: A Compact Among Nations to End Human Poverty* (New York: Oxford University Press, 2003).

Watson, M., 'International capital mobility in an era of globalisation: adding a political dimension to the "Feldstein–Horioka Puzzle"', *Politics*, 21: 2 (2001), pp. 81–92.

Watson, M., *Foundations of International Political Economy* (Basingstoke: Palgrave, 2005).

Weiss, L., *The Myth of the Powerless State* (Ithaca, NY: Cornell University Press, 1998).

Weiss, L. (ed.), *States in the Global Economy: Bringing Domestic Institutions Back In* (Cambridge: Cambridge University Press, 2003).

Whelan, C. T. (ed.), *Values and Social Change in Ireland* (Dublin: Gill & Macmillan, 1994).

Whelan, C. T., R. Layte, B. Maitre, B. Gannon, B. Nolan, D. Watson and J. Williams, *Monitoring Poverty Trends in Ireland: Results from the 2001 Living in Ireland Survey* (Dublin: Economic and Social Research Institute, 2003).

Whitaker, T. K., *Economic Development* (Dublin: Stationery Office, 1958).

Index

active state 6, 100, 113
agriculture 44, 101, 107–9, 134, 144–6
Ahern, Bertie 173, 175–6, 182, 186
Allen, K. 44, 50–1, 119–21, 123, 141
A. T. Kearney 8 n.8, 65, 67, 174
auxiliary state 100–4
Axford, B. 17–18

baby boom 77
Barry, F. 48
Breen et al. 100

Cameron, D. 20
capitalism 12, 20, 73, 99, 141–2, 197, 199
capital mobility 11–12, 15, 19, 23–4, 73–4
Castells, M. 12
Celtic tiger 36–62
  see also discourse
Cerny, P. 19, 120, 141
change, conceptions of 98–9
Chortoreas, G. and T. Pelagidis 26
civil service 101, 106, 109, 111
class 44, 127, 141, 170, 186–7
competition state 6–7, 19, 113, 120–1, 123–4, 128, 130, 132–4, 200
competitiveness 7–8, 12, 15, 18–19, 38, 80, 120, 128, 133, 142, 150, 156–7, 199–201
  see also discourse

complex globalisation thesis 17–19, 25–6, 141–2
consensus 171–2, 181–3, 188
contingent globalisation thesis 22–8
convergence
  economic 47–9, 84
  policy 12, 16, 19–21, 24–5, 27, 150, 199
corporation tax 16, 21, 23–4, 38–9, 72–4, 111, 130, 132, 156, 158
  see also industrial policy
corruption scandals 185
Cox, R. 19
crisis 82, 104, 121, 146–7, 169, 171, 181–2, 186
Cumann na nGaedheal 101, 145, 168

Daly, M. and N. Yeates 124
de Valera, E. 103, 168–70
developmental state 12, 129–33
  see also East Asian tigers
Dicken, P. 17–19
discourse
  Celtic tiger 52–3, 86, 174
  competitiveness 167, 172–4, 177–9, 181, 183, 188
  European integration 167–8, 170–1, 176–7, 179–80, 183–5, 188
  globalisation 4, 17, 19, 24, 27, 29, 63–4, 167–8, 172–88
  importance of 21–5, 28–9, 167–8
  nationalist 168–71, 180

paper tiger 54, 185
Schmidt's conceptual framework
  cognitive function 178–9
  communicative function 183–7
  co-ordinative function 181–3
  normative function 180–1
distributive state 119–29

East Asian tigers 12, 37, 43–7, 54
Economic Development 170
economic growth 36–96
  measures of 40–2
  prior to 1990s 36–7
  sustainability 44–7
education 74–6, 102, 106–7, 109, 112, 170
electoral issues 24, 53, 183–7
employment 38, 40, 43–7, 68, 76–8, 86, 108–12, 134, 145–7, 158
  see also unemployment
European integration 70–2, 156–60
  Common Agricultural Policy (CAP) 108
  European Monetary Union (EMU) 21, 24–5, 48–9, 157–8
  Nice Treaty 159, 185, 195n.104
  Single European Market (SEM) 48, 70–1, 84, 110, 134, 157–8
  Stability and Growth Pact 24, 157–8, 176
  structural funds 54, 71–2, 84, 87
  see also discourse; regional trade blocs

falsification 25–6
Fianna Fáil 53, 101–2, 107, 109, 133, 145, 168–71, 174, 176, 185–7
Fine Gael 53, 169, 171–2, 186
fiscal policy 82–5, 48, 112, 121, 130, 157, 171
  see also public expenditure
foreign direct investment 11–13, 66–9, 74, 76, 87

Garrett, G. 19–21, 82
Giddens, A. 17
globalisation, definition 25–8
gravity models 24
Gray, J. 10, 141
Greider, W. 10, 141

Hall, P. and D. Soskice 19, 21
Haughey, Charles 171–2
Hay, C. 17, 21–4, 27, 98, 183
healthcare 101–3, 108–9, 111, 126–8, 134
Held et al. 17–19, 25
Hirst, P. and G. Thompson 13, 17, 27
Hobson, J. 20
Honohan, P. and B. Walsh 43
housing 101–2, 107, 110–11, 123, 127–9
hyperglobalist thesis 10–13, 140–1

indigenous industry 43, 46–7, 67–8, 85–6, 107
Industrial Development Agency (IDA) 85–6, 104–5, 108, 110–11, 130–2, 169
industrial policy 85–6, 101–11
industrial relations 54, 102–3, 106–7, 109, 112–13, 122, 171
  see also social partnership
inequality 49–52, 88, 106, 121–3, 129, 141, 173, 187, 200

Jessop, B. 19

Keynesianism 10–13, 71, 83–4, 109–10, 170–1
Kirby, P. 36, 44, 73–4, 119–21, 128, 131–2, 141
Krugman, P. 86

labour supply 77–80
Lemass, S. 103, 170

McCreevy, Charlie 54, 64, 176, 186
migration 37, 77, 147

INDEX

monetary policy 101–4, 106
Murphy, A. 63, 66, 70, 140–1

National Anti-Poverty Strategy 122, 129, 147
national debt 37–8, 40, 82–3, 102, 108–9, 111–12, 147, 171, 173
National Economic and Social Council (NESC) 109, 113, 122, 171–2
Navarro, V., J. Schmitt and J. Astudillo 15–16, 22
neo-liberalism 6, 12, 21, 85, 98, 119–21, 123, 128–9, 133–5, 141–4, 158, 172, 175, 177, 186, 201
new institutionalist thesis 19–22, 27–8, 142

O'Brien, R. 10–11
occupational upgrading 44
O'Connell, P. 44, 78–9, 119, 126, 128–9, 131, 142
O'Conner, J. 141–2
O'Donnell, L. 174–5
Ó Gráda 48, 83–4
O'Hearn, D. 38, 43–7, 66, 73, 129–30, 140–1
Ohmae, K. 10
O'Malley, E. 67–8, 146
Ó Riain, S. 43, 67–8, 119, 126, 128–9, 131, 142
outward investment 46, 155–6

paper tiger 38–47
see also discourse
party system 53, 186–7
planning 101, 106, 110, 112
poverty 49–52, 106, 109–10, 112, 122–3, 129, 173, 176, 193n.79
privatisation 107, 133–4, 157, 172, 185
productivity 37–40, 42–3, 48, 145–6, 172
Programme for Economic Expansion 105–7

Progressive Democrats 176, 187
protectionism 48, 101–7, 145–8, 168–70
public expenditure 12, 15–16, 19–21, 22, 85, 106–7, 109, 111–12, 124–9, 150, 157–8, 171–2, 186

'race to the bottom' 15–16, 21, 73–4
regional trade blocs 13–15, 18, 24–6, 65–6, 69–71, 149, 155, 158
Reich, Robert 10
reification 3, 23, 26–7, 98, 174
reinvested earnings 46, 69, 154–5
Rhodes, M. 19
Rodrik, D. 20
Rosamond, B. 23–4, 183
Rugman, A. 13
Ruigrok, W. and R. Van Tulder 15

sceptical thesis 13–17, 141
Schmidt, V. 21–2, 178
see also discourse
Scholte, J. A. 18
Schumpeterian workfare state 19
Second World War 102–3
service sector growth 44
small state 64–6, 84, 87, 141–3, 147–8, 150, 159–60, 179
social democracy 12, 16, 20–1, 98
social insurance coverage 109–10, 126
social mobility 44
social partnership 47, 54, 80–3, 107, 109, 113, 119–24, 132, 147, 158, 172–3, 175, 181–3
software sector 68, 111
spatial scales 39n.90
state expenditure 15–16, 19, 23, 73, 84–5, 103–4, 106–9, 111–12, 124–9, 147, 150, 157–8, 200
state-sponsored bodies 101–2
see also privatisation
Steinmo, S. 21

structure and agency 4, 12, 19, 21, 13, 26, 28, 87, 143, 197–8, 201

Taylor, G. 81, 121, 142
Teague, P. 82, 121
trade openness 11, 13, 20, 54–6, 64–6, 134, 142–3, 147–51
transfer pricing 38–40, 43
triadisation 13–14, 26, 65
  see also regional trade blocs

unemployment 37–8, 40, 45, 49–50, 78, 109, 112, 122, 168, 172–3, 182–3

Verdun, A. 24–5

Wade, R. 13, 15
Weiss, L. 19–20
welfare state 12, 16, 19, 22–3, 101–4, 109–10, 124–9, 142
Whelen et al. 50–1
Whitaker, T. K. 170
workplace change 81–2

Zysman, J. 13